# The Millennium Development Goals

# The Millennium Development Goals

Raising the Resources to Tackle World Poverty

Edited by
**FANTU CHERU** and **COLIN BRADFORD JR**

## ZED BOOKS
LONDON AND NEW YORK

*in association with*

The Helsinki Process
on Globalisation and Democracy

*The Millennium Development Goals:*
*Raising the Resources to Tackle World Poverty*
was first published in 2005 by
Zed Books Ltd, 7 Cynthia Street, London N1 9JF, UK and
Room 400, 175 Fifth Avenue, New York, NY 10010, USA.
www.zedbooks.co.uk

in association with
the Helsinki Process on Globalisation and Democracy,
Ministry for Foreign Affairs of Finland.
Ministry for Foreign Affairs, PO Box 176, Katajanokanlaituri 3,
FIN-00161 Helsinki, Finland
www.helsinkiprocess.fi

Cover designed by Andrew Corbett
Set in 10/12 pt Photina by Long House, Cumbria, UK
Printed and bound in Malta by Gutenberg Ltd

Distributed in the USA exclusively by Palgrave Macmillan, a division of
St Martin's Press, LLC, 175 Fifth Avenue, New York, NY 10010.

A catalogue record for this book
is available from the British Library

US Cataloging-in-Publication Data
is available from the Library of Congress

ISBN   Hb 1 84277 734 3
       Pb 1 84277 735 1

# Contents

# List of Figures, Tables and Boxes

## Figures

## Tables

## Boxes

# About the Contributors

**Tony Addison** is the Deputy Director of UNU–WIDER.

**Daniel Adom** is Human Settlements Officer at UN–Habitat.

**Nancy Birdsall** is President of the Center for Global Development, Washington, DC.

**Colin Bradford** is a Visiting Fellow at The Brookings Institution.

**Fantu Cheru** is Professor of Development Studies at the American University, Washington, DC.

**Brian Deese** is a Researcher at the Center for Global Development, Washington, DC.

**Martin Khor** is Director of the Third World Network, Malaysia.

**George Mavrotas** is a Research Fellow and Project Director at UNU–WIDER.

**Mark McGillivray** is Senior Research Fellow at UNU-WIDER.

**Ann Pettifor** is Director of the Jubilee Research/new economics foundation, UK.

**Kunibert Raffer** is Professor of Economics at the University of Vienna.

**Rathin Roy** is a member of the Poverty Group at UNDP, New York.

**Andrés Solimano** is Regional Adviser, United Nations Economic Commission for Latin American and the Caribbean (ECLA).

**Anna Tibaijuka** is Executive Director, UN–Habitat.

**David Tipping** is Human Settlements Officer, UN–Habitat.

**Jan Vandemoortele** is Director of the Poverty Group, UNDP.

**Raimo Väyrynen** is President of the Finnish Academy of Sciences.

# Members of the
# Helsinki Process Track 2:
# Global Economic Agenda

**Convenor**

*Fantu Cheru*, Professor of International Development, American University, Washington, DC. (Ethiopia/USA)

**Advisor of the Track**

*Colin Bradford, Jr.* Visiting Research Fellow, The Brookings Institution, Washington, DC. (USA)

**Members**

*Tony Addison*, Deputy Director of the World Institute for Development Economics Research (WIDER) of the United Nations University, Finland (United Kingdom)

*Regina Amadi-Njoku*, the ILO Regional Director of Field Programmes in Africa, Côte d'Ivoire

*Marti Hetemaki*, Permanent Under-Secretary of State, Ministry of Finance, Finland

*Anthony Hill*, Ambassador, Jamaica

*Jose Olivio Miranda Oliveira*, Assistant Secretary General of the International Confederation of Free Trade Unions, Brazil

*Maureen O'Neil*, President of the International Development Research Center (IDRC), Canada

*Aida Opoku-Mensah*, Team Leader of the United Nations Economic Commission for Africa's ICTs for Development Programme implementing the African Information Society Initiative (AISI), Ghana/Ethiopia

*Knut Sorlie*, Assistant Director, Confederation of Norwegian Business and Industry, Norway

*Anna Tibaijuka*, Executive Director of the United Nations Settlements Programme (UN-Habitat).

# Foreword

The Helsinki Process on Globalisation and Democracy was launched in 2003 after a conference held in that city in December 2002 had called for a global dialogue to bridge divisions between various stakeholders and discover the common ground. One of the most vigorous strategies issuing from the conference was to further synthesise the energy and commitment of various actors in the implementation of the Millennium Declaration.

In facilitating the process the Finnish and Tanzanian governments recognised its key idea: that various stakeholders – governments, civil society, the business community, international organisations, academia and even the media – can play a major role in accelerating global problem solving and implementing global commitments. Different stakeholders have such diverse resources at their disposal that through joint and well-coordinated action they can make a notable difference in addressing complex, globally manifested problems such as environmental degradation or poverty. Whilst governments are able to agree on norms and legal frameworks, business actors often have the technical solutions and know-how to address the problem efficiently. Civil society, typically, has as its strength the ability to enrich civic dialogue on priorities and thus to mobilise awareness and political will. Acting together, the stakeholders can manifest a new era in agreeing upon and implementing the global agenda.

In order to advance dialogue and the setting of stakeholder priorities, the Helsinki Process established three Tracks, which worked simultaneously and reciprocally. Entitled *New Approaches to Global Problem Solving*, *Global Economic Agenda* and *Human Security*, the Tracks were asked to prioritise issues from the vast global agenda that would win credible support for implementation from the stakeholder groups or, in the opinion of the invited experts, bring particular added value from multi-stakeholder engagement. They explored new ways in which to construct global governance and advance global leadership, discussed how to mobilise finances from both developed and developing countries to meet the Millennium Development Goals, and prioritised policies around the central tactic of empowering communities at risk.

In this publication the reader will encounter some of the vital expert contributions to the Track on *Global Economic Agenda*. We would like to take the opportunity to thank Fantu Cheru and Colin Bradford for leading and advancing the Track and for editing this publication, Sami Lahdensuo for coordinating the background research for the Track, and all the researchers and writers for their vital contributions. The research in this volume adds depth to the work of the Helsinki Process and is of interest to wider audiences. We would also like to thank Zed Books, and Robert Molteno in particular, for making the research available to this wider circle of readers.

It is our impression that those who have engaged in the dialogue between stakeholders in the Helsinki Process have been genuinely inspired by the experience. Some of the results of that inspiration can be found in this book and in the report of the Track on the *Global Economic Agenda* (the latter can be found at www.helsinkiprocess.fi). That being said, it is equally true that the dialogue has been challenging. Engaging in it has required openness and honesty as well as a will to learn and respect one another. In order to succeed in an enterprise of this kind, it is vital that differences are respected, that the focus is steadily maintained on issues shared rather than on those that divide, and that collaboration and dialogue are built on the strengths of different stakeholders and not on their weaknesses. Furthermore, it is important that the dialogue takes place in an action-oriented context. If it is approached simply as an exercise in searching for common ground, without any ambition to act together to implement the findings, the level of achievement is likely to remain lower.

The first Helsinki Process helped to end the Cold War, whilst the second has contributed towards bridging the divide between North and South and bringing more democracy into international relations. The aim now is to set development on a new course. The continuing process, started in 2002, is bringing on board a growing number of government, NGO and business community participants.

*Jakaya M Kikwete*
*Minister for Foreign Affairs and*
*International Cooperation*
*Tanzania*

*Erkki Tuomioja*
*Minister for Foreign Affairs*
*Finland*

# Introduction

FANTU CHERU and COLIN BRADFORD JR

## The linkages between governance, mobilisation, and human security

We live in a divided, polarised world. Half of the five billion people living in the developing world live on less than US$2 a day. Massive global poverty signifies too many deep failures in the prevailing market-oriented system of global governance, the global economy and policy reform efforts. Economic growth is too slow, income distribution too unequal, and poverty reduction too constrained to generate a sense of progress and hope. The rules of the game and the protection afforded to human rights seem skewed to favour the haves over the have-nots. There is increasing frustration, disillusionment and distrust.

As a result, the planet is at risk. Even those who are well-off feel insecure in a polarised world. Human security has become a widespread global concern of all rather than a condition affecting only the poor and disadvantaged. Crime, violence, conflict, terrorism and instability spread unexpectedly into cities and neighbourhoods around the world. No one is exempt. Everyone has a stake in changing the dynamics of globalisation, which appear to be disadvantaging the global majority.

There are three levels of the challenge for achieving change: global governance; mobilising resources; and clarifying the policy agenda. These three levels are embodied in the three tracks of the Helsinki Process: global governance; the global economy; and human security. In this book on financing development, we begin by connecting the three levels in relation to the primary focus here on mobilising resources for the Millennium Development Goals (MDGs). The linkages between the three levels of the challenge are essential to achieving change: no one of the three sets of issues can achieve results without the other two. One of the main reasons for the tensions defining the current conjuncture is precisely the failure to implement new paths for governance, resource allocation and policies that would yield greater global democracy, equity and security.

Human security for all in the current era embraces a broad agenda. There is the 'hard power' side of this agenda, rooted in the need to address violent conflict, terrorism, drug trafficking, money laundering, crime, genocide, civil war, failed states and illegal arms sales, including nuclear proliferation. These require international cooperation among intelligence services, police, military forces and geopolitical policy makers. Then there is the 'soft' side of the same agenda, rooted in the need to address issues of global health, the environment, education, gender equality, poverty reduction, governance, institutions, and economic growth and financial stability. These require new forms of cooperation and coordination among and between (1) ministers of finance, health, environment, education, labour, and social affairs in developing countries; (2) trade, finance and development cooperation ministries in industrial countries; and (3) the major international institutions. Finding lasting solutions to these global problems should not be left to the intergovernmental system. Considerable effort must be made to ensure that the voices of the marginalised majority and other societal actors, including the private sector, are included in the discussion of alternative policies.

The nuance is that whereas global poverty is not the direct cause of violence and terrorism, global inequality in opportunities and income have fed a process of political reaction to the perceived injustices of globalisation that challenges the legitimacy of international policies, and the institutions, ideas and powers behind them. As a consequence, the anti-globalisation debate in the streets since Seattle, in the eyes of many, fuses with the alienation of the terrorist or criminal whose anger and frustration are fed by power disparities. This joining of the two streams of dissent creates linkages between the two sides of the global agenda.

In this context, the MDGs provide a powerful organising device for international action to change the current patterns of globalisation and generate forces for greater democracy, equity and security. The goals were derived democratically from a series of UN summit conferences in the early 1990s involving governments, civil society and private sector leaders from all UN member nations (Bradford 2002).[1] The Monterrey Consensus in March 2000, which welded industrial country actions to actions by developing countries in a new global partnership, represents a major break from the previous convergence of thinking on development in the Washington Consensus. Whereas the Washington Consensus was purely economic, the MDGs are multisectoral. Whereas the Washington Consensus was formed in the 1980s to identify policy reforms to restore financial stability, the MDGs were formed in the 1990s, when there was a realisation that economic growth and stability would not be sustainable unless the overall trends were socially, environmentally and politically sustainable.

Therefore, rather than the imperatives of policy reform being limited to macroeconomic policies, the new imperatives are multisectoral and inter-sectoral, defining a completely new development agenda that is holistic, balanced and humanistic rather than specialised, deflationary and techno-cratic. This new agenda creates major new challenges for governments in developing and industrial countries and for international institutions and global governance. The MDGs provide a set of specific benchmarks that can be used as mobilising devices for scaling up reforms, resources and policies by all actors to change the patterns of globalisation.

## The challenge of mobilising development finance to achieve the MDGs

Huge obstacles remain in the way of mobilising predictable external finance to meet the MDG goals. The central issue of official financing is the declining volume in official development assistance (ODA) relative to rising demand from poor countries. To bridge this ever-widening gap, fundamental progress is required on three fronts.

### ⋊ Mobilising finance

For a large number of low-income countries, ODA will continue to be a major source of foreign capital. Yet the donor countries find it difficult to increase their aid levels, let alone live up to their commitment to provide at least 0.7 per cent of their GNP in aid. It is therefore imperative to seek innovative ways of mobilising public and private sources of finance for development to complement efforts to increase official aid. UN agencies and many think tanks have been exploring new sources of development financing for covering the shortfall. The most widely discussed proposals, as discussed by Atkinson (2003; 2004), include taxes on international currency transactions (the so-called Tobin tax), carbon emissions and the international arms trade, and a general tax on the sum of exports and imports. These proposals have been re-emphasised by the recently released Chirac–Lula Commission, which presented its findings to the UN General Assembly in September 2004.[2]

Other proposals discussed in this book include Special Drawing Rights (SDR) and the sale or revaluation of gold stocks held by the International Monetary Fund (IMF). However, as Atkinson rightly observed, a number of relevant issues need to be addressed properly before these proposals can bear fruit. These include possible crowding-out effects on other critical global problems such as terrorism, peace-building, etc. given current aid flows, revenue-raising potential and political economy considerations (Atkinson 2003; 2004). If political will can be found to adopt some of these proposals, enormous sums of money can be mobilised by the international community to eliminate the worst forms of human deprivation.

## Reforming the global trading system

Two of the world's most urgent problems are the global commodities crisis and the distorting nature of global agriculture trade. The two issues are interconnected: a major part of commodities exported by developing countries are agricultural products. The effects of distortions caused by continued vigorous protectionism by the developed countries through subsidies and tariff escalation have been devastating to the economies of commodity-dependent developing countries. The commodities crisis has been a major cause of the persistence of or increase in poverty in the developing world. Resolving this problem is thus crucial to achieving the MDGs.

The issue of mobilising finance for development cannot therefore be separated from the urgent need to support the completion of the work of the Doha Development Round of trade negotiations. With a level playing field, trade can be of much greater effect than aid in reducing poverty. Achieving the MDGs would require, at the very least, the introduction of mechanisms to achieve fair and stable prices for commodities and improving market access for exports from developing countries. Needless to say, the current international agricultural trade regime is tilted precipitously in favour of rich countries; the many rules that must be rebalanced in agriculture are deeply entrenched and guarded by powerful political interests in the developed world (Khor 2001). Trade can facilitate development only when fundamental reforms are made to the underlying global trade structure.

## Debt cancellation

Since the onset of the debt crisis in the early 1980s, living standards for the majority have suffered in the face of rising unemployment and mass poverty. The continued outflow of resources in the form of debt repayment squeezes out spending in critical areas of social development. Piecemeal debt relief initiatives by the developed countries, while reducing some debt, have failed to bring a permanent solution to the debt problem. Most highly indebted poor countries (HIPCs) currently service their debts at the cost of widespread malnutrition, premature death, excessive morbidity and reduced prospects for economic growth (Cheru 2002). Growing debt service squeezes out spending in critical areas such as health and clean water. If the resources were freed up and successfully redirected towards basic human needs, there could be significant improvements in human welfare.

Significant debt reduction is necessary for the recovery and resumption of growth in many indebted countries and for achieving many of the MDGs. Money matters. Vaccination, drug therapies, doctors' and teachers' salaries, basic sanitation systems, and other underpinnings of basic human welfare cost real dollars. While the average Frenchman or German has approximately US$2,500 devoted by the government to public health, the sobering figures in sub-Saharan Africa include Kenya (US$8), Uganda (US$9), Burkina Faso (US$54) and Ethiopia (US$3). The same gap is evident in education spending. It would be impossible to meet the internationally agreed targets of the MDGs without freeing the poorest countries from the shackles of debt. At the same time, debt reduction, or even cancellation, cannot have lasting results without tackling the trade dynamics that have perpetuated debt accumulation for so many countries.

## Rising to the challenge

The essence of the challenge in front of the international community is to know which proposals for increasing the net resource flows to developing countries have the greatest potential to generate additional increments of finance. The answer seems to be that different proposals have greater chances of implementation for different actors and donors, depending on their circumstances. No one proposal seems to solve the problem or be the rallying point around which everyone can agree. Not even the comprehensive and highly imaginative International Financial Facility (IFF) proposed by the UK galvanises a broad enough segment of opinion in industrial countries.

When one looks closely at the variety of proposals being discussed, one concludes, as Helmut Reisen at the Organisation for Economic Cooperation and Development (OECD) has put it, that 'no proposal for an innovative approach is without at least one serious side risk'. Since no single proposal rises above the rest, and since all actors and agents face differing circumstances, Reisen's proposal to 'pursue a combination of innovative approaches of funding, rather than a single form' seems to make sense (Reisen 2004).

He recommends, in considering the original proposal that the IFF should raise US$50 billion in additional finance required for the achievement of the MDGs by 2015, that the IFF carry some but not all of the burden. Then this might be combined with the Global Premium Bond proposal advocated by the World Institute for Development Economics Research (WIDER) and with the use of public guarantees, especially for infrastructure where the private sector is involved, as put forward by the Camdessus Report on water financing. Expanded debt reduction through IMF gold sales or revaluation, for example, would add significant resources to finance development in poor countries. The impact of voluntary contributions both from corporations and private individuals is likely to grow as corporate social responsibility takes its course within the international private sector companies in developing countries and as development awareness and education increase. Other proposals might fit other donors and recipients better. Each should move in its own way but with an eye on making substantial new contributions to the flow of resources needed for the achievement of the MDGs in 2015. The accumulation of new and traditional sources of finance should be coordinated through the global monitoring processes already under way in the United Nations, in the World Bank's World Development Index (WDI), and in the OECD's Development Assistance Committee (DAC).

This search for new sources of finance should not ignore the fact that the most traditional source of development finance, ODA, is still the most important. There are two aspects here, both pointed out by Reisen. The first is that this form of assistance is 'the most straightforward'. The second is that 'given the recent post-Monterrey donor pledges and initiatives, the extra effort needed to double ODA is no longer out of reach'. As DAC chair Richard Manning put it before the Bank–Fund Development Committee ministers in April 2004, 'there is now growth momentum in official development assistance'. At their High-Level Meeting (HLM) in April 2004, OECD member country development cooperation ministers declared: 'As we approach the UN review in 2005, we are resolved to build on the new impetus to gear aid volume and effectiveness, as well as other development-related policies, to achieving the MDGs and to ensure that our publics are properly informed on the outcomes of these efforts' (OECD DAC 2004: 3). Nevertheless, Richard Manning warned Development Committee finance ministers that 'commitments do look very demanding in relation to current performance for a number of donors'. As Reisen points out, 'whether from traditional or innovative approaches, funding the MDGs will imply a budgetary problem: the transfer to poor countries must ultimately be borne by the private sector in the donor countries'. There is no easy way out. In the end, someone has to pay.

It makes no sense for industrial countries to provide more official aid while simultaneously failing both to remove obstacles to the growth of agriculture exports from poor countries and to alleviate the pressure of debt payments which drain domestic resources in poor countries from investment in health, education and the environment. A holistic approach is required by industrial countries to improve policy coherence, as much as an intersectoral approach is required by developing countries to achieve the synergies embedded in the MDGs. Through a systemic approach to mobilisation in global governance and a holistic approach to national policies, it is possible to marshal reforms, resources and policies to achieve the MDGs by 2015 as a benchmark in transforming the patterns of globalisation.

The ten essays in this volume were commissioned by the Helsinki Process as part of the deliberations of the Global Economic Agenda track, whose final output – entitled *Mobilising Resources for the Millennium Development Goals* – was launched simultaneously in Porto Alegre, Brazil and Davos, Switzerland in January 2005. The quality of the volume was strengthened by the contributions of three of the authors who were key figures in the UNU–

WIDER project on Innovative Sources of Development Finance, which published its research result as *New Sources of Development Finance* (Atkinson 2004). We are indebted to Tony Addison and George Mavrotas of WIDER for their intellectual guidance and support. We also want to recognise the contributions of Sami Lahdensuo, Programme Manager and Secretary for Track II, for his invaluable contributions throughout the process. Last but not least, we would like to extend our sincere thanks to Ana Carmen Neboisa, a graduate research assistant at the School of International Service, for doing all the technical and computer-related work involved in the production of this book.

## Notes

1 MDGs began life in the mid-1990s as the International Development Targets of the OECD's Development Assistance Committee, part of an effort to restore the credibility of aid.
2 Report of the Technical Group on Innovative Financing Mechanisms, *Action Against Hunger and Poverty*, chaired by Presidents Chirac (France) and Lula (Brazil), with the support of the governments of Spain and Chile (September 2004).

## References

Atkinson, A. (ed.). 2004. *New Sources for Development Finance*. Oxford: Oxford University Press for UNU–WIDER.

—— 2003. *Innovative Sources for Development Finance: Overarching Issues*. WIDER Discussion Paper No. 2003/88. Helsinki: World Institute for Development Economics Research of the United Nations University.

Cheru, Fantu. 2002. 'Debt, Adjustment and the politics of effective response to HIV/AIDS in Africa'. *Third World Quarterly*, 23, 2: 299–312.

Bradford, Colin I. Jr 2002. *Toward 2015: from Consensus Formation to Implementation of the Millennium Development Goals. The Historical Background: the Consensus Formation Phase: 1990–2002*. World Bank Background Paper, available from cbradford@brookings.edu.

Khor, Martin. 2001. 'Some Key Issues in Cancun'. *TWN Briefings for Cancun*, 1.

Manning, Richard. 2004. Statement by OECD Development Assistance Committee Chair, Development Committee Spring Meeting, Washington, 24–25 April.

Reisen, Helmut. 2004. *Innovative Approaches to Funding the Millennium Development Goals*. OECD Development Centre Policy Brief No. 24, Paris: OECD, pp. 27–8.

OECD DAC. 2004. Statement adopted by Members of the OECD's Development Assistance Committee. High-Level Meeting, 15–16 April, p. 3.

# 1

## Global Inequality, Poverty and Justice: Empirical and Policy Issues

### RAIMO VÄYRYNEN

### The relevance of inequality

Observations about degrees of trends in global inequality have both conceptual and empirical dimensions. In addition, these dimensions of inequality have political, institutional and normative aspects that obtain added significance through their links with the process of globalisation. In fact, inequality has become a major issue in the debates concerning globalisation and its effects on individuals, social groups, regions and nation states. The merits of globalisation are assessed, to a large degree, on the basis of whether it enhances or diminishes poverty and inequality.

In effect, poverty and inequality have become major yardsticks of the legitimacy of the globalisation process. This is evident in the Millennium Declaration and the Millennium Development Goals (MDGs) enunciated by the UN General Assembly in 2000. A similar benchmark for the success of globalisation has been set up by the World Commission on the Social Dimension of Globalisation in its recent report.

> Our primary concerns are that globalisation should benefit all countries and should raise the welfare of all people throughout the world. This implies that it should raise the rate of economic growth in poor countries and reduce world poverty, and that it should not increase inequalities or undermine socio-economic security within countries. (WCSDG 2004)

The Commission accepts inequality as a fact of life, but is opposed to its increase as a result of the opening up of national markets.

Most social theories consider equality as a necessary condition of the good life, or at least regard marked inequality as a hindrance to it. Obviously, in particular in liberal theory, equality is often confined to the political sphere, while the market system is expected to produce economic efficiency through some degree of inequality. In the past, social theories have focused primarily on the essential badness (but sometimes on the essential goodness) of inequality. Beitz (2001) notes this level of preoccupation with inequality as offering direct reasons for asserting fundamental ethical requirements. On the other hand, he speaks of derivative reasons that treat inequality as a bad thing, not in itself but because of its adverse consequences. It appears that, in recent debates, derivative reasons have assumed a central position. This ties in with the debates on globalisation, in which (in)equality is clearly a derivative reason that reflects the expansion of the market to most spheres of society.

## Conceptual and ethical issues

The first issue to be addressed here is conceptual in nature: how terms such as inequality, polarisation, poverty and justice relate to each other. Inequality is a measure of how various assets are distributed within a given system of units: as a rule, the greater the share of the rich, the smaller the share of the poor; and the weaker the middle category, the greater the degree of inequality as measured by the Gini index and similar formulas. It should be borne in mind, however, that the same value of the Gini index can be obtained from different kinds of income distribution that may, moreover, have different political connotations. In addition, the Gini index, measuring aggregate inequality, is unable to detect changes in the underlying income distribution. Therefore, it can sometimes be justified to use simpler measures, such as the ratio of total income going to the richest and the poorest 20 per cent of the world population.

Polarisation comes close to the concept of inequality, although one can make a distinction between them by saying that polarisation seems to focus more on the upper end of the distribution of assets. The concept refers literally to a pole that constitutes a central point in the system around which assets are accumulated and other actors are organised. In that sense, polarisation is akin to the concept of accumulation that, though a collective term, singles out certain dominant actors that have been able to amass power and wealth. Polarisation, however, also refers more specifically to the lower end of the distribution, where resources have remained limited despite being shared by a large number of people.

Inequality, polarisation and accumulation are collective or contextual concepts; they cannot be applied to a single individual or group. This means that they are systemic concepts and have system-wide consequences. On the other hand, poverty is an individual concept; for instance, every single individual living on less than a dollar or two a day can be described as poor. Such an individualisation of poverty should not be taken too far, however. Poverty is also a systemic concept as it affects the entire community; the rich and poor cannot avoid their interdependence. This view has significant political and policy implications: poverty cannot be eradicated without considering the functions that poor people have in society and touching upon the privileges of the richest strata (Oyen 1996).

A focus on inequality also brings in the ethical dimension. Inequality hints at exploitation, an asymmetric transaction between parties in different power positions. The ethical approach refuses to accept the point that 'inequality is nobody's fault and cannot be fixed in our lifetime' (Birdsall 1998). In particular in the study of poverty, power relations are often neglected as they would raise the issue of guilt, pointing at those responsible for the prevailing state of affairs. For this reason, the problem of power may be easier to deal with if the starting point is inequality instead of poverty, as this approach seems to focus more clearly on unfair and exploitative social relations.

Ultimately, the ethical-political perspective leads one to ask whether global inequality is, in the last instance, the mere reflection of a comprehensive Western hegemony in international relations or a natural state of affairs. Seen from this perspective, the practical struggle for global justice entails the development of feasible mechanisms by which, gradually, the superiority of industrialised countries can be diluted (Miller 1999; Dalmayr 2002; Goodin 2003).

It nevertheless appears that, while the justification of inequality can be debated, it is difficult to present a high degree of polarisation and lopsided accumulation as morally acceptable conditions. The terms of the debate easily lead to the identification of 'robber barons' and 'filthy rich' who are condemned, often not without reason, as being 'bloodsuckers' on the common people. This primitive political comment leads to the perennial issue of justice in debates concerning inequality, poverty, polarisation and their mutual relationships.

Recent policy debates have focused heavily on poverty and its reduction. One can even speak of an anti-poverty norm that has come to dominate international debates (if it has not been so conspicuous in actions). Moreover, there are extensive empirical data available on the number and percentage of people living below the poverty line, which has usually been defined as having less than one or two dollars a day available for personal consumption. In particular, the World Bank and the United Nations Development Programme (UNDP) have been active since the 1990s in dealing with the issue of poverty and means to reduce it (World Bank 2001; UNDP 2000)

In other words, many but not all people are poor because others are rich; poverty is not a natural state of affairs, but a function of deep inequities in the national and global systems. The poor and the rich may be physically segregated from each other, but there is a systemic connection between them. Obviously, this connection is both politically and empirically complex as both poverty and inequality are multidimensional concepts and phenomena that are difficult to define and measure (Nederveen Pieterse 2002; Alkire 2002).

## The choice of methods

The results of any inquiry involving inter-country comparisons are critically affected by the choice between different methods and measures. Deaton (2004) speaks with justification about the mixture of science and politics in the study of poverty. One choice needs to be made between average *per capita* figures and those weighted by population, purchasing-power parity (PPP) and actual exchange rates. The choice between these alternatives depends on the premises and purposes of analysis. If the main concern is the development of economic power relations between countries, and thus the distribution of power among the nation states, the choice of these states as units of analysis and the unadjusted real GDP *per capita* can be justified. This approach is consistent with the traditional power-politics model of international relations.

On the other hand, if the target of the study is to explore relative welfare conditions of people living in various countries, the methodological choices should be different. First, the experiences of each country should be weighted by population size, as we are interested primarily in the welfare of the people and not in the economic power of states. Second, we should pick up PPP versions of the GDP *per capita*, as these figures reflect different price levels of individual countries. In poorer countries, available income usually provides access to a bigger bundle of goods and services. In other words, standard GDP *per capita* understates the true income of least-developed countries. Presumably the choice of this approach results in a somewhat lower degree of inequality than the alternative method (Wade 2001).

Perhaps the biggest controversy concerns the choice between the estimates of poverty derived from the national accounts, and thus income figures, on the one hand, and consumption data based on household surveys on the other. The reliance on direct household surveys leads to much higher rates of poverty, and their lower decline, than the use of national accounts. One of the reasons for this is that even poor people might be able to save something and hence consumption figures result in a higher poverty rate (*Economist* 2004).

It is important to bear in mind that empirical results depend on methodological premises and choices; therefore, there are no absolute truths about poverty and inequality. All too often, the analysis deteriorates into litanies of evil inequality derived from secondary analyses, where measures and methods are mixed up without much concern for their underlying differences (Pieterse 2002; Weissmann 2003). This is not to say that the world is not an unequal place, and often grotesquely so, but that effective policy-making requires more thorough and thoughtful analyses.

Another choice to be made in empirical studies is whether income differences should simply be measured between countries, or whether intra-country differences should also be considered. A common finding in several empirical studies is that, in overall global inequality, inter-country variations play a much greater role than intra-country differences. In other words, it is more decisive for your social position whether you were born in a poor or rich country than whether you were born to a poor or rich family (Bourguignon and Morrisson 2002).

No doubt, different aspects of being an underdog reinforce each other. The worst economic fate, determined by an almost complete lack of opportunities, is to be born to a poor family in a poor country. However, the point remains that global and domestic inequalities are different phenomena and should not be conflated. In fact, some of the richest countries, especially the UK and the US, are among the most unequal in the world, while some poorer countries can be relatively equal.

This raises the perennial issue of how the domestic distribution of assets and income is associated with the structure of the global order. Structuralists tend to see domestic conditions as reflections of global inequality, because national elites are usually associated with the global economy and its benefits, even though subordinated to its operation. On the other hand, the poor, especially in the rural areas, are disconnected from the global system and, therefore, are doubly discriminated against. Thus, some empirical studies have divided China and India internally into two different 'countries', urban and rural, with markedly uneven average incomes. This raises another perennial issue: whether association with or separation from the world economy is conducive to low incomes and poverty (more on this later).

## A historical perspective

The traditional model leads one to ask how the average income of different countries has developed over time. Maddison (2001) has done the most detailed and reliable research on this matter, covering the last two millennia. One of his main points is that the year 1820 was a major turning point, after which economic development, while obviously fluctuating, has become much more dynamic. In 1820, the GDP *per capita*, measured in 1990 US dollars, was about US$1,200 dollars in Western Europe and North America, and roughly half that in Eastern Europe, Asia and Latin America. The figure for Africa was a little over US$400 dollars and remained essentially unchanged at that level from 1000 AD to the early twentieth century (the same is true for much of Asia over an even longer period of time).

The marked divergence started in the second half of the nineteenth century. In 1950, Western Europeans had reached the average income of US$4,500 dollars – though there were major country-to-country variations – while the North Americans had double that average income. Latin America had reached the *per capita* income of US$2,500, Eastern Europe US$2,100, and Japan US$1,900 dollars, while the rest of Asia languished at US$635 and Africa at US$850 dollars. By 1998, *per capita* income differences had grown even more steeply. North America was still leading the league at US$27,000 dollars, while Western Europeans and the Japanese were earning

US$18–20,000. East Europeans and Latin Americans had fallen far behind, with an average income of some US$5,500, and most of Asia and Africa were even further back, with *per capita* incomes of US$3,000 and US$1,350, respectively (Maddison 2001).

The big picture emerging from these statistics is clear: during the last two hundred years or so, there has been a major divergence in the average income levels of main regions. As a result, global income inequality has been growing historically. This growth has not been even, of course, but several countries and regions have been going through spurts of growth in *per capita* terms, including the US in the nineteenth and twentieth centuries, the Soviet Union from the 1930s to the 1970s, Japan after the 1950s, and China and India even more recently. On the other hand, Africa in particular has been a victim of slow development through the entire past two centuries. Thus, in the main, the West has been the victor in the global competition for economic welfare, while the leading Asian economies have staged a certain comeback, moving closer to the leading position they held in the fifteenth century.

Long-term intra-country distributions of income are extremely difficult to obtain, but Williamson's work (1996; 1998) provides some insights into this question. At the turn of the twentieth century, large flows of migrants critically shaped the degree of equality in the Atlantic economy. Inequality decreased dramatically in the European countries that were the main source of these emigrants, while it increased in the receiving countries such as Australia, the US and Canada. These changes resulted from the convergence of factor prices, as predicted by conventional trade theory. With deglobalisation, protectionism and economic crises, especially in the 1930s, convergence in income levels ceased and inequality increased sharply, in particular in poorer countries.

For the post-Second World War period, scholarly work suggests, in a nutshell, that if each country is treated equally and income is measured by the real GDP *per capita*, the world's income distribution has become more skewed over time. This reflects simply the fact that the distance between richer and poorer countries has continued to grow, but not in a unilinear manner. If the income per worker, rather than per person, is measured relative to the US level in 1960 and 1988, it emerges that the degree of polarisation among all states has been growing, and in quite a predictable manner. On the other hand, at the top of the global income distribution there has been a convergence in income levels, as the Asian countries especially have been catching up to the US and European countries. In other words, the core of the global economy has become somewhat more homogeneous and consolidated, while the globe as a whole has become more polarised.

## Where are we now?

Thus, there has been continuing divergence at the bottom of the league table, where several peripheral countries have even gone backwards in terms of relative economic development. The growth disasters and social crises have concentrated, first of all, in sub-Saharan Africa, where human suffering shows little sign of abating. However, if countries are weighted by their population size, the main findings are different. Two hitherto poor but populous countries, China and India, have been growing even more quickly than the US and other industrialised countries. As a result, the degree of global income inequality among nations has declined since 1960, or at least since 1978 (Jones 1997; Schultz 1998).

Similar findings are reported in a study of 38 poor and 26 rich countries. As already observed, among the rich countries, a convergence of income levels occurred in 1950–92. On the other hand, among poor countries, there has been a greater diversity of individual country experiences: some countries, especially in Asia, have made progress while others have stagnated (Sarkar 2000). Deep inequality continues to be one of the hallmarks of the current world economy.

The rising living standard of the average Chinese or Indian person means that the income of a typical citizen in developing countries has been rising relative to the level of personal income in industrialised countries. This does not, of course, mean that all countries and individuals are better off now than they were, say, a quarter-century ago. In reality, average income in many African countries has declined during this period. However, poverty in China has decreased to a quite significant degree. Estimates suggest that the share of people living on less than US$1 a day decreased in China from about one-third of the population in 1970 to less than 3 per cent in 1998. Similarly, the share of Chinese subsisting on less than US$2 a day decreased in the same time period from three-quarters to one-fifth. This positive trend coincided, however, with an increase in economic inequality in China.

Another dramatic shift happened in India, where the share of people living on less than US$1 a day decreased from 33 per cent in 1970 to less than 2 per cent in 1998. Although the incidence of poverty also decreased in Bangladesh and Pakistan, South Asia continues to be, in absolute terms, one of the seedbeds of world poverty in the world. It should also be borne in mind that, from the 1970s onwards, Indonesia has waged a very successful battle against poverty, although the financial crisis since 1997 has been a major setback. With the weakening of social safety nets, many Indonesians have slipped back into poverty. Among the major countries in the South, Nigeria is the saddest case: there, the share of people living on less than US$1 a day increased from 9 per cent in 1970 and 17 per cent in 1980 to 46 per cent in 1998. In Brazil, too, the incidence of poverty and income inequality continues to be very high (Sala-i-Martin 2002a). Milanovic (2002a) argues that Sala-i-Martin's choice of data and methods leads to flawed results.

Poverty reduction does not mean equality, however. As mentioned, there is evidence that the degree of inter-regional and social inequality has increased in China, in contrast to India where poverty reduction has happened in tandem with relatively stable income distribution (meaning that the rich have benefited as well). In China, inequality has increased since the market reforms, in both the urban and rural areas, and between them. This deterioration in equality has been contrasted with Indonesia, where, as mentioned above, adjustment was combined successfully with growth and equity from the late 1970s until the Asian financial crisis in the late 1990s (Stewart and Berry 1999).

Although there is some disagreement on the strength of the trends in income inequality within China, the following conclusion appears to be valid: 'Over the last twenty years, the incomes of the Chinese have grown, poverty rates have been reduced dramatically and income inequalities within the most populous nation in the world have increased'. Clearly, the poorest 20 per cent of Chinese citizens have benefited much less from the heady economic growth than their 'average' compatriots, not to speak of the real rich of the country (Sala-i-Martin 2002a).

This fact has a major influence on the distribution of world income. An empirical study, based on household data, concludes that the increase in world inequality up until 1993 depended on two Chinese factors. First, rapid economic growth in urban China reduced the wealth gap between it and the middle-income and rich countries. In addition, the widening gap between urban and rural China and, to a lesser extent, urban and rural India also contributes to the growth in global inequality. While it is estimated that 80 per cent of global inequality is due to inter-country differences in mean income, internal inequality, especially in China, also has a global impact (Milanovic 2002b).

In sum, global performance in the reduction of poverty and inequality appears to have been uneven. This requires us to make an effort at a more comprehensive assessment of where the trends in global economic and social welfare are pointing. Relevant data come from different sources, especially from the World Bank and other international institutions, and from academics. The institutional data can be considered relatively reliable, although two types of criticism have consistently emerged. First, various surveys are criticised for producing inconsistent conclusions because the different methods of estimation and time periods used produce wide margins of uncertainty. This criticism obviously applies to many national surveys as well. However, independent studies have tended to confirm that, with some *caveats*, most empirical findings have not been too wide of the mark. This could also be said about the controversial issue of the poverty rate in India – it does, indeed, seem to have declined quite significantly since the 1970s (Deaton 2002).

Another type of criticism pertains to the ideological agenda that the World Bank researchers are assumed to pursue. Criticism concerns, for instance, the applicability of the PPP measure to poverty assessment, and the comparability of the Bank's data over time. A part of this criticism is justified, but it also applies to most other research efforts, reflecting the inherently inadequate and incomplete nature of data on poverty and inequality. Perhaps a more serious criticism is that the Bank and its research teams are out to prove that globalisation – the open world economy – is the cause of a positive economic circuit that leads from international trade to economic growth and from there to reduction in poverty and inequality. Critics argue, for instance, that even if China and India technically would fit this pattern, they hardly pursue the neoliberal policies that the World Bank supposes to be conducive to diminishing poverty and inequality (Kiely 2004).

The main message of the World Bank is well reflected in a summary article by two of its key scholars in the field. Based on empirical data, they argue that the trend towards greater inequality lasted until the turning point of 1975, after which poverty and inequality have been reduced. Also, they claim that the number of people living in absolute poverty continued to grow until about 1980, when the trend was reversed. The main reason for these positive trends is that 'because increased trade usually accompanies more rapid growth and does not systematically change household-income distribution, it generally is associated with improved well-being of the poor'. The World Bank scholars do not argue, however, that economic globalisation alone would be able to produce the desired social effects. For these effects to be realised, one needs 'complementary measures' to support globalisation, including good institutional governance, the provision of education and health care, more development support, and less protectionism in labour-intensive sectors by the developed countries (Dollar and Kraay 2002; World Bank 2002).[1]

The real situation is more complicated, however. In fact, the World Bank relies, in its estimates of poverty, on the analysis based on household surveys that provide higher rates of poverty than alternative methods. In fact, the *Economist* has argued that the World Bank estimates, produced primarily by Martin Ravallion, exaggerate the degree of global poverty and its decline. In Ravallion's view, poverty has been largely defeated in China, but not in many other countries (*Economist* 2004).

The next step, before policy conclusions, is therefore to test the criticism that alleged positive trends in the reduction of poverty and inequality are fabricated by the methods and data used. Without going into technical details, it may be stated here that Sala-i-Martin (2002a; 2002b) has arrived at an estimate that the number of people living in severe poverty (less than US$1 a day) increased from 554 million in 1970 to close to 600 million in 1976, and then declined to 352 million in 1998. Using the US$2 definition, the corresponding figures were 1,320, 1,430 and 973 million, respectively. In the period 1970–98, the share of people in severe poverty declined from 17.2 per cent to 6.7 per cent. In another paper, using somewhat different data and techniques, the same author arrives at roughly similar conclusions: that the number and share of poor people in the world have declined significantly, even though they continue to be an embarrassingly common phenomenon in many parts of the world (Sala-i-Martin 2002a; 2002b).

Another benchmark against which we can measure the validity of the World Bank studies is a research paper by Chen and Ravallion (2000), themselves working for the Bank. As mentioned, their effort relies on household survey data on consumption poverty from 83 countries, using local currencies at PPP. Their global estimate indicates that the number of people living on less than US$1 per day increased from 1.18 billion in 1987 to 1.30 billion in 1993, then decreased to 1.20 billion in 1998. However, if China is excluded, the number of people living in absolute poverty increased rather steadily from 880 million in 1987 to 986 million in 1998. In relative terms this meant, however, a small proportional decline in the share of very poor people from 28.5 per cent to 26.2 per cent of the world population (if China is included, the decline is from 28.3 to 24.0 per cent).

Inter-regional variation, however, is quite extensive. The poverty gap index decreased in 1987–98 in East Asia, South Asia and the Middle East, increased in Eastern Europe and Central Asia, and remained about constant in Latin America and sub-Saharan Africa. If US$1 a day is used as the benchmark, the index in Africa was more than twice as high as in South Asia and five times higher than in East Asia. The differences were smaller if the benchmark was, instead, US$2 a day.

Chen and Ravallion (2000) also carried out an interesting counterfactual estimate of how much the Asian financial crisis would increase the poverty headcount if the trend continued uninterrupted. Contrary to various World Bank estimates, they found that the financial crisis in East Asia, excluding China, would increase the number of poor people by 22 or 33 million, depending on whether the US$1 or US$2 criterion of poverty was used.

The main difference between the estimates of Sala-i-Martin and Chen and Ravallion is that the number of poor people is much higher in the latter than in the former estimate, in particular if US$1 per day is used as the criterion. The figures used by the World Bank in its influential *World Development Report* (2001) on poverty are the same as those used by Chen and Ravallion, and hence probably derived from their calculations.

Moreover, Chen and Ravallion estimate the decline in absolute numbers of poor to be much slower. If China is left out, the numbers even increase – showing the pivotal importance of China's size and mix of policies in assessing trends of global poverty and inequality. Another implication of China's relative success in poverty reduction is that severe poverty is increasingly concentrated in other regions. The combined sub-Saharan African and South Asian share of people living on less than US$1 a day increased from 58.5 per cent in 1987 to 67.8 per cent in 1998. Any international action to eradicate poverty in the world must place special emphasis on these regions.

## Poverty vs inequality

As was pointed out earlier, poverty and inequality are two different matters and may co-vary independently of each other. Therefore, it is important to review various research findings concerning the degree and trends of inequality. The most ambitious study of global inequality among world citizens was conducted by Bourguignon and Morrisson, who cover the period 1820–1992. They observe that world inequality, estimated by several measures, increased continuously from 1820 to 1950, pausing only between 1910 and 1929. Global income distribution improved slightly in the first decade after 1950 and has remained quite stable since 1970 (Bourguignon and Morrisson 2002).

Thus, historically the world has been an unequal place and, over time, the situation has become worse rather than better. Inequality has not been severe enough, however, to prevent the gradual victory over poverty, which has decreased, especially in relative terms: in 1820 the share of world population living in extreme poverty was 80 per cent of the total, but by 1992 it had decreased to 24 per cent. The rise in the world population has meant, however, that the absolute number of poor people has increased until recently.

Bourguignon and Morrisson estimate that if world economic growth had been even across the countries for the entire historical period, the number of extremely poor people would be 150 million now, instead of 1.3 billion. The pivotal importance of economic growth is revealed by their conclusion that 'differences in country economic growth rates practically explain all of the increase in world income inequality and in the number of poor people'. There is ample evidence, however, that empirical investigation of the relationship between economic growth and poverty reduction is fragile, and that results depend heavily on research design (Ghura *et al.* 2002).

The conclusion, thus, is that the world is an unequal place where, in absolute terms, inequality and poverty have been increasing historically. However, in the post-Second World War era their deterioration has been halted and there has even been some improvement. Regional differences continue, however, to be stark, and in the subcontinents of South Asia and sub-Saharan Africa, especially, poverty continues to wreak havoc. Yet this does not prove that globalisation is a main cause of poverty and inequality. This calls for a separate scrutiny.

Among the industrialised countries, the degree of wage inequality varies considerably, the UK and the US being the most unequal societies, especially if compared with the countries of Northern Europe. This is reflected by the fact that across the entire wage distribution the growth of earnings has been stronger in most OECD countries than in the US. Empirical studies suggest that international trade has contributed little to income inequality in recent decades. This does not mean, of course, that there has been no migration of jobs to low-wage countries; on the contrary, the international division of labour has been in continuing flux. The primary reason for this has been the change in labour demand rather than international trade *per se*.

Owing to technological change, demand has favoured skilled workers at the expense of the less-skilled labour force, which has faced the growing risk of unemployment. The deunionisation of labour has contributed to the same tendency. However, the composition of labour demand cannot explain all wage differences, which are determined by a multitude of factors. In fact, the decline in cross-national transaction costs – ranging from transportation costs to cutbacks in tariffs – has been an important factor facilitating the transfer of low-skilled jobs from the centre to the periphery. This has enhanced skill intensity in both of these regions and tended to increase wage differences among different groups of workers. The reason behind this change is not international trade alone, however, but a combination of domestic and transnational factors (Blanchflower and Slaughter 1999; Wood 2002).

A critical issue is how international trade, foreign direct investment and short-term capital flows affect economic growth and the distribution of its results. It has been rightly pointed out that these three economic flows represent different aspects of globalisation and also have quite different consequences. International trade is more stable than capital flows, especially the short-term ones, and hence causes less unpredictable disturbances in the countries involved. In this view, the impact of international trade is mostly positive, while capital flows can also have adverse social consequences (Bhagwati 2004).

Historically, globalisation has contributed to economic growth, while protectionism has correlated with global economic stagnation. Thus a more open international economy is a positive factor, at least for the majority of countries, although it may also cause undesirable relations of dependence and social dislocation. In the aggregate, the degree of openness of the world economy does not seem to have any direct connection with trends in inequality. Economic studies have argued on both sides of the issue: globalisation has been found to result in both increased and decreased inequality.

During the first wave of globalisation, from 1870 to 1914, there was a convergence of income among the growing and globalising societies, while the distance to the rest of the world increased. On the other hand, household inequality at the beginning of the twentieth century climbed to a higher level than ever before: globalisation and growing income inequality seemed to go hand in hand. A main reason for this trend during the long period from 1820 to 1950 was the slow growth of the Asian region on the one hand and the rapid economic expansion of Europe and North America on the other. In addition, average national income was equalised among the European countries and they were also catching up with the United States (Bourguignon and Morrisson 2002).

The increase in income inequality continued during the authoritarian and protectionist period from 1914 to 1945. In combination with slow growth, rates of poverty and inequality went back to the level where they had been in the middle of the nineteenth century. In the period from 1945 to 1980, income differences among the industrialised countries decreased, but increased between them and the developing countries. Various social redistribution schemes reduced income differences in Northern societies, but had little positive influence in the South. On the global level, the degree of inequality in 1970 was about the same as it had been right after the Second World War.

More detailed evidence from developing countries shows beyond any doubt that in Latin America different waves of economic liberalisation have had a strong negative impact on income distribution. In some cases – such as Argentina, Bolivia and Venezuela – liberalisation has resulted in violent encounters between the government and protesters. In Africa, the situation has been somewhat more ambiguous. In most countries, income distribution seems to have worsened both in the urban and rural sectors, but in some cases the trend has been offset by improved agriculture–industry terms of trade (Stewart and Berry 1999). In Africa, the gap between urban and rural areas is not as wide as it is in China, although Africa is, after Latin America, otherwise the most unequal region.

Since 1980, income differences among the industrial and emerging economies have decreased, while failed and other unsuccessful countries have fallen increasingly behind. More specifically, global income inequality increased considerably in the 1960s, but has experienced a downward trend since. This is the case especially if the role of each country in global income distribution is weighted by the size of its population, as this brings in China and India as decisive factors. However, the global economic system remains deeply polarised, although the composition of income distribution among states is changing. Nothing suggests that the gap between the richest and poorest countries of the world will start decreasing any time soon.

Trends in domestic income inequality tend to vary. There is, however, substantial evidence that it has been growing in recent decades in many Asian, Latin American, East European, and some African and industrialised countries. Clearly, the forces of inequality are stronger than those of equality. Even in the short period from 1988 to 1993, the share of world income earned by the poorest decile of the world population fell by a quarter, while the share of the richest decile increased by 8 per cent, and the share of the richest 1 per cent by even more.

Empirical studies suggest that economic openness, or globalisation, does not have any systematic relationship with the degree of domestic inequality, especially in developed countries. However, globalisation has clearly contributed to the massive increase in inequality in China and also appears to be associated with greater inequality in many of the least-developed countries (World Bank 2002; Bhatta 2002). On the other hand, many deglobalised countries have a high degree of inequality as traditional hierarchies and authoritarian practices keep large groups of people subordinated without the benefits they could derive from the market. The fact is that the share of developing countries in world trade has been declining, despite the increase of their manufactured exports: most of these countries have great difficulty in gaining access to the markets of developed countries, which are protected by tariffs and other restrictive practices (Kiely

2004). Without a more active and balanced engagement in the world economy these countries have a very slim chance of better growth and equality.

The conclusion, then, appears to be that both the absolute and the relative incidence of poverty, while still pervasive, are declining in the world. This means that, on the global level, the Millennium Development Goal of poverty reduction may well be attainable by 2015. In some regions, especially in sub-Saharan Africa, Eastern Europe and the CIS states, the target seems to be moving away, however. A few success stories from these regions are not enough to reverse the dismal trend (UNDP 2004). It should be borne in mind, though, that not all assessments agree on the decline of global poverty. We have noted that Chen and Ravallion, and the World Bank with them, see little progress in the 1990s.

It appears that, by encouraging economic growth and the spread of technology and knowledge, globalisation has helped, in a limited way, to reduce poverty in many countries. However, poverty continues to worsen in countries suffering from war and humanitarian crises, and those either cut off from the world economy or integrated with it in a lopsided manner due, for instance, to the dominance of raw material or fuel exports. Overall, as pointed out by Chen and Ravallion, 'the 1990s did not see much progress against consumption poverty in the developing world'.

A main reason for this is that growing inequality has wiped out the gains to the poor from economic growth. Either initial inequality, or its subsequent increase, tends to undermine the positive effects of poverty-reducing growth. If inequality is high, the benefits of economic growth tend to go to the highest strata of the society and those on the bottom rungs of income distribution will continue to lag behind (Chen and Ravallion 2000). Thus poverty reduction can work only if the trend towards international and national inequality is arrested.

Yet the degree of global inequality has remained pervasive, and has even continued to increase. In domestic contexts, inequality levels have been uneven and have been affected by the policies pursued by individual governments. While globalisation has helped to reduce poverty in the aggregate, it has been unable to have a similar impact on international and national inequality and may even have increased inequality in the most vulnerable societies. Empirical investigations suggest that international trade has a weak negative association with equality, while foreign direct investment might be linked to its slight improvement (Bhatta 2002). In general, however, there are good reasons to agree with the statement that 'it is extremely difficult to assess the impact of liberalisation on income distribution' (Stewart and Berry 1999).

The critics of globalisation argue that inequality is built into the nature of 'disciplinary neoliberalism' which imposes political constraints on all national or international redistributive policies. There is even an effort to 'constitutionalise inequality' by new rules and institutions banning the exercise of political alternatives (Gill 2002). While this point is exaggerated, it refers to a central dilemma: global economic growth cannot be made more balanced, nor poverty alleviated, until the growth in international and national inequities is reversed. Global redistribution of resources is a key to sustainable globalisation.

This task has been formulated as a moral imperative. In a nuanced analysis, Pogge (2002) argues that world poverty should not be thought of in terms of helping the poor, an activity engaged in by the most charitable among us. Instead, he stresses the need to address the nature of the global order and make sure that it is not benefiting us through the harm it imposes on poor people. Thus a main task of developed countries and their citizens is the responsibility to protect the poor from the unjust effects of global rules.

## Future work

There is no lack of recommendations on how the markets and state institutions should be made more responsive to poor people, and globalisation thus more inclusive. It is difficult to avoid the impression that there are at least two, almost diametrically opposed, approaches to poverty reduction. The *public policy approach* pays most attention to the redistribution of resources by taxation, social transfers and other means, from the top to the bottom of the income pyramid. On the international level such a policy of equalisation also focuses on the transfer of resources by development assistance, taxation of international transactions, and other political measures.

In this approach public policy is basically a welfare policy that aims to meet the basic needs of poor people and keep income differences within reasonable limits. A weakness of the public policy approach is that its implementation requires an effective and impartial public administration that implements faithfully the relevant policy decisions. Such an administrative structure rarely exists in poor and unequal countries, nor is there international machinery to manage and redistribute taxes on transactions. Apart from the efficiency concerns, there is also predictable neoliberal political opposition to the policy of national and international equalisation.

Another dominant approach to poverty reduction advocates *market-oriented reforms*. Its key conviction is that by removing unnecessary political constraints on the free operation of national and international markets, the poor will ultimately benefit from wealth creation and the trickle-down effect. The evidence in favour of this argument is at best limited. Economic growth is no doubt needed to reduce poverty, but in a context of power asymmetries and economic inequality the efforts to alleviate poverty produce only limited results. Thus, neither the public policy nor the market approach can alone provide adequate direction for sufficient reduction in poverty and misery.

This conclusion is by no means new; indeed, there is almost a consensus behind it. The recognition of this fact has resulted in a 'newspeak' on the need for empowerment, private–public partnerships, networking and new entrepreneurship. The basic idea is to mobilise the private sector, perhaps especially small or medium-sized enterprises (SMEs), and integrate their activities into the everyday lives of the poor sections of the population. This calls for access to skills, employment, communication, market opportunities and microcredits as well as new socially conscious and impartial legislation. What is needed is an enabling social and political environment where companies operate in a responsible manner (UNDP 2004).

This approach, while offering several useful guidelines as the elimination of poverty without an active market society, is not a feasible goal. The poor are involved everyday in markets; the challenge is how to make them serve the cause of poverty reduction better. This cannot happen without partnership, nationally and internationally, between the private and public sectors. Such a partnership must provide a chance for the reasonable freedom of the market to operate, but the market actors must, on the other hand, accept the fact that the reduction in both poverty and inequality requires public intervention in the operation of the market system. The necessary compromise is very difficult to reach as it requires a lot from the decision makers on both sides of the fence.

On this basis national and international strategies have been devised to provide complementary policies by which the adverse effects of globalisation on poverty and inequality can be prevented or mitigated (World Bank 2001). These strategies fall into three main categories:

1 Comprehensive provision of resources for equal development (including domestic sources of funding, international trade, development assistance, private flows and debt relief);

2 Restructuring existing international rules and institutions in a manner such that the interests of developing countries, and especially the poor people in them, are better protected than today; and

3 Development of innovative means to support developing countries and their efforts at better political governance and economic policies. Bad policies produce bad markets and vice versa.

These strategies are very broad and they can have positive effects only if the norm of poverty reduction is taken seriously and made a cornerstone of international policy. Poverty alleviation cannot succeed, however, unless it is closely linked with the attack on inequality and polarisation, both on the national and international levels.

It is not necessarily very helpful to make politics out of poverty, as this may lead to flawed analysis and bad policies. It is important to note that inequality is an important reason for poverty and an obstacle to its reduction. When we speak of polarisation, the key issue is not the existence of a few super-rich people, but the shape of the entire income distribution. To make the world more livable for everyone, redistribution is a necessity. This should be done primarily by domestic means, but in the context of the present global structure, redistribution of resources also requires international support.

## Note

1 Galbraith *et al.* (2002) criticise various aspects of the Dollar and Kraay article, including their data on inequality, the operationalisation of globalisers and causal interpretations. See also Ravallion 2004.

## References

Alkire, Sabina. 2002. 'Dimensions of Human Development'. *World Development*, 30, 2: 181–205.

Beitz, Charles R. 2001. 'Does Global Inequality Matter?' *Metaphilosophy*, 32, 1–2: 95–112.

Bhagwati, Jagdish. 2004. *In Defence of Globalisation*. New York: Oxford University Press.

Bhatta, Saurav Dev. 2002. 'Has the Increase in World-Wide Openness to Trade Worsened Global Income Inequality?' *Papers in Regional Science*, 81, 2: 185.

Birdsall, Nancy. 1998. 'Life is Unfair: Inequality in the World'. *Foreign Policy*, 111: 73–94.

Blanchflower, David G. and Matther J. Slaughter. 1999. 'The Causes and Conse-quences of Changing Income Inequality', in Albert Fishflow and Karen Parker (eds.), *Growing Apart: the Causes and Consequences of Global Wage Inequality*. New York: Council on Foreign Relations, pp. 67–94.

Bourguignon, François and Christian Morrisson. 2002. 'Inequality among World Citizens, 1820–1992'. *American Economic Review*, 92, 4: 727–44.

Chen, Shaohua and Martin Ravallion. 2000. 'How Did the World's Poor Fare in the 1990s?' World Bank Research Paper, Washington, DC: World Bank. http://econ.worldbank.org/docs/1164.pdf.

Dalmayr, Fred. 2002. 'Globalisation and Inequality. A Plea for Global Justice'. *International Studies Review*, 4, 2: 137–51.

Deaton, Angus. 2002. 'Is World Poverty Falling?' *Finance and Development*, 39: 2
—— 2004. 'Measuring Poverty'. Princeton University, January. http://www.wws.princeton.edu/~deaton/papers.html.

Dollar, David and Aart Kraay. 2002. 'Spreading the Wealth'. *Foreign Affairs*, 81, 1: 120–33.

*The Economist*. 2004. 'More or Less Equal?' *The Economist* (13 March): 73–5.

Galbraith, James K., Joe W. Pitts III and Andrew Wells-Dang. 2002. 'Is Inequality Decreasing? Debating the Wealth and Poverty of Nations'. *Foreign Affairs*, 81, 4: 178–83.

Ghura, Dhansehwar, Carlos A. Leite and Charalambos Tsangarides. 2002. 'Is Growth Enough? Macroeconomic Policy and Poverty Reduction'. IMF Working Paper WP/02/118. Washington, DC: International Monetary Fund.

Gill, Stephen. 2002. 'Constitutionalising Inequality and the Clash of Globali-sations'. *International Studies Review*, 4, 2: 47–66.

Goodin, Robert E. 2003. 'Globalising Justice', in David Held and Mathias Koenig-Archibugi (eds.), *Taming Globalisation. Frontiers of Governance*. Cambridge: Polity, pp. 68–92.

Human Development Report. 2003. *Millennium Development Goals: a Compact to End Human Poverty*. New York: Oxford University Press/UNDP, pp. 50–3.

Jones, Charles I. 1997. 'On the Distribution of the World Income'. *Journal of Economic Perspectives*, 11, 3: 19–24.

Kiely, Ray. 2004. 'The World Bank and Global Poverty Reduction: Good Policies or Bad Data?' *Journal of Contemporary Asia*, 34, 1: 3–20.

Maddison, Angus. 2001. 'The World Economy: a Millennial Perspective'. Paris: Organisation for Economic Cooperation and Development, 44–48, 264.

Milanovic, Branko. 2002a. 'The Ricardian Vice: Why Sala-i-Martin's Calculations of World Income Inequality Are Wrong'. Washington, DC: World Bank. November.

—— 2002b. 'True World Income Distribution, 1988 and 1993: First Calculation Based on Household Surveys Alone'. *Economic Journal*, 112, 1: 51–92.

Miller, David. 1999. 'Justice and Global Inequality', in Andrew Hurrell and Ngaire Woods (eds.), *Inequality, Globalisation and World Politics*. Oxford: Oxford University Press, pp. 187–210.

Pieterse, Jan Nederveen. 2002. 'Global Inequality: Bringing Politics Back In'. *Third World Quarterly*, 23, 6: 1036–9.

Pogge, Thomas W. 2002. *World Poverty and Human Rights: Cosmopolitan Responsibilities and Reforms*. Cambridge: Polity Press.

Oyen, Else. 1996. 'Poverty Research Rethought', in Else Oyen, S. M. Miller and Syed Abdus Samad (eds.), *Poverty: a Global Review*. Oslo: Scandinavian University Press, pp. 3–17.

Ravallion, Martin. 2004. 'Pessimistic on Poverty?' *The Economist* (10 April): 70.

Sala-i-Martin, Xavier. 2002a. 'The World Distribution of Income (Estimated from Individual Country Distributions)'. Working Paper 8933, Cambridge, MA: National Bureau of Economic Research, pp. 9–12 and 38–43.

—— 2002b, 'The Disturbing "Rise" of Global Income Inequality'. Working Paper 8904, Cambridge, MA: National Bureau of Economic Research, pp. 16–20.

Sarkar, Prabirjit. 2000. 'North–South Uneven Development. What the Data Show'. *Review*, 23, 4: 439–57.

Schultz, T. P. 1998. 'Inequality and Distribution of Personal Income in the World: How It Is Changing and Why'. *Journal of Population Economics*, Vol. II, Issue 3, pp. 307–44.

Stewart, Francis and Albert Berry. 1999. 'Globalisation, Liberalisation, and Inequality: Expectations and Experience', in Andrew Hurrell and Ngaire Woods (eds.), *Inequality, Globalisation and World Politics*. Oxford: Oxford University Press, pp. 174–80.

UNDP. 2000. *Poverty Report 2000: Overcoming Human Poverty*. New York: United Nations Development Programme.

—— 2004. *Unleashing Entrepreneurship: Making Business Work for the Poor*. New

York: United Nations Development Programme.

Wade, Robert. 2001. 'Winners and Losers'. *The Economist* (28 April): 74–6.

Weissmann, Robert. 2003. 'Grotesque Inequality: Corporate Globalisation and the Global Gap between Rich and Poor'. *Multinational Monitor* (July/August): 9–17.

Williamsson, Jeffrey G. 1996. 'Globalisation, Convergence and History'. *Journal of Economic History*, 56, 2: 277–306.

—— 1998. 'Growth, Distribution and Demography: Some Lessons from History'. *Explorations in Economic History*, 35, 2: 256–8.

Wood, Adrian. 2002. 'Globalisation and Wage Inequalities: a Synthesis of Three Theories'. *Weltwirtschaftliches Archiv*, 138, 1: 54–82.

World Bank. 2001. *Attacking Poverty: World Development Report 2000/2001*. New York: Oxford University Press/World Bank, pp. 21–6.

—— 2002 'Globalisation, Growth and Poverty. Building an Inclusive World Economy'. New York: Oxford University Press/World Bank, pp. 24–31, 46–51.

World Commission on the Social Dimension of Globalisation (WCSDG). 2004. *A Fair Globalisation. Creating Opportunities for All*. Geneva: International Labour Organisation, p. 35.

# 2

## Development Financing through ODA: Trends, Financing Gaps, and Challenges

### TONY ADDISON, GEORGE MAVROTAS
### and MARK MCGILLIVRAY[1]

The final declaration of the 2002 UN Financing for Development conference in Monterrey emphasised the importance of mobilising more resources (both official and private) to meet internationally agreed development objectives. The Millennium Development Goals (MDGs) are now the central goals guiding policy and action in this area. Private financial flows, including portfolio flows and foreign direct investment, are essential for stimulating the private investment that is in turn vital for reducing poverty through employment and livelihood generation. Official flows finance public infrastructure and services that encourage private investment, as well as public spending on services that are essential to improving human development indicators. Official flows therefore complement private flows and enhance their effectiveness. If development finance works well and poor countries develop successfully, their reliance on official development assistance (ODA) will decline over time and private flows will assume the primary role of driving economic growth. That growth will in turn deliver the rising revenue base to fund public spending on human development, and eventually domestic revenues can replace ODA as the main source of finance for public spending. But before they reach self-sustaining economic growth, poor countries need ODA to accelerate their development, since they are often unattractive to international investors. This is especially so in sub-Saharan Africa where ODA accounted for almost 90 per cent of total capital flows over the years 1991–2002 (OECD 2004).

This chapter deals with key priorities in connection with the Helsinki Process on the theme 'Development Finance for Millennium Development Goals' which is part of Track II of the Process, the Global Economic Agenda. It addresses the most traditional source of development finance, namely ODA, but also a new proposal for development financing, the International Finance

Facility (IFF). In what follows we discuss key issues in this area and set out some priorities that need to be addressed within the context of the Helsinki Process. The chapter also discusses recent ODA projections and scenarios in relation to implementing the MDGs. In suggesting priorities we have tried to bear in mind the urgency of the issues as well as their political feasibility, reflecting discussion during the Track II meetings.

## The rationale for aid

The last few years have seen important developments within the aid scene and a changing landscape for aid. The 1996 report of the OECD's Development Assistance Committee (DAC) on *Shaping the Twenty-first Century: the Contribution of Development Cooperation* set out new priorities for aid (OECD 1996). In particular it strengthened the link between aid and poverty reduction through the International Development Targets, especially the commitment to halve absolute poverty by 2015, thereby laying the foundations for the MDGs. The World Bank study *Assessing Aid*, published in 1998, exercised a considerable, albeit controversial, influence on bilateral donors, and stimulated a new and vigorous research literature on aid effectiveness (see World Bank 1998 and further discussion below). The UN system also became increasingly active in development finance, starting with the report of the panel chaired by President Ernesto Zedillo of Mexico, which estimated that an additional US$50 billion would be required annually to achieve the international development goals (UN 2001); the Monterrey Financing for Development conference followed in 2002. Since then there has been a UNU–WIDER study on creating new and innovative sources of finance, which was presented to the UN General Assembly in 2004 (Atkinson 2004) and the UN Millennium Project report, which will guide the Millennium summit to be held later in 2005 (UN Millennium Project 2005). Meanwhile, the Declaration on Aid Harmonisation by aid donors in Rome in February 2003, the UK's IFF proposal, the UK-sponsored Africa Commission, the US Millennium Challenge Account, and the Action Against Hunger and Poverty Initiative of the governments of Brazil, Chile, France and Spain are all major steps forward.

While it would be too bold to claim that there is anything approaching a complete consensus on development finance (the United Kingdom and the United States differ over the IFF, for example) we can nevertheless discern some broad contours of agreement. First, and most fundamentally, there is now widespread agreement that aid works. More specifically, it is agreed that in most aid-receiving countries growth would be lower in the absence of aid and, by implication, poverty would be higher. This is not, however, to imply that aid could not have worked better or that reforms to aid design and delivery are not required. Second, while the MDGs certainly need considerably more development finance for their achievement, aid-recipient countries must also do their best to mobilise domestic resources by improving taxation and revenue-raising institutions and by encouraging the growth of the domestic financial system (which can then mobilise domestic savings to finance private-sector investment which is vital for the employment generation necessary to meet the MDG poverty targets). Third, countries and their donor partners must work to improve aid effectiveness, both in achieving poverty reduction through economic growth (and raising the benefits of growth for the poor by investing in their capabilities and livelihoods) and by financing pro-poor public spending on services and infrastructure targeted on poor people and their communities (especially in the areas of primary health care, primary education, and safe water and sanitation).

Fourth, aid must work to strengthen fiscal management, since without effective, accountable, and transparent public expenditure management we cannot expect increased aid or domestic revenues to achieve the necessary increase in pro-poor expenditures (McGillivray and Morrissey 2004; Reinikka and Svensson 2004). Improved fiscal management is in turn integral to the broader but imperative task of state building itself, since without resources all of the present weaknesses that bedevil government administrations in poor countries will continue, in particular the corruption and low morale that result from inadequate salaries and the inability to recruit and retain essential skills (Kayizzi-Mugerwa 2003). Fifth, public money in the form of aid must do its best to leverage additional private money as well, through increased foreign direct investment, commercial bank lending and portfolio flows (aid in the form of technical assistance in the areas of commercial law, banking and finance is therefore important). Sixth, additional aid will enhance the benefits of debt relief under the Heavily Indebted Poor Countries (HIPC) Initiative. Indeed, if more debt relief is offset by lower aid (as some observers fear) then debt relief will have only modest benefits for growth and poverty reduction (Hansen 2004).

In summary, these five broad areas of agreement represent a substantial foundation upon which to go forward in designing more effective aid policies and in mobilising political and public support for increased aid flows. Still, there remains a fundamental scepticism in some quarters – notably in the conservative media in the United States – regarding aid's ability to generate growth and development. In part this scepticism rests on a misreading of the history of aid in which examples of failed aid programmes – notably aid given in the 1970s and early 1980s to African dictatorships such as Mobutu's Zaïre and Siyad Barre's Somalia – are used to condemn aid in general and aid to Africa in particular (thereby also ignoring African success in advancing democratisation over the last decade, which changes the political context for using aid effectively). But individual examples of aid failure no more demolish the case for aid than individual business failures demolish the case for promoting entrepreneurship. Scepticism also arises from a profound ideological distrust of the role of the state in development, and therefore of any form of finance, such as official aid, that goes to states. But this ignores historical examples of successful aid programmes, notably that of US assistance in reconstructing South Korea following the Korean War, as well as the limitations of private charity as a form of development finance. Although philanthropy is very important as a means of helping individuals and local communities in poor countries, philanthropy cannot finance large-scale infrastructure (ports, highways, etcetera) and national-level programmes of education and health.

We would submit that aid policy needs to be based on rigorous research to understand aid's development effects and not on the selective use of country examples or on ideological bias. Indeed, when one examines the research that has been undertaken a clear conclusion can be reached, namely that aid is broadly effective in raising growth (Morrissey 2001; McGillivray 2003; and Clemens *et al.* 2004 for reviews of the literature). In so far as growth generates more employment and livelihood opportunities for the poor – and this of course needs every possible form of enhancement, from micro-projects up to large-scale spending on education and health – then aid can be said to reduce poverty. A large measure of consensus therefore exists within the research community over aid's effectiveness. Where there has been disagreement among researchers is over the role of recipient-government policy in making aid effective; the World Bank's *Assessing Aid* study, and the associated work by Burnside and Dollar (2000) and Collier and Dollar (2004) emphasises the importance of a 'good' policy environment to aid effectiveness, while Hansen and Tarp (2000) and Guillamont and Chauvet (2001) cast doubt on the statistical robustness of the World Bank's results. Irrespective of whether policy is important for aid effectiveness, it must be emphasised that both groups of studies agree that aid works, in one way or another.

More fundamentally, we need to unpack the concept of 'good policy', a phrase that tends to be trotted out in donor circles without much reflection on what it actually means. There is a large measure of consensus that the maintenance of basic macroeconomic stability (that is, avoiding hyper-inflation) and the avoidance of certain types of gross price distortion (in particular those that lower agricultural producer incentives) are conducive to growth in poor countries. This does not imply, however, that the growth benefits of such policies are necessarily large: countries can achieve macro-economic stability but see only modest gains in *per capita* income if structural impediments to growth – lack of infrastructure, limited human capital, and weak institutions – remain in place. Thus in agriculture, one of the most crucial sectors for Africa's overall development, output and income may recover following the elimination of gross price distortions, but recovery will start to 'top out' as smallholders reach their production frontiers (the maximum level of output that they can hope to achieve with the best use of their resources). What then become crucial are the policies and investments (some financed by aid) that push their production frontier out: new seeds and crop technologies; better systems of input delivery; and support and investment in the livelihoods of Africa's female farmers (see Sachs 2005 for a recent restatement of the importance of appropriate technologies to tropical development). The devil of good policy is then in the detail of *sectoral* policies and, critically, in the creation of effective *institutions* that develop and implement 'good policy'. Institutions in turn require resources, and aid has a valuable role to play in institution building.

## ODA: recent trends and projections

Anyone with an understanding of aid's development effectiveness must review trends in aid flows with a heavy heart. One basic fact stands out, and that is the parsimony of the wealthy: whilst the economies of the developed countries have more than doubled in size over the past 30 years, they have in recent years spent a smaller proportion of their GNP on ODA than at any time since the 1960s. ODA measured as a share of the OECD–DAC members' combined gross national income (GNI) was 0.25 per cent in 2003, well below the average of 0.33 per cent achieved over the period 1980–92 (OECD 2005). This yielded ODA of US$69 billion in 2003, whereas if aid donors were to meet the UN ODA target of 0.7 per cent, some US$175 billion would result – more than double the present level, and more than enough to fill the present gap in financing the MDGs. There are of, course, notable and honourable exceptions such as Denmark, Luxembourg, the Netherlands, Norway and Sweden, which have met, and indeed exceeded, the 0.7 per cent target (OECD 2005). But the world's two largest aid donors by volume, the United States and Japan, have ODA–GNI ratios of only 0.15 and 0.20 per cent respectively (OECD 2005). And Finland has the lowest aid ratio among the Nordic donors (0.35 per cent).

Moreover, the country aid allocations of some major donors are not in line with their professed commitment to the world's poor. Thus in the case of European development cooperation, the EU accounts for more than 50 per cent of the world's total ODA, with about 75 per cent of the total EU ODA provided by its member states (see Grimm 2004).[2] Yet, despite being a major player in development, the EU listed no SSA countries, no least developed country and only two non-European countries (Morocco and Tunisia) amongst its top ten recipients of aid in 2001.

Figure 2.1 shows the trend in aid flows to sub-Saharan Africa from 1960 to 2002. Beginning in the early 1990s, sub-Saharan Africa saw a fall in the volume of aid which has remained below its 1990 level until only recently. Aid to sub-Saharan Africa fell as world aid contracted and as donors allocated away from the region and towards Europe and East Asia, resulting in a real 8.8 per cent aid loss for Africa during the 1990s (OECD 2004). This decline in Africa's share of total aid is not what we would expect, given the region's progress in democratisation over the decade and the intensive efforts by African governments to turn their economies around through policy reform.

As Figure 2.1 shows, sub-Saharan Africa has shared in the recent recovery of world aid flows, which saw total ODA increase from US$58.3 billion in 2002 to US$69 billion in 2003 (OECD 2005). The aid picture has become somewhat more positive and donors are expected to increase their aid until

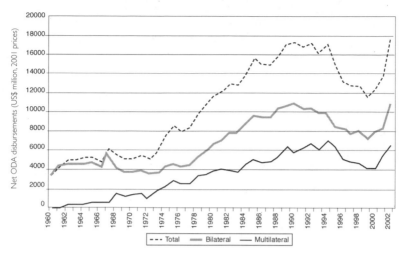

Figure 2.1 Aid flows to sub-Saharan Africa, 1960–2002

2006, the target date for commitments made at the Monterrey Conference on Financing for Development. In this regard, a number of countries have recently committed to raising their ODA–GNI ratios, including Sweden and Norway, which aim to achieve 1 per cent by 2006 and 2006–2009 respectively (up from their 2003 ratios of 0.79 per cent and 0.92 per cent). Belgium, Canada, Finland, France, Ireland, Spain, the UK and Switzerland have also promised to raise their aid. The OECD–DAC expects that, if all these promises are fulfilled, ODA will pass US$100 billion (at 2003 prices and exchange rates) by 2010 (OECD 2005).

Nevertheless, despite the recent increase in aid volumes it is apparent that some donors are 'talking up' what are in fact modest commitments, and the blunt fact remains that donors as a whole are devoting less to aid (as a proportion of their national income) than they did twenty years ago. The lengthy dip in aid volumes to sub-Saharan Africa during the 1990s has set back the prospects of achieving the MDGs in the region, since more could have been done for the poor if aid flows had been higher over the last decade. This amounts to missed opportunities to invest in basic health care, primary education, and safe water and sanitation. Donors must bear some of the responsibility for countries where human development indicators regressed rather than progressed in the 1990s, since financial constraints limited the ability of countries to take urgent action (particularly in meeting the enormous challenge of HIV/AIDS, which is devastating southern Africa in particular).

## The International Finance Facility (IFF)

As we noted earlier, there has recently been much discussion regarding the creation of new and innovative sources of finance to supplement ODA and to

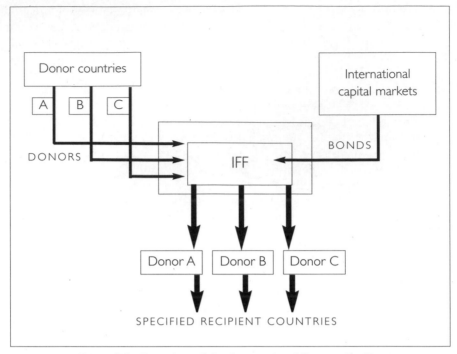

**Figure 2.2 Overview of the International Finance Facility**

Source: HM Treasury–DfID 2003.

meet the large financing gap that now exists for the MDGs (Atkinson 2004). Here we discuss one of the most prominent proposals, namely the International Finance Facility as set out by Her Majesty's Treasury and the Department for International Development (DfID) in January 2003 (HM Treasury–DfID 2003). Our analysis of the advantages and disadvantages draws on Mavrotas (2005).

The IFF aims to accelerate financing for the MDGs by frontloading aid, thereby guaranteeing long-term, but conditional, donor funding for the poorest countries. Long-term pledges of a flow of annual payments to the IFF would leverage additional money from the international capital markets (through a securitisation process), achieving a flow of US$50 billion for 2010–15, building up from 2006 and falling to zero by 2020. Figure 2.2 provides an overview of the IFF and its processes.

The IFF has several advantages. The first is its *revenue-raising potential*. The Facility could double existing ODA from US$50 billion to US$100 billion per year during the crucial years of 2010–15, thereby meeting much of the MDG financing gap. The IFF's second advantage is that it delivers a *predictable and stable aid flow* that minimises the significant and negative effects associated with the present situation of often unpredictable and volatile aid flows (Fielding and Mavrotas 2005). Aid is often among the most volatile sources of foreign-exchange income (Gemmel and McGillivray 1998; Pallage and Robe 2001) and aid volatility has significant and negative effects on growth (Lensink and Morrissey 2000; Bulí and Hamann 2003). Third, unlike the US Millennium Challenge Account, the IFF does not deal with recipient countries on a bilateral basis only; it therefore enhances *multilateralism* in aid provision. Finally, the *securitisation principle* for raising finance through the international capital markets is tried and tested.

In summary, the IFF can significantly raise aid flows: the amount is equivalent to an average aid ratio of 0.47 per cent of donor GNP, a substantial increase from the current level (but still below the 0.7 per cent UN target that would yield US$175 billion at present levels of donor GDP). But one of the IFF's potential strengths – the fact that it is based on multilateral aid provision – is also the source of its weakness: to work, the IFF requires substantial political agreement for its creation and then sustained donor co-operation over the Facility's lifetime. Moreover, for the IFF to increase the *total* amount of development finance, commitments must be *additional* to those for existing aid programmes. This entails additional organisational costs to monitor any international treaty governing the creation and operation of the IFF. But it would be difficult (if not impossible) to guarantee that the money committed through the IFF would be additional to ODA flows, given the long lifetime of the scheme.

EU countries are politically the most likely to press ahead if the UK can persuade them (France and Italy are supportive), but one as yet unresolved problem is whether the IFF is consistent with the EU's stability and growth pact, which aims to contain the fiscal deficits and debt levels of member states (Germany appears to be wary on these grounds). The UK intention is to have the IFF bonds accounted for on the books of a new IFF agency, but if the bonds are counted as liabilities in the accounts of participating governments then their debt-to-GDP ratio will rise. This will pose a problem for several EU members, including Germany, that have effectively breached the fiscal ceilings (the so-called 'Maastricht criteria') set by the EU's stability and growth pact, and which are under political pressure to reign in their debt levels. The US is very sceptical but UK Chancellor Gordon Brown is hoping to get approval for a US$4 billion pilot version of the IFF at the Group of Eight summit in Scotland in July 2005.

There is also an issue of donor coordination on disbursing the IFF funds. Since the bilateral and multilateral channels for delivering IFF money will vary (see Figure 2.2), and since each of these channels attaches different conditions to the use of the funds, in practice recipients will be faced by a variety of donor conditionalities. Hence the multilateralism of the IFF would be reinforced on the disbursement side of the operation if donors work together (and with their country partners) to create a greater consensus on aid conditionality and disbursement practices. This would also increase the ability of recipients to absorb aid and to use it effectively, since they would

not have to devote so many scarce resources to meeting the varying conditionality and reporting practices of donors.

## New priorities and challenges in the area of ODA

Following our discussion of aid effectiveness, and having reviewed aid trends
and projections as well as the IFF, we now turn to consider two major new
priorities and challenges in the area of ODA. These are the role of aid in
fragile states and the absorption of aid as well as aid heterogeneity.

### Aid in fragile states

In addition to the global economic agenda, the Helsinki Process in its work
has also focused on the urgent issues of peace and governance, while the
recent report of the UN High Level Panel on Threats, Challenges and Change
has highlighted the interactions between security and development (UN
2004). Meanwhile, the work of Collier and Hoeffler (2004) for the Copenhagen
Consensus has quantified the immense cost of civil wars for economic development. The cost of a civil war in a typical developing country is at least US$
64.2 billion, including the value of lost output as well as the value of the lost
life and health (Collier and Hoeffler 2004: 135). This is roughly equal to the
total flow of aid (US$69 billion) in 2003.

Conflict is an especially important issue in Africa, which in the 1990s saw
19 major armed conflicts ranging from civil wars to the 1998–2000 war
between Eritrea and Ethiopia (Addison 2003). In addition to the tragic loss of
life, war is another claim on scarce aid resources. Humanitarian ODA assistance stands at about US$5.5 billion per year and has been at that level since
1999 (currently 10 per cent of ODA compared to 3 per cent over the period
1970–90). However, official data significantly understate total spending on
humanitarian programmes – recent data indicate that humanitarian aid is
twice as high as the official aid figures seem to suggest (US$10 billion in
2001 if spending coming from non-DAC donors, NGOs, UN agencies and
international organisations is included).

By the end of the 1990s there was a marked reluctance among donors to
get involved in the conflict countries, beyond humanitarian assistance (the
major exception was the Balkans, which benefited from the diversion of aid
from Africa). Inevitably, the poorer conflict countries score low marks when
judged by World Bank criteria of 'good policy' and, with the end of the Cold
War, the United States was increasingly indifferent to Africa – the region
with some of the worst civil wars. However, the geopolitics of aid shifted once
again with the 9/11 terrorist attacks on the United States and the subsequent overthrow of the Taliban regime in Afghanistan, pushing 'nation
building' back to the top of the mainstream aid and foreign policy agenda
(Fukuyama 2004). This has, in turn, led to a new and recent debate within
the donor community on aid to so-called 'fragile states': those in, at risk of or
rather shakily emerging from, conflict (Addison and McGillivray 2004).

The debate so far has taken some strange twists and turns. Donors, having convinced themselves of the World Bank view that 'good' policy is essential to aid effectiveness (see our earlier discussion), are now closely involved in a set of countries with histories of policy turmoil – from which, nevertheless, they cannot walk away. Thus, whereas the international community, including the United States and Europe, could largely ignore Afghanistan's distress prior to 9/11, it must now get Afghanistan back on its feet – otherwise Al Qaeda will quickly re-establish itself (thereby destabilising neighbouring Pakistan as well). Consequently, net ODA to Afghanistan from all sources has risen from US$0.4 billion in 2001 to US$1.5 billion in 2003 (OECD 2005). Likewise, in the Pacific region Australia has a strong political interest in strengthening the Solomon Islands and Papua New Guinea, both of which receive large amounts of Australian aid.

From the perspective of the MDGs the fragile states are critical, since they are, almost by their very definition, the least likely to meet the MDG targets. And if they show little progress in reducing poverty – or indeed if their poverty increases (which is conceivable) – then they are likely to become politically more unstable, thereby offering excellent opportunities for local warlords, organised crime and international terrorists. Poverty provides a ready recruiting ground, as the so-called 'new wars' in West Africa demonstrated in the 1990s (Kaldor 1999). This poses a major dilemma for donors since *reconstructing* pre-existing state institutions is a less demanding task than *transforming* state institutions, but the latter is essential for development and stability if countries have histories in which state institutions were used to heavily favour one ethnic or regional group over another. State transformation is a much more invasive task than simple state reconstruction, and one which raises major ethical dilemmas for donors (Addison 2000; Addison and McGillivray 2004). Nowhere is this more evident than in Iraq, where net aid is about US$2.3 billion (OECD 2005).

## The absorption of aid and aid heterogeneity

While the evidence shows that aid is positively associated with growth (see our discussion earlier) it does appear that aid is subject to diminishing returns: as aid increases relative to the recipient's GDP, its effect on growth is positive, but there comes a point after which the growth effect turns negative (see for instance Collier and Hoeffler 2002; Hansen and Tarp 2000; Lensink and White 2000). The range of estimates for the point at which diminishing returns sets in is very broad, ranging from 15 to 45 per cent of recipient GDP (McGillivray 2003). Diminishing returns to aid have been interpreted as indicating limited absorptive capacities, with recipient governments being constrained in the amounts of aid they can use effectively (Clemens *et al.* 2004; Heller and Gupta 2002). It may be the case that very large amounts of aid have a distorting effect akin to that of other large resource inflows if the real exchange rate appreciates – thereby reducing the private sector's incentive to produce internationally traded goods (the so-called 'Dutch Disease' effect of commodity booms). This is still a matter of debate and certainly countries such as Mozambique and Uganda that have received very large aid inflows and pursued sound macroeconomic policies to manage aid do not appear to have suffered adverse effects on their main 'tradeable sector', which is agriculture; agricultural output and exports have shown strong recoveries in both cases (DfID 2002).

Aid absorption is a key issue for the IFF which aims to mobilise major aid financing and to disburse it over a comparatively short period. But doubling aid in real terms by 2015 (as the IFF sets out to do) would raise the aid-to-GDP ratio of only 14 countries, with a combined population of 109 million, above 20 per cent, and this is at the lower end of the bound (15 to 45 per cent) in which diminishing returns are believed to kick in. More fundamentally, one must be careful in using cross-country studies to develop 'rules of thumb' that set a ceiling on aid-to-GDP ratios for individual recipients. Countries vary greatly in their institutional capacities to manage aid (including its macroeconomic effect) and, perhaps more importantly, well-designed aid programmes will attempt to raise that institutional capacity and remove bottlenecks to aid effectiveness. Thus investing in improving budgetary planning and management in recipients should pay dividends for donors and governments alike, by enabling aid flows to move rapidly and effectively through the fiscal system and into expenditures on services and infrastructure (Fozzard and Foster 2004). And successful institutional development is likely to increase the positive impact of public expenditure on the growth process (Jones and Shaw 2001).

Moreover, different types of aid will vary in their effects on growth (Clemens *et al.* 2004). One of the main features of the vast quantitative literature on aid effectiveness has been the employment of a single figure for aid. However, this is likely to be misleading for reaching conclusions on aid effectiveness, since we can distinguish at least four different categories of aid: project aid with a rather lengthy gestation period, programme aid that disburses rapidly as free foreign exchange, technical assistance, and food aid and other commodity aid which add directly to consumption (Cassen 1994, White 1998 and Mavrotas 2002a, b). To the above four types of foreign aid, emergency or relief aid must be added as a separate category, given its increasing importance in recent years (Addison 2000).

Well-designed aid programmes must pay close attention to the timing and sequencing of each component of the total aid package. Thus two countries with the same aid-to-GDP ratio may have radically different *compositions* of aid, where the country circumstances and capacities determine the mix. For example, within the category of 'post-conflict' countries there are large differences between countries – as between Afghanistan and Sri Lanka for instance – reflecting the depth of damage that conflict inflicted on core state institutions and capacities. In Afghanistan donors and the government must rebuild the finance ministry and central bank virtually from scratch, whereas in Sri Lanka the civil war did comparatively little damage to key economic institutions. So, in Afghanistan aid flows will tend to focus on humanitarian assistance, NGO projects to rebuild the livelihoods of poor communities, and technical support to rebuild core state institutions, whereas in Sri Lanka the aid mix can contain a greater proportion of budgetary support.

## Conclusions

This chapter has explored a range of issues in the area of aid and its relationship to the Millennium Development Goals. Our first key message, from the studies of aid effectiveness, is that aid is broadly positive for economic growth. This is certainly not to imply that all aid programmes and projects work in all countries and at all times, for this is certainly not the case. But it is to say that pessimism about aid effectiveness as a whole is not warranted when the evidence from research is carefully examined. From this follows our second key message, namely that in so far as growth reduces poverty, and aid promotes growth, aid is vital to poverty reduction through growth. This is not to say that growth always reduces poverty, for much depends upon the social structure; in particular the access of the poor to assets such as land and other natural capital as well as skills that enable them to engage productively in the growth process. But well-designed aid programmes can contribute to raising the participation of the poor in a market economy, and thus their benefits from its growth. This is a vital message to carry forward into the public debate on aid which has, for too long, been captured by aid pessimists, whereas the general public in developed countries is often highly sympathetic to aid provided it can trust that its money is being well used (Lankester 2004).

The chapter's third key message is that while the recent recovery in aid volumes is very welcome, the decline in aid for much of the 1990s – and the reallocation of aid away from sub-Saharan Africa, the region which is most dependent on official flows – have made the MDGs harder to achieve. This has endangered the ability of the MDGs to meet their true test, which in our view is to reduce poverty significantly and improve human well-being in small and vulnerable economies, especially in sub-Saharan Africa. Of the 31 'top priority countries' where urgent action is needed to achieve the MDGs, 25 are in Africa (UNDP 2003). Again, this is an important point to get over to the general public in the developed world, which, according to surveys, believes that governments are giving much more aid to poor countries than they actually are.

Given the slowness in hauling aid volumes back up from the low of the 1990s, we need more promising, forward-looking and creative proposals such as the IFF to inject a sense of *urgency* into the debate on development finance. Since politics is perhaps, in the final analysis, more important than economics in driving forward initiatives such as the IFF, we need to see more coalitions of politicians and civil society movements from both North and South on these issues. In that regard, the recent 'Action Against Hunger and

Poverty' initiative of the governments of Brazil, Chile, France and Spain is exemplary. This is the chapter's fourth message.

Related to the previous point is the growing need to put emphasis on aid coordination by moving fast towards the implementation of the recent Rome declaration on country ownership, donor alignment with country strategies and aid harmonisation to reduce transaction costs (Manning 2004). Introducing new schemes and synergies in the area of development cooperation is vital: donors as a whole or in groups acting together in aid projects, or inventing new schemes of cooperation to combine several priorities and then provide aid to a group of countries that implement a common project. Linking these efforts to recent regional initiatives (the New Partnership for Africa's Development – NEPAD – for example) is equally important. This is our fifth message.

Our sixth and final message is that we need to know much more about which *types* of aid work best and in what circumstances. Only then can donors and recipients begin to optimise the mix of different types of aid, and build the institutions that make the most effective use of these resources. This applies particularly to fragile states, where donors are likely to increase their engagement over the next few years, and where the depth of poverty and the need to meet the MDGs are amongst the most urgent issues facing the international development community.

## Notes

1  We would like to thank Colin Bradford, Fantu Cheru and Sami Lahdensuo for very helpful comments and suggestions on an earlier draft. We are also grateful to Nicola Bullard, Martti Hetemaki, Jaakko Iloniemi, Kunibert Raffer, Richard Samans, Andres Solimano, Jan Vandemoortele and participants in the Helsinki Track II meting in Geneva (25–27 March 2004) for useful comments and background discussions.
2  See also Wolf (2002) for a comprehensive analysis of EU aid to ACP countries.

## References

Addison, T. 2000. 'Aid and Conflict', in F. Tarp (ed.), *Foreign Aid and Development: Lessons Learnt and Directions for the Future*. London: Routledge, pp. 392–408.

—— (ed.) 2003. *From Conflict to Recovery in Africa*. Oxford: Oxford University Press for UNU–WIDER.

—— (ed.) 2004. *New Sources for Development Finance*. Oxford: Oxford University Press for UNU–WIDER.

Addison, T. and M. McGillivray. 2004. 'Aid to Conflict-Affected Countries: Lessons for Donors'. *Conflict, Security and Development*, 4, 3: 347–67.

Atkinson, A. B. (ed.) 2005. *New Sources of Development Finance*. Oxford:

Oxford University Press for UNU–WIDER.

Bulí, A. and J. Hamann. 2003. 'Aid Volatility: an Empirical Assessment'. *IMF Staff Papers*, 50: 65–89.

Burnside, C. and D. Dollar. 2000. 'Aid, Policies and Growth'. *American Economic Review*, 90, 4: 847–68.

Cassen, R. 1994. *Does Aid Work?* Oxford: Oxford University Press (2nd edition).

Clemens, M., S. Radelet and R. Bhavnani. 2004. 'Counting Chickens When They Hatch: the Short-term Effect of Aid on Growth'. Working Paper No. 44, Centre for Global Development, Washington, DC.

Collier, P. and D. Dollar. 2004. 'Development Effectiveness: What Have We Learnt?', *Economic Journal*, 114: F244–71.

Collier P. and A. Hoeffler. 2002. 'Aid, Policy, and Growth in Post-Conflict Societies'. Policy Research Working Paper No. 2902, World Bank: Washington, DC.

—— 2004. 'Conflicts', in B. Lomborg (ed.), *Global Crises, Global Solutions*. Cambridge: Cambridge University Press, pp. 129–56.

DfID. 2002. 'The Macroeconomic Effects of Aid'. London: Department for International Development.

Fielding D. and G. Mavrotas. 2005. 'The Volatility of Aid'. Discussion Paper 2005/06. Helsinki: UNU–WIDER.

Fozzard, A. and M. Foster. 2004. 'Changing Approaches to Public Expenditure Management in Low-Income Aid Dependent Countries', in T. Addison and A. Roe (ed.), *Fiscal Policy for Development, Poverty Reconstruction and Growth*. Basingstoke: Palgrave-Macmillan for UNU–WIDER, pp. 97–129.

Fukuyama, F. 2004. *State Building: Governance and World Order in the Twenty-first Century*. Ithaca NY: Cornell University Press.

Gemmell N. and M. McGillivray. 1998. 'Aid and Tax Instability in the Government Budget Constraints in Developing Countries'. CREDIT Research Paper 98/1, University of Nottingham: Nottingham.

Grimm, S. 2004. 'European Development Cooperation to 2010: What Scenario for the Future?', Overseas Development Institute (ODI) Briefing Paper, January.

Guillamont, P. and L. Chauvet. 2001. 'Aid and Performance: A Reassessment'. *Journal of Development Studies*, 37, 6: 66–87.

Hansen, H. 2004. 'The Impact of External Aid and External Debt on Growth and Investment', in T. Addison, H. Hansen, and F. Tarp (eds.), *Debt Relief for Poor Countries*. Basingstoke: Palgrave Macmillan, pp. 134–57.

Hansen, H. and F. Tarp. 2000. 'Aid Effectiveness Disputed'. *Journal of International Development*, 12: 375–98.

Heller, P. and S. Gupta. 2002. 'More Aid – Making It Work for the Poor'. *World Economics*, 3, 4: 131–46.

HM Treasury–DFID. 2003. *International Finance Facility*. London, January.

Jones, S. and U. Shaw. 2001. 'Development Effectiveness and Assessment

Issues'. Contribution to *Working Paper on Development Effectiveness*. London: Department for International Development.

Kaldor, M. 1999. *New and Old Wars: Organised Violence in a Global Era*. Cambridge: Polity.

Kayizzi-Mugerwa, S. 2003. *Reforming Africa's Institutions: Ownership, Incentives and Capabilities*. Tokyo: United Nations University Press for UNU–WIDER.

Lankester, T. 2004. 'International Aid: Experience, Prospects and the Moral Case'. *World Economics*, 5, 1: 17–39.

Lensink R. and O. Morrissey. 2000. 'Aid Instability as a Measure of Uncertainty and the Positive Impact of Aid on Growth'. *Journal of Development Studies*, 36, 3: 31–49.

Lensink, R. and H. White. 2000. 'Assessing Aid: a Manifesto for Aid in the Twenty-first Century?' *Oxford Development Studies*, 28, 1: 5–18.

Manning, R. 2004. 'Development Challenge'. *OECD Observer*, 243 (May).

Mavrotas, G. 2002a. 'Foreign Aid and Fiscal Response: Does Aid Disaggregation Matter?' *Weltwirtschaftiliches Archiv (Review of World Economics)*, 138, 3: 534–59.

—— 2002b. 'Aid and Growth in India: Some Evidence from Disaggregated Aid Data'. *South Asia Economic Journal*, 3, 1: 19–49.

—— 2005. 'The International Finance Facility Proposal', in A. B. Atkinson (ed.), *New Sources of Development Finance*. Oxford: Oxford University Press for UNU–WIDER, pp. 110–31.

McGillivray, M. 2003. 'Aid Effectiveness and Selectivity: Integrating Multiple Objectives in Aid Allocations'. *DAC Journal*, 4, 3: 23–36.

McGillivray, M. and O. Morrissey. 2004. 'Fiscal Effects of Aid', in T. Addison and A. Roe (eds.), *Fiscal Policy for Development: Poverty, Reconstruction and Growth*. Basingstoke: Palgrave Macmillan, pp. 72–96.

Morrissey, O. 2001. 'Does Aid Increase Growth?' *Progress in Development Studies*, 1, 1: 7–50.

OECD. 1996. *Shaping the Twenty-first Century: the Contribution of Development Cooperation*. Paris: Organisation for Economic Cooperation and Development, Development Assistance Committee.

—— 2004. 'International Development Statistics On-line', Paris: OECD.

—— 2005. *Development Cooperation Report*. Paris: OECD Development Assistance Committee.

Pallage S. and M. Robe. 2001. 'Foreign Aid and the Business Cycle'. *Review of International Economics*, 9: 636–67.

Reinikka, R. and J. Svensson. 2004. 'Efficiency of Public Spending: New Microeconomic Tools to Assess Service Delivery', in T. Addison and A. Roe (eds.), *Fiscal Policy for Development: Poverty, Reconstruction and Growth*. Basingstoke: Palgrave Macmillan, pp. 218–36.

Sachs, J. D. 2005. *Ending Poverty: Economic Possibilities for Our Time*. London: Penguin Press.

UN. 2001. *Report of the High-Level Panel on Financing for Development (chair*

*Ernesto Zedillo*). New York: United Nations.

—— 2004. *A More Secure World: Our Shared Responsibility*. New York: United Nations.

UNDP. 2003. *Human Development Report*, New York: Oxford University Press for UNDP.

UN Millennium Project. 2005. *Investing in Development: a Practical Plan to Achieve the Millennium Development Goals*. New York: United Nations.

White, H. 1998. *Aid and Macroeconomic Performance: Theory, Empirical Evidence and Four Country Cases*. London: Macmillan.

Wolf, S. 2002. 'EU Aid for ACP Investment'. Discussion Paper No. 192, Hamburg Institute of International Economics.

World Bank. 1998. *Assessing Aid: What Works, What Doesn't, and Why*. Oxford and New York: Oxford University Press.

# 3

## Making Sense of MDG Costing

### JAN VANDEMOORTELE and RATHIN ROY[1]

*There is an evil in extreme impatience as well as in extreme patience with social ills.*

Alfred Marshall, *Principles of Economics*, 1890

Millennium Development Goal (MDG) costing is necessary for integrating global development goals into national poverty reduction strategies. But the price tag of the MDGs depends on strategic choices about the ways and means for reaching the targets. Since the technical experts seldom agree on the optimal path towards the MDGs, it is best to approach MDG costing through a participatory process of political economy, driven by tailored targets for 2015 expressed in intermediate targets and actionable propositions. When estimating MDG costs, the key words must be flexibility, humility and learning. None of the existing methods yield robust or accurate cost estimates. In making sense of MDG costing, more attention must be paid to country-level estimates than to global ones; to the short-to-medium time horizon than to the long-term one; to relative cost estimates than to absolute ones; to domestic sources of funding than to foreign aid; and to national ownership than to donorship. Three practical steps are proposed for aligning the poverty reduction strategy papers (PRSP) and the medium-term expenditure framework (MTEF) with MDG targets. They are based on the premise that for the sake of the MDGs, prudence is silver but ambition is golden.

## Global targets, local progress

The MDGs stipulate quantitative reductions in the various dimensions of human poverty by 2015, ranging from hunger, disease and ignorance to gender discrimination and environmental degradation.

By and large, the numerical targets were set on the premise that the progress observed in the 1970s and 1980s at the global level would continue over the lifetime of one generation – covering the 25 years between 1990 and 2015. Were such progress to be maintained for child survival, for instance, the average under-five mortality rate in developing countries would be reduced by two-thirds between 1990 and 2015. While this target is valid at the global level, it is not necessarily so for each and every country.

Global targets are valid but not all nations can meet them because country-specific circumstances differ significantly from global trends. The Philippines, for instance, is closer to reflecting the global trends than, say, Chad is. Countries that face an acute HIV pandemic cannot be expected to achieve the same progress in human development as countries that do not face such a challenge.

Target setting at the national level is more about adaptation than about adoption. The spirit of the Millennium Declaration is not to impose a uniform set of targets on each and every country. The MDG targets must be tailored and customised to reflect national circumstances and priorities. In describing his country's recent progress towards universal primary education, Tanzania's President stated, 'I am now convinced that the MDGs can only be attained through a global compact, anchored in national policies that take into account local circumstances' (*International Herald Tribune*, 13 July 2004).

Setting country-specific targets does not mean that the global targets will be abandoned or watered down. The global targets will not be undermined if some countries set lower national targets because others will set targets that exceed the global ones – so-called 'MDG-plus' targets. In the aggregate, global targets will still be met because global progress is an average of country-specific performances.

The global trends on which the MDG targets are based are, after all, the result of aggregating millions of very different trends across individuals, families, communities and countries. National development planning and target setting cannot be driven by such aggregations and abstractions. Global targets abstract away a country's history, deep-seated social and gender disparities and other specific challenges. Global targets cannot be interpreted as one-size-fits-all objectives; the Millennium Declaration does not assume homogeneity across national borders. Moreover, the imposition of global targets inherently undermines national ownership, which remains weak in several countries. Creating the space to tailor the MDG targets is essential for generating a stronger sense of ownership among national stake-holders.

At the same time, tailoring national targets cannot become a euphemism for abandoning the political commitment made at the Millennium Summit to 'spare no effort to free our fellow men, women and children from the abject and dehumanising conditions of extreme poverty' (Millennium Declaration 2000). Setting country-specific targets that lack in ambition and in urgency would be an escape clause from that commitment.

Thus the focus must gradually shift from global targets to local progress. The efforts to set region-specific targets in South Asia is a step in that direction. Global targets need to be complemented by tailored and customised targets at the national and sub-national levels as benchmarks for success. The question is not whether a country or a community is on track *vis-à-vis* the global targets; it is whether the greatest and fastest possible progress is being made – given the specific constraints faced by that country or community and given the level of external support. It is not about being on track globally but about accelerating progress locally.

## Power of quantification

The MDGs have moved quickly to the centre of the international develop-ment agenda, in large part due to the power of quantification. For the first time, we have an internationally agreed agenda for human development that can be monitored in quantitative terms. Estimating the financial cost of operationalising the MDG agenda is driven by that same power. Sayings such as 'if it cannot be measured, it cannot be managed' and 'if it cannot be counted, it does not count' are popular expressions of the power of quanti-fication. Social science increasingly adopts the motto that 'nothing can be known unless it can be quantified'.

Several attempts are under way to estimate the cost of achieving the MDGs – at the global level and in several countries, as well as sectorally. One of the first estimates was made by the Zedillo Commission in preparation for the international conference on Finance for Development in 2002. It estimated that realising the MDGs at the global level would require at least an extra US$50 billion per year.

Attempts to quantify the cost of realising the MDG agenda use very different methods. Not only do they calculate the cost of operational inter-ventions differently, but they handle issues of absorptive capacity, 'good' policies and the Dutch disease in degrees of detail that vary. A review of these methods and approaches shows that MDG costing is not an exact science. None of the existing cost estimates is robust, since they all rely on assumptions that remain uncertain – however plausible they may be. Each methodology seems to be driven by an implicit agenda – whether to make the case for more aid, to caution *vis-à-vis* absorptive capacity or to promote 'good' policies.

Notwithstanding the imperfect methodologies, the importance of MDG costing is beyond doubt. MDG costing provides a quantitative basis for defining anti-poverty strategies and programmes, as well as for forecasting needs and gaps and for mobilising additional resources. But the method-ologies that underpin such attempts have severe limitations. By reviewing them in some detail, we do not imply that MDG costing is a futile exercise. The question is not whether to attempt MDG costing or not; it is how best to do it and for what purpose. Cost estimates have been valuable for the purpose of advocacy *vis-à-vis* pro-poor budgeting and more foreign aid.

## Methodological issues

Like the targets themselves, the relevance of MDG costing lies mainly at the national and sub-national levels. The primary purpose of estimating the price tag of the MDGs is to align the national budget, sectoral plans and foreign aid with the country-specific targets. Flexibility is crucial because MDG costing must be premised on two basic and interrelated assertions, namely that:

1   it cannot be known in advance with any reasonable degree of certainty how the MDGs will be achieved in a particular country or community; and

2   it cannot be known in advance with any sensible degree of precision how much it will cost to meet the MDGs in that country or community.

At the outset, it is important to admit that our knowledge about important aspects of MDG costing equals, at best, our ignorance. The severe limitations associated with any costing methodology must be acknowledged; it must be accepted that ultimately the exact cost of achieving the MDG targets is unknowable. Thus, MDG costing must be addressed with humility, flexibility and from a point of view of learning. The degree of uncertainty about the outcome of existing methodologies cannot be over-emphasised. Five main weaknesses deserve to be highlighted.

*First*, different approaches, delivery mechanisms and policies exist for reaching the MDGs. Each of them has different unit costs and different cost functions. Generic drugs, for instance, are less expensive than brand-name medicines; home-based care is less costly than institution-based care; day schools are less pricy than boarding schools; community-driven initiatives and grassroots involvement lower the cost of delivering education, health care and water supply. Some interventions, such as promoting hand-washing, combine high impact with low cost; others are more costly, especially the development and rehabilitation of basic infrastructure.

The cost-effectiveness of specific interventions will depend on the institutional and policy environment. Selecting the best delivery mechanism and defining the appropriate policy framework will typically reduce costs. But their optimal choice cannot be known *ex ante*. The notion of 'good' policies – which is integral to several approaches to MDG costing – involves judgement and assumes that they are value-free and are applicable across all borders.

*Second*, most MDG cost estimates use a one-size-fits-all approach, based on fixed coefficients and linear relationships. They seldom allow for economies or diseconomies of scale. Although adjustments are sometimes made for non-linear relationships, there is no sound basis for choosing one specification of non-linearity over another. 'Average' unit costs are commonly used but they seldom provide an adequate basis for estimating total costs. The cost of expanding the coverage of a service in health and education by an extra ten percentage points, for instance, will depend on whether the country's coverage moves from 50 to 60 per cent or from 90 to 100 per cent.

Marginal costs are not always better because the determination of the extra cost will depend on the entire cost function. We need to know the cost of all additional units; not just the cost of the next unit. But the cost function as a whole is unobservable.

Neither can a quantitative approach address the qualitative and efficiency aspects of implementing the MDG agenda. Speculations about the nature of the cost function can only undermine the reliability of the results. The problem is likely to grow as cost estimates are projected further into time – making once-and-for-all estimates for the next ten years rather pointless.

In addition, it cannot be assumed that the cost will be unrelated to the scale of operations. A major effort to reach the education target, for example, may increase the demand for trained teachers so as to push their wages upwards – thereby increasing the cost of achieving universal primary education.

Moreover, constant growth elasticities of poverty and fixed incremental capital-output ratios are crude approximations because they change in time and in space. This is not a statistical quirk but reflects real differences across counties in endowments, in histories, in income distribution, in poverty levels and in development trajectories. Any time series confirms that the relationship between economic growth and the level of poverty is highly unstable.

*Third*, because the MDG targets are interrelated, adding up their individual costs will lead to serious over-estimations of the total cost. In technical terms, this is called 'positive externalities'. The MDGs are also characterised by 'joint production'.

Positive externalities mean that the outputs generated for one target serve as inputs to other targets. Girls' education, for instance, helps to reduce child mortality and HIV infection. Ignoring these important interlinkages can lead to significant over-estimations of the total MDG cost. The existence of such synergies is beyond dispute; what is a matter of debate is the exact quantification of their cost implications. There is no consensus because the magnitude and character of the externalities themselves are not always clear. For instance, quantifying the cost of addressing gender discrimination, and its impact on all MDG targets, is enormously challenging.

Joint production means that one input simultaneously affects several targets. Nurses, doctors and hospital beds, for instance, help to achieve several MDG targets – such as child and maternal mortality and malaria control. When one input affects several targets at once, then the cost function for a separate MDG target cannot be defined. The cost of achieving the entire set of MDGs cannot be estimated without understanding the manner in which specific inputs help to advance multiple goals. Since joint production is ubiquitous, it can bias MDG cost estimates in a major way.

*Fourth*, absorptive capacity will determine the efficiency and effectiveness of reaching the MDGs. When extra money cannot be adequately absorbed, it will lead to greater inefficiencies. However, intangible factors play an important role in determining absorptive capacity. Country-specific campaigns against hunger or for education have shown that absorptive capacity is not fixed – not even in the short-term. In addition, the structural reforms and institutional capacity needed to improve management and fight corruption all require extra money. Additional resources can significantly relax absorptive constraints because insufficiencies and inefficiencies are not independent but very much interdependent. Thus, extra resources can be a prerequisite for enhancing absorptive capacity, not the other way round.

*Finally*, the HIV pandemic and other emergencies – such as conflict – will have an obvious impact on the total cost of achieving the MDGs but it cannot be quantified with any degree of confidence. We know, for example, that achieving universal primary education will cost more when many teachers are HIV-positive. But we have no way of knowing how much more.

In addition to these methodological limitations, data weaknesses often add to the unreliability of MDG cost estimates.

## Costing without confidence

Given the methodological challenges and data weaknesses, it is not surprising that MDG cost estimates vary greatly – globally, nationally and sectorally. It is particularly difficult to have much confidence in global cost estimates, with existing estimates ranging from an extra US$30 billion per year to over US$100 billion.

Among the many examples that could be used, we highlight the case of Uganda, for which several cost estimates exist for achieving universal primary education. UNICEF, UNDP, the World Bank and the UN Millennium Project sponsored such work – with all estimates relating to the early 2000s. Each of the four studies follows a different approach and makes various assumptions about issues such as the pupil–teacher ratio, the proportion of the budget for teaching materials, and the level of teachers' salaries. None of these assumptions appears exaggerated or implausible. Yet, the four studies yield very different unit costs for one year of primary education in Uganda – ranging by a staggering factor of 5:1. When cost estimates for the education target appear so questionable, then we can only wonder how reliable estimates can be for targets whose price tag is more difficult to quantify – and, by extension, how reliable aggregate cost estimates can possibly be.

This example illustrates that nobody should be gullible about any cost estimate. All estimates must be interpreted with caution and scrutinised carefully; nobody should be subject to irrational exuberance about their precise nature. In our view, there is no robust or 'best' way of costing the MDG targets.

## Making sense of MDG costing

Despite the many methodological and data-related problems that bedevil the exercise, MDG costing is important and must be pursued. However, we caution against an approach that pretends to give policy makers, politicians and the public a precise price tag for achieving the MDGs – nationally, globally or sectorally.

In contrast with a technocratic approach, MDG costing must be placed within the ambit of the national political economy, driven by tailored targets for 2015 that are expressed in intermediate targets and actionable propositions that can be achieved within the next two to three years. The political economy that underlies MDG costing cannot be addressed through a purely quantitative approach. Cost estimates must be made context-specific – including *vis-à-vis* the social and political situation – and must be based on strategic choices for prioritising the ways and means of realising the MDG agenda in that specific context. As technical experts seldom agree on the optimal path towards the MDGs, the most reasonable course is to follow a participatory process that is driven by the key stakeholders and supported – not supplanted – by technocrats.

An excessive focus on getting the numbers right runs the risk of leading to a situation of 'analysis-paralysis', whereby the merits of the different costing approaches will forever be challenged and their results heatedly debated or strongly opposed – thereby postponing action in terms of budget restructuring and aid allocations. Since it is better to be broadly right than to be precisely wrong, MDG cost estimates are best seen as orders of magnitude, expressed as a range rather than a single figure.

In making sense of MDG costing, five elements deserve special attention: (1) relative versus absolute costing; (2) domestic versus external funding; (3) financing versus costing; (4) short- and medium-term versus long-term costing; and (5) ownership versus donorship.

### Relative vs absolute costing

Cost estimates can be derived either as absolute amounts or in relation to national income or the national budget. A relative approach that is used as a rule of thumb, and flexibly *vis-à-vis* the level of income, is preferable to the use of a fixed dollar amount. UNESCO's statistical yearbook, for instance, indicates that absolute expenditure on education ranges widely across countries. When expressed in absolute dollar figures, industrialised countries spend about 40–50 times more per student than low-income countries. But when expressed as a percentage of national income, the range narrows considerably – with most countries spending 3–6 per cent of national income on education.

Others prefer absolute cost estimates. For instance, it is estimated that public health spending should be at least US$40 per person per year to guarantee basic health care. However, the principal cost item for delivering health care services is labour, whose cost is closely related to the level of economic development of the country. Salaries for nurses and doctors vary enormously across national borders because they relate to the level of national income. Hence, a fixed dollar amount in health spending will buy considerably more health care in China than in Chile, for example. The same is true for education and other services.

Admittedly, certain cost items can be expressed in absolute terms – such as imported medicines – but this does not justify absolute costing as the norm. Teachers, nurses and doctors are not freely mobile across borders; the cost of their labour cannot be assumed to be uniform. Thus, MDG costing is best driven by relative costing.

It could be argued that any cost estimate can be described either as a relative share or as an absolute amount; but more is at stake than a simple accounting convention. Relative estimates give a better indication of a country's efforts to meet agreed targets than absolute cost estimates do.

### Domestic vs external funding

More and better aid, as well as steeper debt relief, will be critical for achieving the MDGs, especially – but not exclusively – in the least developed and low-income countries. But as the case is being made for doubling global foreign aid, individual countries are not always given the space for setting more expansionary fiscal policy to accommodate these external resources.

In addition, different disbursement mechanisms are needed to reduce the vulnerability of a country's anti-poverty programme to non-compliance with a variety of conditionalities – which frequently turned them into 'stop-go' programmes in the 1980s and 1990s. Proposals such as 'fixed and variable' tranches are meant to make aid flows less volatile and more predictable.

Several costing exercises assume that most of the funding gap *vis-à-vis* the MDGs will be covered by foreign aid. We consider that the bulk of the extra investment will need to come from domestic sources – through savings and taxation as well as through private–public partnerships. It would be erroneous to assume that most of the funding gap can be financed from external sources.

This does not diminish the value of foreign aid and debt relief. Since pro-poor policies are never neutral *vis-à-vis* the country's income distribution, they are bound to meet stiff resistance. For instance, foreign aid can help in easing the resistance to inter- and intra-sectoral reallocations in the national budget, which will be required in most cases for reaching the MDGs.

### Financing vs costing

Ultimately, the only correct answer to the question of 'How much will the MDGs cost?' is 'more' – albeit that the exact amount cannot be known. Hence, MDG costing must always go hand in hand with MDG financing – examining the potential of various sources of funding, including general taxation, cost recovery for non-basic services, private-public partnerships, foreign aid and debt swaps. A combined financing strategy that is based on domestic and external resources will give concrete expression to the MDGs as a global deal and as a framework for mutual accountability.

Pro-poor resource generation – a subject that receives scant attention in most PRSPs – is at the heart of the debate on MDG costing. Most PRSPs now make a stronger case for pro-poor public expenditure – partly as the result of the UN's advocacy and analytical work on the 20/20 Initiative. While they emphasise the gains in allocative efficiency that stem from expenditure-switching measures, few pay adequate attention to the link between development goals and revenue targets.

During the 1990s, the tax system has been eroded and has become less pro-poor in many countries. But historically high-performing countries in terms of human development have mobilised adequate levels of public revenue. Tax reforms are urgently needed to generate more domestic resources for the MDGs, and to generate them more equitably – a venture that will require rethinking restrictive fiscal targets and tight inflation targets. Ceilings on public finance have to be set in line with the country-specific targets; short-term fiscal constraints cannot be allowed to eclipse the long-term MDG vision.

## Short- and medium-term vs long-term costing

Given the methodological and data weaknesses, it would be pointless to estimate the MDG costs covering the entire period until 2015. It is infinitely more important to estimate the cost implications of the MDGs for the next two to three years than to estimate them for the next ten. The longer the time horizon, the less reliable such estimates become; each additional year lessens their potential accuracy.

The question of how much the MDGs will cost must be framed within a short-to-medium time horizon, within a two-to-three-year rolling framework. The PRSP and the MTEF provide such rolling frameworks. Unfortunately, they are not being used for the purpose of forecasting needs, identifying gaps and mobilising resources. An independent evaluation of the PRSPs (World Bank 2004) notes, 'Many PRSPs have not been reliably costed and fail to provide strategic prioritisation' and 'the hard choices in prioritising actions over the short to medium term have not been made in most PRSPs'. The report also concludes: 'PRSPs ... focus largely on leveraging public expenditures to reduce poverty and have not uniformly delineated non-expenditure-related policies or actions ... such as tax/revenue policies'.

Three practical steps are required to align the national poverty reduction strategy with the MDGs. First, set tailored targets for 2015 and beyond. Second, express them in intermediate targets and actionable propositions for the short and medium term so as to generate a stronger political momentum, because they will have to be achieved by the current leadership – which is not the case for 2015 targets. Third, estimate the cost of the intermediate targets so they can drive the macroeconomic and sectoral policy frameworks as well as the national budget. Steps 2 and 3 are more technical in nature, while step 1 must be driven by a process of political economy.

Intermediate targets and actionable propositions for the next two to three years can cover a variety of things, ranging from immunising children to iodising salt, training teachers and building schools and feeder roads, drilling boreholes and planting trees, treating HIV/Aids patients and distributing bed nets, and abolishing user fees for basic social services; as well as improving statistics because they fuel the power of quantification that underpins much of the MDG agenda. Issues of absorptive capacity and Dutch disease need to be addressed, too. But flexibility will be key because it cannot be known in advance with any degree of certainty or precision how exactly the MDGs will be achieved in country-specific circumstances.

Setting intermediate targets presupposes that the shape of the trajectory for reaching a particular target by 2015 is known in advance. Frequently, the trajectory is assumed to be linear, but for some targets it can be argued that progress will be fastest in the early years when the so-called low-hanging fruits can be harvested, and that it will slow down as the country gets closer to the target. For other targets, it can be assumed that initial progress will be slow until institutional and human capacities are developed, gender discrimination is addressed and physical infrastructure is in place. The former implies that the trajectory will be logarithmic in nature; the latter indicates that it will be exponential in shape. Ultimately, the exact shape will depend on country-specific and target-specific circumstances. But alternative trajectories must be considered besides the linear one, because a straight line seems to be the exception rather than the rule.

### Ownership vs donorship

Many perceive the attempts to quantify the price tag of the MDGs as driven by external partners, based on the central planning of a bygone era. Such perceptions need to be acknowledged because they undermine national ownership. For the targets to trigger real change on the ground, a stronger constituency must be mobilised. Global and long-term cost estimates are unlikely to prompt local actors. Country-specific, intermediate and costed targets are more likely to mobilise people and influence national decision makers.

The periodic consultations between a developing country and its external partners – either in the form of a consultative group or a round-table meeting – provide an opportunity for substantive discussions about the content and financing of the national strategy for reducing poverty. However, these meetings often focus narrowly on compliance with rules and conditionalities that stem from donorship rather than debating the strategic choices and policy orientations that reflect national ownership.

A peer-and-partner review is proposed to make the periodic consultations with external partners less donor-centric and more substantive, focused on ambitious country-specific MDG targets. The current mode whereby a developing country faces a large number of bilateral donors and multilateral institutions is not conducive to an equal exchange and a frank debate about an ambitious anti-poverty programme.

The peer-and-partner review would involve peer countries and a more select group of partner countries to review the anti-poverty strategy, programmes and financing plans. When Nepal, for instance, meets with its external partners, it could be joined by representatives from Bangladesh, Cambodia, India and Sri Lanka; and perhaps from another landlocked country such as Bolivia or Lesotho. A person of distinction could join the consultative process – preferably from a civil society organisation. The peer-and-partner review would help to reduce the extent of donorship and deepen the sense of national ownership by advancing a home-grown poverty reduction strategy geared to meeting ambitious MDG targets.

To turn the peer-and-partner review into a practical proposition, a number of steps will be required, such as consulting with a few developing countries, bilateral donors and multilateral organisations about important details; initiating the process in a few pilot countries on a voluntary basis; choosing the participating peers and partners; linking the review to similar initiatives (such as the New Partnership for Africa's Development), based on existing documents such as the PRSP. The challenge is to keep the process light and flexible, supported by a small functional secretariat – possibly composed of the World Bank, DAC and UNDP.

## Conclusion

MDGs imply a certain boldness of perspective. Business-as-usual will not turn the noble targets into a practical reality by 2015. For the MDGs' sake, the PRSP and MTEF need to make a quantum leap in scale and in ambition. Yet, making that leap does not necessarily require MDG costing over the entire trajectory to 2015 – summarised in a single dollar figure. While it is not possible to obtain reliable cost estimates for the long term, MDG costing is essential for aligning the national budget and aid allocations with global development goals. The price tag and the financing plan of the MDG targets can only be ascertained realistically within the country's own development plan and national budget, within a short-to-medium time horizon.

Relative cost estimates tend to be more relevant than absolute ones. In most cases, domestic resources will be more important, more reliable and more sustainable than foreign aid and debt relief. A financing strategy that combines domestic and external resources will give concrete expression to the MDGs as a global deal, based on the principles of shared responsibility and mutual accountability. Governments will renew their efforts at reforming policies and at mobilising domestic revenue and private–public partnerships, while the external partners will increase their support for ambitious but country-specific MDG agendas.

Finally, MDG costing can enhance the strategic nature of the periodic consultations between a developing country and its external partners. Too often, their emphasis is on compliance with rules and conditionalities rather than on substantive discussions about policies and programmes. A peer-and-partner review can make such consultations less asymmetric and more substantive. It can help lessen donorship and strengthen national ownership by advancing home-grown pro-poor policies, centred on ambitious inter-mediate targets that drive the national budget and take account of absorptive capacities.

## Notes

1 We are indebted to Sanjay Reddy and Antoine Heuty for their review of the strengths and weaknesses of existing methodologies of MDG costing. We benefited from insightful discussions with Tony Addison, Sudhir Anand, Ann Pettifor and David Sahn. We received valuable comments and suggestions from Khalid Abu-Ismail, Diane Elson, Selim Jahan, Kamal Malhotra, Tanni Mukhopadhyay, Gustave Nebie, David Parker, Sanjay Reddy, Guido Schmidt-Traub, Anuradha Seth and Eduardo Zepeda. The usual disclaimers apply. The views expressed are not necessarily those of the United Nations Development Programme.

## Reference

World Bank. 2004. *The Poverty Reduction Strategy Initiative. An OED review.* World Bank Operations Evaluation Department. Washington, DC.

# 4

## Foreign Direct Investment, Innovative Sources of Development Finance and Domestic Resource Mobilisation

### TONY ADDISON and GEORGE MAVROTAS[1]

Development finance is a large canvas, with a wide range of issues, each of which is surrounded by considerable economic and political complexity (and controversy). Accordingly, the debate has an inevitable tendency to compartmentalise itself into discussion of the individual types of development finance, thereby distracting attention away from the very important complementarities and synergies that exist *between* financial flows. Thus, within the area of external development finance, official flows such as grant aid and concessional loans are often discussed separately from private flows such as foreign direct investment (FDI) and portfolio flows. This is unfortunate, since some of the most creative proposals to increase the flow of external finance to poor countries operate at the intersection of official and private flows, notably the UK's proposal for an International Finance Facility and the Finnish proposal for a global lottery.

The debate also tends to compartmentalise itself into one discussion about external finance (official and private) and another about domestic government finance (taxation and other forms of domestic revenue mobilisation). This is also unfortunate, since it tends to downplay the very interactions between external and domestic finance that are important for policy. For example, the quality of the domestic taxation system will affect the flow of FDI to a country (by creating incentives and disincentives for foreign investors), and it will affect the returns (both social and private) that we can expect from both official and private external financial flows. Similarly, the creation of a deep domestic financial market will mobilise domestic savings while attracting foreign savings in the form of portfolio flows, and both outcomes can fund private investment.

More broadly, some recent proposals to increase funding for development involve measures of global taxation, in particular taxes on environmental 'bads' such as the emission of greenhouse gases, where there is a 'double dividend' in the form of an improvement in global environmental quality as well as a stream of revenues (that could be used to fund both national development programmes as well as global public goods that benefit poor and rich countries alike). These proposals cross over the traditional boundaries of national public finance and global development finance. They are therefore a particularly interesting set of initiatives, but ones that raise larger and wider issues of global economic governance.

Our purpose in this chapter is therefore to sketch out the issues on this larger canvas, beginning with foreign direct investment, a major source of development finance and economic growth for some, mainly larger, developing countries and one that, in our view, needs to be urgently expanded in the poorer and smaller countries. We then summarise the main results of a UNU–WIDER project on new and innovative sources of development finance (including global taxes) undertaken at the behest of the UN General Assembly. The chapter also discusses the importance of domestic resource mobilisation, both through the domestic financial system and by government revenue mobilisation. We conclude that there is considerable scope for further innovation in development finance, if the political will exists.

## Foreign direct investment

It would be fair to say that there is a wide spectrum of views over FDI and developing countries, ranging from many in the business world who take a largely uncritical attitude to FDI to those in the development community who have deep misgivings about international business in general, and their operations in developing countries in particular.[2] Our own view is that given the limited availability of official financial flows, it is essential to encourage private capital flows within a well-designed policy framework that maximises the contribution of private flows to national development goals. That policy framework needs in turn to emanate from a national vision that sets out the ways in which foreign private capital should contribute to development. Such a consensus can only be built through national debate and discussion, involving as wide a group of actors as possible, from legislators to businesses to local communities.

Recent years have witnessed a proliferation of international investment agreements (IIAs), affecting the parameters for national policy making on FDI. However, as the 2003 *World Investment Report* (UNCTAD 2003b) argues, a new approach is urgently required so that the benefits from entering into IIAs and the need to secure sufficient policy space are properly balanced. There is a need to find a development-oriented balance when negotiating the objectives, content, structure and implementation of future IIAs. The development dimension is often absent from IIAs and must be an integral part of the new IIAs. This will then support national policies in host countries to attract more FDI and to increase its benefits (UNCTAD 2003b).

Countries in the past have used a number of FDI performance criteria such as local content, export and technology transfer requirements. However, these experiences seem to suggest that such measures have not always been effective. It would be better to concentrate on getting the fundamentals right, including the policy environment and the development of the local skill and technology development system. Ensuring coherence between trade and investment policies is equally important, since the liberalisation of FDI policies without trade liberalisation may reduce the gains from FDI, especially with respect to export growth (ILO 2002).

### The development impact of FDI

Employment creation is central to achieving the first Millennium Development Goal: to halve the proportion of people living on less than US$1 per day. FDI can make a significant contribution to employment growth. First, FDI is a source of capital accumulation, both physical capital and human capital (when FDI enhances skills through training). Provided that FDI projects are well-designed – reflecting the policy framework discussed above – their rate of return will raise economic growth, thereby adding to the growth of employment, an indirect effect which is additional to the jobs created by FDI projects themselves.

Second, FDI can generate much-needed revenues for governments to spend on MDG-focused infrastructure and services. These revenue effects are both direct (through the corporate taxes paid by the enterprises themselves as well as revenues from FDI in the natural resource sectors) and indirect (when FDI raises economic growth and therefore the economy's total tax base). This benefit from a private external capital flow to the stream of public revenues is an example of the synergy between flows that we discussed at the outset of this chapter. Hence, FDI can contribute to the MDGs by reducing income poverty (through its employment effect) and, via its revenue effects, as a source of finance for public spending on human development, particularly in the areas of basic health care, primary education and safety nets for the poor (on the latter see Klein *et al.* 2001). FDI may also help reduce adverse shocks to the poor stemming from financial instability if, as the evidence seems to suggest, FDI flows are more stable than other private capital flows (Ffrench-Davis and Griffith-Jones 2003).

FDI's development benefits are *potentially* strong, but whether this potential is realised or not very much depends on the host country having a clear vision of how FDI fits into its overall development strategy. Thus FDI can be used to diversify the economy, thereby reducing over-dependence on a few commodity-based sectors: by creating new manufacturing and service sectors, for example, particularly in exports and in services that use the new information and communication technologies (ICTs). Both Malaysia and Mauritius have used FDI successfully in this way, including public investment in infrastructure, training and skills to attract FDI into sectors producing goods and services with a high value-added component.

An active government policy with regard to *vertical* FDI, which entails the relocation of intermediate stages of production to take advantage of lower costs, is especially important. A common view is that vertical FDI is largely driven by a search for unskilled labour at the lowest cost. However, the share of low-skilled labour is only 5–10 per cent of total production costs in industrial countries, and clothing and footwear is the only sector in which low-skilled labour costs remain significant at one-third of total production costs (Kotler *et al.* 1997: 187). If low wage levels were the main attraction for foreign investors, then Africa would dominate vertical FDI, but in fact Africa receives very little FDI outside of the mineral sector (see next section). Instead, human capital and infrastructure are the main driving factors for vertical FDI. The quality of the host country's human capital stock strongly influences FDI flows as well as the value-added of the associated technology transfer (Keller 1996; Noorbakhsh *et al.* 2001; Saggi 2002). Large investments in education and training have enabled Malaysia, Singapore, Taiwan (and now China) to move up the value-added 'ladder' from manufacturing that is intensive in unskilled labour. These countries have created highly effective partnerships with foreign investors to import, and then eventually create, high technology. The global telecoms industry is an example of this process.

Good-quality ICT infrastructure and skills are now vital to integrating local producers into international 'B2B' (business-to-business) networks, and to attracting vertical FDI in services as well as manufacturing (Addison and Heshmati 2004). Routine tasks such as customer support and data processing in financial services, as well as higher value-added tasks such as design and product development together with software development, are examples. Multinationals providing business services and consultancy are now significant investors in India where they can draw on local ICT skills to develop business solutions for international clients. ICT capacity also influences *horizontal* FDI to produce manufactures and services for sale in the host country market, particularly in large markets such as Brazil, China and India, where ICT is increasingly used to manage supply chains (with greater efficiency and lower inventories reducing business costs).[3] National capacities to adapt ICT to local needs (languages, preferences and regulations) are fundamental. South Korean companies producing locally for the Indian consumer-goods market are heavy users of local ICT skills, and ICT has been central to organising the global expansion of South Africa's companies (in the brewery sector, for example).

Mineral-rich countries face particularly difficult challenges in managing FDI – a crucial issue for sub-Saharan Africa, since much of the FDI to the region is concentrated in the mining sector. Many of these countries do not have well-articulated development goals for using mineral wealth, either by directing the revenues to poverty reduction or by investing to diversify the non-mineral economy (the latter being especially important since the mineral sectors themselves are capital-intensive and do not generate a large amount of direct employment). Moreover, large-scale corruption has been a serious problem in the sector. FDI in the natural-resource sectors must be subject to an open and transparent process in which contracts for lucrative concessions are awarded on merit (governments must also ensure that the stream of revenues produced by such investment is properly accounted for in national budgets). Governments must also exercise care in any inducements they offer to attract foreign investors, particularly in the area of fiscal incentives (such as tax holidays) and in concessions of land and other natural capital for which poor communities may have usage and ownership rights (Addison and Mavrotas 2003). Unfortunately, many of the oil-rich countries have performed very badly in the areas of fiscal management and the protection of community interests; FDI in their natural-resource sectors has therefore been disappointing. One promising step forward is the Extractive Industries Transparency Initiative (EITI), which aims to increase revenue accountability through full corporate and government disclosure. EITI will help civil societies challenge governments to spend these revenues on development.

Hence, FDI is a useful, but not a miracle-working, ingredient for development. This is reflected in empirical research on the relationship between FDI and economic growth. For developing countries as a whole, there is a positive but weak relationship between FDI as a share of GDP and gross fixed capital formation (UNCTAD 2003a: 77). The empirical evidence overall seems to suggest that although FDI may affect growth, growth itself is also a crucial determinant of FDI (Chowdhury and Mavrotas 2003; Hansen and Rand 2003). This may be explained by the attractiveness to foreign investors of a growing market in enterprises that produce manufactures and services for domestic consumers and producers (an important motive for horizontal FDI in the larger economies of Brazil, China and India). Thus, in so far as national development strategies achieve higher growth, they will attract more FDI, thereby creating a virtuous circle of investment and growth.

## Trends in foreign direct investment

The history of the global economy shows distinct phases, some of which have been more encouraging for FDI flows than others. Globalisation's first wave, one hundred years ago, featured considerable FDI to Europe's colonies in Africa and Asia as well as to Latin America's independent states; the stock of foreign investment in developing countries was US$19 billion by the eve of the First World War, and up to 60 per cent of this consisted of FDI (Svedberg 1978).

Globalisation's present wave encompasses a number of trends which should, in principle, be very positive for FDI in developing countries. These include: the emergence of globally integrated production and marketing networks; the associated reduction in transactions costs from the spread of ICTs; and a policy environment that is now more favourable to foreign investors. The latter is evident in the proliferation of bilateral investment treaties, a greater acceptance of the merits of outward-orientated development strategy (albeit within a continuing and vigorous debate on what form this should take), the

Table 4.1  FDI flows to developing countries, 2001–3*

| Host region/economy | 2001 | 2002 | 2003* |
|---|---|---|---|
| World | 823.8 | 651.2 | 653.1 |
| Developed economies | 589.4 | 460.3 | 467.0 |
| Developing economies | 209.4 | 162.1 | 155.7 |
| Africa | 18.8 | 11.0 | 14.4 |
| Ghana | 0.1 | 0.1 | 0.9 |
| Morocco | 2.8 | 0.4 | 1.2 |
| Mozambique | 0.3 | 0.4 | 1.0 |
| South Africa | 6.8 | 0.8 | 0.2 |
| Latin America and the Caribbean | 83.7 | 56.0 | 42.3 |
| Argentina | 3.2 | 1.0 | -0.3 |
| Brazil | 22.5 | 16.6 | 9.1 |
| Chile | 4.5 | 1.6 | 3.1 |
| Mexico | 25.3 | 13.6 | 10.4 |
| Venezuela | 3.4 | 1.3 | 3.3 |
| Asia and the Pacific | 106.9 | 95.1 | 99.0 |
| China | 46.8 | 52.7 | 57.0 |
| Hong Kong | 23.8 | 13.7 | 14.3 |
| India | 3.4 | 3.4 | 3.4 |
| Thailand | 3.8 | 1.1 | 1.6 |
| Vietnam | 1.3 | 1.2 | 1.3 |

Source: UNCTAD (2003b).
* UNCTAD estimates. Note: World FDI inflows are projected on the basis of 109 economies for which data are available for part of 2003. Data for 2003 for most economies are estimated by annualising either quarterly or monthly data. The proportion of inflows to these economies in total inflows to their respective region or sub-region in 2002 is used to extrapolate the 2003 data for each region or sub-region.

policy advice and influence of the multilateral development banks which favour FDI, and the generally positive experiences of countries that have encouraged FDI (Brooks *et al.* 2003).

The world should therefore be experiencing something of a boom in FDI to developing countries. Yet recent years have seen a declining trend in FDI, when compared with the high volume of FDI inflows to the developing world in the 1980s and the 1990s. Data from the UN Conference on Trade and Development (UNCTAD 2003b) and World Bank (2003) show a downturn in FDI inflows. Global FDI inflows, already down by over 40 per cent in 2001 to US$823.8 billion, fell by 20 per cent to US$651 billion in 2002 (Table 4.1).

In the case of the developing world, the overall picture is worse for the period 2001–3, since the 23 per cent decline in 2002 (US$162.1 billion as compared to US$209.4 billion in the previous year) is expected to continue in 2003, sinking to US$155.7 billion in that year, as Table 4.1 suggests. Although FDI flows typically recover quickly after a downturn, the duration of the present downturn is a serious concern since only once in the past

Table 4.2  Annual averages of net FDI inflows to developing countries and
selected regions, 1970–99 (US$ million)

| Region | FDI net inflows | | | Growth rate (%) | |
| --- | --- | --- | --- | --- | --- |
| | 1970s | 1980s | 1990s | 1970s–80s | 1980s–90s |
| East Asia and Pacific | 749 | 3,967 | 43,347 | 430 | 993 |
| Latin America and Caribbean | 2,498 | 5,714 | 3,748 | 129 | 556 |
| Middle East and North Africa | −129 | 806 | 3,836 | −725 | 376 |
| South Asia | 61 | 256 | 2,278 | 323 | 789 |
| Sub-Saharan Africa (SSA) | 773 | 1,102 | 3,509 | 43 | 218 |
| All developing countries | 4,013 | 12,059 | 10,308 | 201 | 755 |
| SSA's share (%) | 19 | 9 | 3 | | |

Source: World Bank (2003) and Asiedu (2004).

(1982–3) has a downturn lasted for two consecutive years (UNCTAD
2003b).

Looking at FDI across the regions we see that Africa experienced the
steepest decline in 2002 (41 per cent) followed by Latin America and the
Caribbean (33 per cent), for which region 2003 was the third consecutive
year of declining inflows (UNCTAD 2003b). In the case of Asia and the
Pacific, FDI flows declined for the second consecutive year, from US$107
billion in 2001 to US$95 billion in 2002.

This fall-off in FDI stands in contrast to the impressive growth rates of the
1980s and the 1990s. Indeed, the growth rate of net FDI flows to the
developing world in that period reached on average 755 per cent, with some
regions registering even higher rates (East Asia and the Pacific and South
Asia, for example – see Table 4.2).

A fundamental issue is the geographical concentration of FDI in a small
group of countries: East Asia and Latin America received more than 70 per
cent of total FDI in developing countries, with China alone receiving almost
25 per cent of the total (World Bank 2002, 2003). Note that China was the
top recipient of FDI inflows in the world after Luxembourg, with US$53
billion in 2002 (UNCTAD 2003b).

FDI in sub-Saharan Africa has increased over time, thus indicating absolute
progress (Table 4.2). However, the growth rate of FDI in SSA is substantially
lower than the developing-country average, and therefore the region's share
of global FDI has declined over time (Asiedu 2004). This trend of relative
decline is worrying in view of the importance of FDI to employment generation and growth, which we discussed earlier. A recent UNCTAD survey of
the executives of multinational corporations (UNCTAD 2000) suggests that
the state of (physical) infrastructure is one of the key inhibiting factors when
they contemplate FDI projects in sub-Saharan Africa, along with limited access
to finance, high administrative costs, the tax regime, poor access to global
markets, low levels of skill, and the regulatory and legal framework governing

FDI. These disadvantages to foreign investment more than offset the low price of labour in Africa.

Infrastructure itself can be financed through FDI. Infrastructure attracted considerable private capital flows in the 1990s, reaching a peak of over US$ 120 billion in 1997 and thus exceeding ODA flows to infrastructure that year. However, the Asian financial crisis of 1997 had a dramatic effect on private capital flows to infrastructure during the period, and they fell by almost 50 per cent over 1997–9. For the whole decade, however, total private investment in infrastructure (US$550 billion) was more than three times as much as total ODA flows (UNCTAD 2001; PPI Database 2000). Unfortunately, Africa largely missed out on the spectacular increase in private sector financing of infrastructure, since 80 per cent of the private capital flows (in the form of FDI and portfolio flows) going into infrastructure went to just six upper-middle-income countries: Brazil (which received almost one-third of the total), Argentina, Mexico, South Korea, Malaysia and Hungary. This means that ODA flows remain the principal source of finance for infrastructure for most developing countries, and particularly for sub-Saharan Africa (UNCTAD 2001).

As we noted earlier, the research literature concludes that the level of skills and the quality of the human capital in host countries are of paramount importance for attracting FDI as well as other private flows (Lizondo 1990; Noorbakhsh et al. 2001; de Mello 1997). With education/GDP spending ratios not exceeding 3–4 per cent on average in many African countries, Africa is clearly not in a good position to attract FDI outside of the mineral sector. Hence investment in education and training would not only contribute directly to the MDGs, but would also encourage FDI into Africa (Addison and Mavrotas 2003). Human capital investment also raises the returns on investments in ICT, where ICT is also increasingly important in attracting FDI. Overall, Africa needs an integrated approach in order to attract more FDI. UNCTAD has recently proposed an African Investment Initiative so that interested intergovernmental and civil society organisations in the region can coordinate with the New Partnership for Africa's Development (NEPAD) (UNCTAD 2003b). This could improve the national/international investment framework, support national investment promotion efforts, promote information dissemination and public–private dialogue in the area of FDI, and facilitate business linkages.

## Innovative sources of development finance

The stagnation in aid flows in the 1990s stimulated an increasing interest in the possibilities of finding new and innovative sources of finance (Clunies-Ross 1999). This task has become particularly urgent with the launch of the MDGs: estimates of the additional annual funding required to meet the MDGs by 2015 range from US$50–76 billion and upwards (Devarajan et al. 2002; UN 2001; Vandemoortele and Roy 2004). Accordingly, there have been two recent studies on new sources of finance. As a result of the Five Year Review of the World Summit for Social Development, the UN General Assembly in September 2000 adopted a resolution calling for a rigorous analysis of proposals for creating new and innovative sources of funding, both public and private. The World Institute for Development Economics Research (UNU–WIDER) in Helsinki undertook the study for the UN Department of Economic and Social Affairs, the project being led by Anthony Atkinson of Oxford University (Atkinson 2005). A second study, which drew upon much of the UNU–WIDER research, was undertaken by the French government (Landau 2004). This study contributed in turn to the Action Against Hunger and Poverty Initiative of the governments of Brazil, Chile, France and Spain, which convened a heads of state meeting at the UN in September 2004. UNU–WIDER's findings were presented at the Second Committee (Economic and Financial) of the UN General Assembly in October 2004.

The UNU–WIDER project first considered a tax on goods generating environmental externalities, and specifically a tax on the use of hydrocarbon fuels according to their carbon content. This has substantial revenue-raising potential: a tax on high-income countries alone could raise revenue of US$ 50 billion (see Sandmo 2005 for a detailed discussion). A tax on foreign currency transactions (also known as the Tobin Tax), covering a range of currency-market transactions, could generate US$15–28 billion for global public use (Nissanke 2005). Both of these taxes have 'double dividends': a Tobin Tax can reduce exchange-rate volatility and the carbon tax will reduce global warming, while both raise revenues for the MDGs. However, it must be emphasised that the UNU–WIDER study concentrated on the financing objective (this was the objective set for it by the UN General Assembly) and so the tax rates that yield these revenue estimates are significantly below those proposed in the general debate. Nevertheless, substantial sums can be raised at quite modest tax rates. The French government has also proposed an airline fuel tax and this was highlighted in President Chirac's presentations to international and European conferences during 2005.

The proposal to create Special Drawing Rights (SDRs) for development purposes, with donor countries making their SDR allocation available to fund development, was also considered by the UNU–WIDER study. An SDR allocation of US$25–30 billion could make a significant contribution to filling the MDG financing gap (Aryeetey 2005). The UK proposal for an International Finance Facility (IFF) can provide a stable flow of US$50 billion annually during the crucial years 2010–15, thereby reducing the volatility of aid flows at the present time (Mavrotas 2005). Long-term pledges of a flow of annual payments to the IFF would leverage additional money from the international capital markets through a securitisation process (IFF bonds). This is an example of the interface between private and official finance that we emphasised in the introduction to this chapter.

The proposal for a global lottery, an idea given impetus by the Crisis Management Initiative (a Finnish NGO led by the former Finnish President

Martti Ahtisaari), was also examined (Addison and Chowdhury 2005). This could raise US$6 billion a year, which is feasible given that gambling in all of its forms is a US$1 trillion per year global business. An alternative proposal in the UNU–WIDER study is to create a global premium bond for development modelled on the very successful UK premium bond that provides funding for the British government (Addison and Chowdhury 2005). Bonds are entered in a monthly prize draw, and the prizes provide an income stream (which depends on the bondholder's luck) with no loss of the initial investment (in contrast to the purchase of an unlucky lottery ticket). This would overcome some of the ethical objections to a lottery product, and a global premium bond could be attractive to the growing number of ethical investors.

Finally, the UNU–WIDER study looked at proposals to increase private financial flows to developing countries. Proposals on remittances are 'new' in the sense that they aim to reduce the transactions costs involved in remitting money back to home countries. Remittances are estimated to be U$80 billion annually (much more than annual aid flows), and they can directly contribute to meeting the MDGs when remittances reach poorer households and communities (Solimano 2005). Philanthropy can mobilise considerable amounts as the response by individuals and corporations to the 2005 tsunami disaster in Asia demonstrates. Tax incentives, global funds, and corporate giving (including measures that encourage payroll giving) can all encourage charitable donations for development purposes (see Micklewright and Wright 2003).

In summary, a range of proposals are now on the table. Inevitably, some will make faster progress than others. The IFF, for instance, has powerful political backing from the UK government, and there is now considerable momentum behind proposals to reduce the transactions costs of making remittances. The issue of global taxes has become intertwined with the larger issues of the UN's role in international economic governance and the reform of the Bretton Woods Institutions (Nayyar 2002). For these proposals the prospects are less hopeful, given the present US administration's retreat from multilateralism. However, the European Union may be able to take greater responsibility for debate and action in this area given the recent positive statements on development finance by the leaders of France, Germany and the UK.

## Domestic resource mobilisation

Domestic resource mobilisation has two dimensions, both important to achieving the MDGs. The first is building the *domestic financial system* (the banking and insurance sector, the stockmarket, and markets for public and private debt). The second is increasing government *revenue mobilisation*.

### Building the domestic financial system
Developing the domestic financial sector will enhance savings mobilisation and thereby provide finance for domestic investment to generate growth. Many poor countries have very low rates of saving, especially in Africa; this

reflects not only their low *per capita* incomes, but also the underdevelopment of their banking systems and therefore the lack of attractive savings opportunities (especially in rural areas). This has been compounded by policies of 'financial repression' that offer very low interest rates to savers (often negative in real terms). The banking system itself has failed to act as an efficient intermediary to convert these savings into loans for borrowers, and many countries adopted policies that steered credit towards large, often politically favoured enterprises, which did not make good use of the funds. Small and medium-sized enterprises often had little access to the formal credit market and had to rely on retained earnings or the informal credit market to finance investment. Given the potential for employment generation by small and medium-sized enterprises, this constraint has hindered employment growth and poverty reduction. In addition to building the financial system as whole, it is also vital to provide micro-credit and to create insurance mechanisms for the poor (see Dercon 2004).

As in the case of FDI, portfolio flows are characterised by a high degree of geographical concentration, with a large share channelled to a small group of countries, mainly in Asia and Latin America. With the exception of South Africa, sub-Saharan Africa has a negligible share. These flows are in any case volatile, which can make countries particularly vulnerable during macro-economic and financial crises. In the aftermath of the recent financial crisis in Asia there has been a revived interest in these types of capital flows and in how appropriate international action could be adopted (via regulatory mechanisms) to protect developing countries from financial crises (Ffrench-Davis and Griffith-Jones 2003).

A substantial number of developing countries have now undertaken financial reform, entailing the liberalisation of interest rates, and measures to improve the efficiency of financial institutions, often involving privatisation and the opening up of the domestic banking market to foreign banks (to bring capital and skills through foreign direct investment into the sector). Although straightforward in principle, these reforms have encountered a number of serious problems in practice, many emanating from weaknesses and inexperience in the central banks charged with regulating and supervising the newly liberalised financial system. As a result the impact on savings and investment has not been as positive as was initially hoped. For example, financial sector reforms were unable to boost the savings rate in Zambia due to the poor design of the reforms themselves and inappropriate and ineffective regulation (Maimbo and Mavrotas 2004).

The Asian financial crisis, and Africa's experience, clearly suggest that whilst financial liberalisation may be desirable, the process must be correctly regulated, which requires the construction of institutional capacity, both public and private (Stiglitz 1999; Brownbridge and Kirkpatrick 1999). This is in turn a costly and time-consuming process, and the poorer countries need considerable technical assistance from donors in this area. In summary, transforming the financial structure of a developing economy has been a more complex process than many expected when countries embarked on reform but, nevertheless, it has a substantial pay-off for economic growth and employment generation if done well (Mavrotas 2004).

## Government revenue mobilisation

Official development assistance funds a large proportion of public spending in many low-income developing countries, particularly in countries recovering from conflict. In many SSA countries, the public investment budget is almost entirely funded by donors. To meet the MDG targets effectively, governments need to mobilise more domestic revenues, and there are opportunities in even the poorest countries to do this. However, governments need to undertake considerable institutional investment to improve often archaic tax administrations (Addison and Levin 2004).

The introduction of VAT in a number of developing countries has been successful in raising more revenue. But it is important to complement VAT with either exemptions and/or excise duties to make it less regressive, thereby reducing the burden on poorer households. Excise duties have received less attention in the reform agenda compared to other instruments, but they can raise substantial revenue and at the same time distribute the burden more equitably. However, one needs to have realistic rates to reduce avoidance and corruption, and they should be seen as a long-term opportunity for raising revenue as the economy develops and the consumption of luxury commodities rises.

One important issue is broadening the tax base. According to the empirical evidence, broadening the VAT base cannot be achieved without increasing the tax burden of the poor. Hence, broadening the VAT base should be a low priority and should be implemented only in those countries where the net fiscal incidence (the net impact of taxation and public spending taken together) is favourable to the poor. Instead priority should be given to the wide divergence between the effective and statutory tax rates. There is considerable scope for raising tax revenue without increasing tax rates by reinforcing tax and customs administration, reducing tax exemptions and fighting fraud and corruption (including within the tax authorities themselves). Improving the collection of direct taxes is also important, and the emphasis should be on reducing tax evasion. In order to protect poorer households it is important to set the income tax threshold at a suitably high level (as has been done in Kenya, for example).

Building institutional capacity has been a crucial component in the reform agenda. First, governments should provide a governance framework within which revenue authorities can perform effectively without continual compromise. Second, governments need to respect the independence of the revenue authority and address the need to maintain incentives for staff within that service. Third, governments also have to recognise that weaknesses in budgetary and expenditure management systems will undermine the potential economic and political returns on investment in the revenue services. Fourth, institutional components have been biased towards organisation, information technology procedures and manpower upgrading, with insufficient attention to accountability, anti-corruption institution building and the cost-effectiveness of administration.

Governments must be careful not to deter private investment, either domestic or FDI, by excessive taxation of corporate profits and over-complex tax systems. Many countries have corporate income tax systems that distort the pattern of investment, favouring large over small and medium-sized enterprises for example, thereby reducing employment growth. Tax incentives for FDI should also be carefully considered; countries must ask themselves whether the benefit of such investment is worth the revenue foregone (Heady 2004). Given that FDI responds positively to the availability of infrastructure, it would in many cases be a better policy not to grant tax breaks to foreign investors, but to use domestic revenues to build infrastructure, particularly in the telecommunications sector, which is increasingly critical to location decisions. Tax policy with regard to FDI is another aspect of the overarching national FDI strategy that is so central, as we argued earlier, to using FDI effectively for development and poverty reduction.

## Conclusions

The synergies and complementarities between different types of external financial flow, as well as the interaction between domestic finance issues and international finance issues, are crucial to making development finance work for the MDGs. In this chapter we have discussed some, but certainly not all, of the important dimensions of the topic, with a particular focus on foreign direct investment, recent proposals for new and innovative sources of finance, and the roles of the domestic banking system and government revenue management. Two key points stand out. First, there is considerable scope for encouraging more FDI into sub-Saharan Africa, and the FDI that Africa does get – concentrated overwhelmingly in the minerals sector – must be put into a tighter national policy framework that directs its use for development and poverty reduction. Second, the proposals for new and innovative finance show varying rates of progress, depending upon the coalitions of countries and civil society organisations that organise themselves in support.

Issues of finance often seem far removed from the day-to-day lives of the poor. Yet mobilising finance in the right way can be a tremendous force for good. The roads that the poor travel down, the markets that they access, and the schools that their children attend are all – in one way or another – the products of development finance. Efforts to encourage more external and domestic development finance should thus have high political priority at both international and national levels. There is considerable scope for further innovation in development finance, if the political will exists. The issues are too important to be left to technical analysis but must be debated in earnest in the major forums for development policy discussion and decision making.

## Notes

1 We would like to thank Colin Bradford, Fantu Cheru and Sami Lahdensuo for very helpful comments and suggestions on an earlier draft. We are also grateful to Martti Hetemaki, Jaakko Iloniemi, Richard Samans, Andres Solimano, Jan Vandemoortele, and participants in the Geneva meeting of the Helsinki Process Track II (25–27 March 2004) for useful comments and background discussions. Finally, the views expressed in the paper are those of the authors and should not be attributed to UNU–WIDER.

2 FDI is characterized by a lasting interest in, or effective management control over, an enterprise in another country; it is distinct from portfolio flows, which consist of equity flows and bond issues purchased by foreign investors.

3 Horizontal FDI in developing countries has traditionally been much less important than vertical FDI. For example, only 4 per cent of production by the affiliates of US multinationals in the European Union is sold back to the United States, whereas the proportion is 18 per cent for developing countries (Shatz and Venables 2000).

## References

Addison, T. and A. Chowdhury. 2004. 'A Global Lottery and a Global Premium Bond', in A. B. Atkinson (ed.), *New Sources of Development Finance*. Oxford: Oxford University Press for UNU–WIDER, pp. 156–76.

Addison, T. and A. Heshmati. 2004. 'The New Global Determinants of FDI Flows to Developing Countries: the Importance of ICT and Democratisation', in M. Bagella, L. Becchetti, I. Hasan and W. C. Hunter (eds.), *Monetary Integration, Markets and Regulation: Research in Banking and Finance*, Volume 4. United Kingdom: Elsevier, pp. 151–86.

Addison, T. and J. Levin. 2004. 'Tax Policy Reform in Developing Countries'. Paper prepared for DANIDA, Helsinki: UNU-WIDER.

Addison, T. and G. Mavrotas. 2003. 'Infrastructure and Development in Africa', in 'TICAD III', United Nations University's policy brief. Tokyo: United Nations Centre.

Aryeetey, E. 2005. 'A Development-focused Allocation of the Special Drawing Rights', in A. B. Atkinson (ed.), *New Sources of Development Finance*. Oxford: Oxford University Press for UNU–WIDER, pp. 90–109.

Asiedu, E. 2004. 'Policy Reform and Foreign Direct Investment in Africa: Absolute Progress but Relative Decline'. *Development Policy Review*, 22, 1: 41–8.

Atkinson, A. B. (ed.). 2005. *New Sources of Development Finance*. Oxford: Oxford University Press for UNU–WIDER.

Brownbridge, M. and C. Kirkpatrick. 1999. 'Financial Sector Regulation: Lessons of the Asia Crisis'. *Development Policy Review*, 17, 3.

Chowdhury, A. and G. Mavrotas. 2003. 'FDI and Growth: What Causes What?' Paper presented at the Sharing Global Prosperity Conference, WIDER, Helsinki, 6–7 September 2003.

Clunies-Ross, A. 1999. 'Sustaining Revenue for Social Purposes in the Face of Globalisation', in UN-DESA, *Experts Discuss Some Critical Social Development Issues*. New York: UN Department of Economic and Social Affairs.

de Mello, L. 1997. 'Foreign Direct Investment in Developing Countries and Growth: a Selective Survey'. *Journal of Development Studies*, 34: 1–34.

Dercon, S. (ed.) 2004. *Insurance Against Poverty*. Oxford: Oxford University Press for UNU-WIDER.

Devarajan, S., M. J. Miller and E. V. Swanson. 2002. 'Goals for Development: History, Prospects, and Costs'. Policy Research Working Paper No. 2819, World Bank.

Ffrench-Davis, R. and S. Griffith-Jones (eds.). 2003. *From Capital Surges to Drought: Seeking Stability for Emerging Economies*. Basingstoke: Palgrave Macmillan.

Hansen, E. and J. Rand. 2003. 'On the Causal Links between FDI and Growth in Developing Countries'. Mimeo, Development Economics Research Group, Institute of Economics, University of Copenhagen.

Heady, C. 2004. 'Taxation Policy in Low-Income Countries', in T. Addison and A. Roe (eds.), *Fiscal Policy for Development: Poverty, Reconstruction and Growth*. Basingstoke: Palgrave Macmillan: 130–48.

ILO 2002. *Investment in the Global Economy and Decent Work*. Working Party on the Social Dimension of Globalisation, GB.285/WP/SDG/2, ILO, Geneva.

Keller, W. 1996. 'Absorptive Capacity: on the Creation and Acquisition of Technology in Development'. *Journal of Development Economics*, 49: 199–227.

Klein, M., C. Aaron and B. Hadjimichael. 2001. 'Foreign Direct Investment and Poverty Reduction'. Paper presented at the OECD Conference on New Horizons and Policy Challenges for Foreign Direct Investment in the Twenty-first Century, Mexico City, 26–27 November 2001.

Kotler, P., S. Jatusripitak and S. Maesincee. 1997. *The Marketing of Nations: a Strategic Approach to Building National Wealth*. New York: Free Press.

Landau, J. P. *et al*. 2004. 'Groupe de travail sur les nouvelles contributions financières internationales: rapport à Monsieur Jacques Chirac le Président de la République'. Paris: Government of France.

Lizondo, J. S. 1990. 'Foreign Direct Investment'. IMF Working Paper No. 63, Washington, DC: International Monetary Fund.

Maimbo, S. and G. Mavrotas. 2004. 'Saving Mobilisation in Zambia: the Role of Financial Sector Reforms'. *Savings and Development Quarterly Review*, forthcoming.

Mavrotas, G. 2004. 'Savings and Financial Sector Development: Assessing the Evidence', in C. Green, C. Kirkpatrick and V. Murinde (eds.), *Finance and Development: Survey of Theory, Evidence and Policy*. United Kingdom: Edward Elgar.

Mavrotas, G. 2005. 'The International Finance Facility Proposal', in A. B. Atkinson (ed.), *New Sources of Development Finance*. Oxford: Oxford University Press for UNU–WIDER, pp. 110–31.

Micklewright J. and A. Wright. 2005. 'Private Donations for International Development', in A. B. Atkinson (ed.), *New Sources of Development Finance*. Oxford: Oxford University Press for UNU–WIDER, pp. 132–53.

Nayyar, D. (ed.) 2002. *Globalisation: Issues and Institutions*. Oxford: Oxford University Press for UNU–WIDER.

Nissanke M. 2005. 'Revenue Potential of the Tobin Tax for Development Finance: a Critical Appraisal', in A. B. Atkinson (ed.), *New Sources of Development Finance*. Oxford: Oxford University Press for UNU–WIDER, pp. 132–55.

Noorbakhsh, F., A. Poloni and A. Youssef. 2001. 'Human Capital and FDI Inflows to Developing Countries: New Empirical Evidence'. *World Development*, 29, 9: 1593–610.

PPI Database. 2000. *Private Participation in Infrastructure Group*. Washington, DC: World Bank.

Saggi, K. 2002. 'Trade, Foreign Direct Investment, and International Technology Transfer: a Survey'. *World Bank Research Observer*, 17, 2: 191–235.

Sandmo, A. 2005. 'Environmental Taxation and Revenue for Development', in A. B. Atkinson (ed.), *New Sources of Development Finance*. Oxford: Oxford University Press for UNU–WIDER, pp. 33–57.

Shatz, H. J. and A. J. Venables. 2000. 'The Geography of International Investment'. World Bank Discussion Paper No. 2338, Washington, DC: World Bank.

Solimano A. 2005. 'Remittances by Emigrants: Issues and Evidence', in A. B. Atkinson (ed.), *New Sources of Development Finance*. Oxford: Oxford University Press for UNU–WIDER, pp. 177–99.

Stiglitz, J. 1999. 'Responding to Economic Crises: Policy Alternatives for Equitable Recovery and Development'. *The Manchester School*, 67, 5.

Svedberg, P. 1978. 'The Portfolio-Direct Investment Composition of Private Foreign Investment in 1914, Revisited'. *Economic Journal*, 88: 763–77.

UN. 2001. 'Report of the High-Level Panel on Financing for Development' (chairperson Ernesto Zedillo). New York: United Nations.

UNCTAD. 2000. *Survey of Multinational Corporate Executives*. World Investment Report, Geneva: United Nations Conference on Trade and Development.

UNCTAD. 2001. *Third United Nations Conference on the Least Developed Countries (LDCIII) – Infrastructure Development Session*. Brussels, 19 May 2001.

UNCTAD. 2003a. *Trade and Development Report, 2003: Capital Accumulation, Growth and Structural Change*. New York and Geneva: United Nations.

UNCTAD. 2003b. *World Investment Report*. New York and Geneva: United

Nations.

Vandemoortele, J. and R. Roy. 2004. 'Making Sense of MDG Costing'. Paper submitted to the Helsinki Process on Globalisation and Democracy for discussion, Track II (Global Economic Agenda).

World Bank. 2002. *Global Development Finance 2002*. Washington, DC: World Bank.

World Bank. 2003. *Global Development Finance 2003*. Washington, DC: World Bank.

# 5

## Remittances by Emigrants:
## Issues and Evidence[1]

### ANDRÉS SOLIMANO

Remittances from migrants are a growing, relatively stable and market–based external source of development finance. Remittances bring foreign exchange, complement national savings and provide a source of finance for capital formation (mainly small-scale projects). Through this mechanism remittances can support economic growth in recipient countries. As remittances depend on flows of people that are often less volatile than capital flows, remittances are expected to be more stable than capital flows such as portfolio investment and international bank credit. Remittances are also an international redistribution from low-income migrants to their families in the home country. These transfers act as an international mechanism of social protection based on private transfers. The sustainability of remittances over time depends on various factors such as the anticipated flow of migration, whether the migrants come alone or with their families, and how this changes over time.[2]

It is also important to recognise that the benefits of remittances for receiving countries have to be compared with the potential costs of emigration for developing countries in terms of losses of scarce human skills that leave home (the so called brain drain phenomenon). So we have a certain trade-off here between generating an inflow of foreign exchange and external savings through remittances and the outflow of skilled individuals.[3]

Remittances are, currently, the second most important source of external finance to developing countries, after foreign direct investment. Moreover, remittances surpass foreign aid. There are 20 main recipients of remittances and these are 20 low-to-medium-income developing countries that capture around 80 per cent of total remittances to the developing countries. The three main recipient countries, in terms of value, are India, Mexico and the Philippines. In turn, the three main source countries of remittances are the United States, Saudi Arabia and Germany.

The international market for remittances is segmented and inefficient (from a social point of view), as reflected by high costs of intermediation. Money transfer operators, who dominate the market, charge high fees and use overvalued exchange rates. Commercial banks of both source and recipient countries have a low share of the global remittances market – although the empirical evidence shows that costs are lower when remittances are sent through banks rather than through money transfer operators.

There is, however, room for leveraging a greater value for remittances if international money transfers were conducted at lower cost. The amount of remittances is below the socially optimal amount associated with a more competitive cost structure in the market for remittances (therefore, there is a deadweight loss for both senders and recipients of remittances). The development potential of remittances is thus diminished by current market realities.

The next section of this chapter discusses global and regional trends in remittance flows and their growing importance as a source of external transfer to developing countries. The third section examines measurement issues and discusses the main micro-motives for remittances and implications for their stability across cycles. The fourth section analyses the development impact of remittances (effects on savings, investment, growth, poverty, income distribution). The fifth section overviews the international market for remittances and provides evidence on costs of sending remittances to various country groups. The sixth section highlights policies to cut the cost of sending remittances and enhance their development impact. The final section presents conclusions.

## Global and regional trends in remittance flows

In a world of volatile capital flows, remittances[4] are a stabilising component of external resource transfers to the developing world. Remittances are the financial counterpart of the migration flows that have grown significantly in the last two decades in response to growing opportunities in advanced economies compared to developing countries. Remittances to the developing world have increased, steadily, from around US$15 billion in 1980 to US$80 billion in 2002. This represents an annual rate of increase of 7.7 per cent (see Table 5.1).[5] At regional level, the highest rate of increase in the flow of remittances is towards Latin American and the Caribbean with 12.4 per cent per annum. Then follow East Asia and the Pacific with 11 per cent per year. The lowest annual rate of expansion in remittances is to sub-Saharan Africa with 5.2 per cent. According to Table 5.1, in 2002 Latin America and the Caribbean had the highest level of remittances with US$25 billion, followed by South Asia (US$16 billion), East Asia and the Pacific (US$11 billion) and the Middle East and North Africa (MENA) (US$14 billion). The lowest level of remittances is to sub-Saharan Africa (US$4 billion).

In terms of distribution of remittances by income *per capita* levels, the developing countries as a group received 65 per cent of world remittances. In

## Table 5.1  Remittances received by region, 1980–2002 (US$ billion)

| Regions | 1980 | 1985 | 1990 | 1995 | 1996 | 1997 | 1998 | 1999 | 2000 | 2001 | 2002* | Annual rate of growth (%) 1980–2002 |
|---|---|---|---|---|---|---|---|---|---|---|---|---|
| East Asia & Pacific | 1.1 | 2.3 | 3.6 | 8.3 | 9.5 | 14.2 | 8.3 | 10.6 | 10.3 | 10.4 | 11.0 | 11.0 |
| Share (%) of remittances in developing countries | 7.1 | 12.7 | 12.4 | 17.3 | 18.1 | 22.6 | 13.9 | 16.4 | 15.9 | 14.4 | 13.8 | |
| Europe & Central Asia | 2.1 | 1.7 | 3.2 | 5.5 | 6.2 | 7.1 | 9.2 | 8.1 | 8.7 | 8.9 | 10.0 | 7.4 |
| Share (%) of remittances in developing countries | 13.5 | 9.4 | 11.0 | 11.5 | 11.8 | 11.3 | 15.5 | 12.5 | 13.5 | 12.3 | 12.5 | |
| Latin America & the Caribbean | 1.9 | 2.6 | 5.7 | 12.8 | 12.8 | 13.6 | 14.8 | 16.9 | 19.2 | 22.6 | 25.0 | 12.4 |
| Share (%) of remittances in developing countries | 12.3 | 14.4 | 19.6 | 26.7 | 24.3 | 21.7 | 24.9 | 26.1 | 29.7 | 31.3 | 31.3 | |
| Middle East & North Africa | 3.8 | 4.6 | 9.3 | 8.6 | 9.1 | 9.4 | 10.3 | 10.5 | 10.9 | 13.1 | 14.0 | 6.1 |
| Share (%) of remittances in developing countries | 24.5 | 25.4 | 32.0 | 18.0 | 17.3 | 15.0 | 17.3 | 16.2 | 16.9 | 18.1 | 17.5 | |
| South Asia | 5.3 | 5.8 | 5.6 | 10.0 | 12.3 | 14.6 | 13.3 | 15.1 | 13.5 | 14.9 | 16.0 | 5.2 |
| Share (%) of remittances in developing countries | 34.2 | 32.0 | 19.2 | 20.9 | 23.4 | 23.3 | 22.4 | 23.3 | 20.9 | 20.6 | 20.0 | |
| Sub-Saharan Africa | 1.3 | 1.1 | 1.7 | 2.7 | 2.7 | 3.8 | 3.6 | 3.5 | 2.0 | 2.4 | 4.0 | 5.2 |
| Share (%) of remittances in developing countries | 8.4 | 6.1 | 5.8 | 5.6 | 5.1 | 6.1 | 6.1 | 5.4 | 3.1 | 3.3 | 5.0 | |
| Developing countries | 15.5 | 18.1 | 29.1 | 47.9 | 52.6 | 62.7 | 59.5 | 64.7 | 64.6 | 72.3 | 80.0 | 7.7 |
| Industrial countries | n.a. | n.a. | n.a. | 37.2 | 35.7 | 40.5 | 41.0 | 40.2 | 40.1 | 39.3 | n.a. | n.a. |
| All countries | n.a. | n.a. | n.a. | 85.1 | 88.3 | 103.2 | 100.5 | 104.9 | 104.7 | 111.6 | n.a. | n.a. |

* Estimates

Note: Remittances are calculated as the sum of workers' remittances and compensation of employees (n.a. = not available).

Source: IMF 2003.

### Table 5.2 Remittances received by country groupings, 1995–2001 (US$ billion)

| Countries | 1995 | 1996 | 1997 | 1998 | 1999 | 2000 | 2001 |
|---|---|---|---|---|---|---|---|
| Upper-middle-income | 13.7 | 13.6 | 14.3 | 16.3 | 15.7 | 16.6 | 17.2 |
| Share of remittances in all countries | 16.1 | 15.4 | 13.8 | 16.2 | 15.0 | 15.9 | 15.4 |
| Lower-middle-income | 20.7 | 21.2 | 24.2 | 24.1 | 27.2 | 28.3 | 30.0 |
| Share of remittances in all countries | 24.3 | 24.0 | 23.5 | 24.0 | 26.0 | 27.0 | 26.9 |
| Low income | 13.5 | 17.8 | 24.2 | 19.1 | 21.8 | 19.7 | 25.1 |
| Share of remittances in all countries | 15.9 | 20.2 | 23.5 | 19.0 | 20.8 | 18.8 | 22.5 |
| All developing | 47.9 | 52.6 | 62.7 | 59.5 | 64.7 | 64.6 | 72.3 |
| Share of remittances in all countries | 56.3 | 59.6 | 60.7 | 59.2 | 61.7 | 61.7 | 64.8 |
| Industrial countries | 37.2 | 35.7 | 40.5 | 41.0 | 40.2 | 40.1 | 39.3 |
| Share of remittances in all countries | 43.7 | 40.4 | 39.3 | 40.8 | 38.3 | 38.3 | 35.2 |
| All countries | 85.1 | 88.3 | 103.2 | 100.5 | 104.9 | 104.7 | 111.6 |
| Share of remittances in all countries | 100.0 | 100.0 | 100.0 | 100.0 | 100.0 | 100.0 | 100.0 |

Note: Remittances are calculated as the sum of workers' remittances and compensation of employees.
Source: IMF 2003.

turn, the lower-middle-income and low-income groups receive a higher proportion than upper-middle-income countries (see Table 5.2).

In 2002, for the group of developing countries, workers' remittances represented, on average, 1.3 per cent of GDP, 55.9 per cent of the flows of foreign direct investment and near 140 per cent of the aid flows (see Table 5.3). These coefficients vary from region to region. The proportion of remittances to gross domestic product is the highest in the MENA region (3 per cent in 2002) and the lowest in the East Asia and Pacific region (0.7 per cent). Remittances as a proportion of foreign direct investment are the highest in the MENA region (466.7 per cent in 2002) and the lowest in East Asia and Pacific (19.3 per cent). In turn, the proportion of remittances to foreign aid is lowest in sub-Saharan Africa, reflecting both lower remittances and high aid flows to this region.

In terms of total resource flows, remittances are the second largest component of external resource flows to developing countries after foreign direct investment (see Table 5.4 and Figure 5.1). Remittances have been larger than aid flows as a source of external development finance since 1997. In 2001, foreign aid represented 18 per cent of total external flows of finance and remittances 25 per cent. Interestingly, as mentioned at the outset, remittances are much more stable than other capital flows – mainly bank credit and portfolio investment – that are identified as volatile components of external resource flows.

The quantitative importance of these volatile components of private capital flows is still significant (near 30 per cent of total resource flows to developing countries, as an average, between 1991 and 2000). These components are

## Table 5.3 Remittances received by developing countries, 1996–2002

| Regions | 1996 | 1997 | 1998 | 1999 | 2000 | 2001 | 2002E |
|---|---|---|---|---|---|---|---|
| East Asia and Pacific | | | | | | | |
| as % of GDP | 1.0 | 1.3 | 0.7 | 0.8 | 0.7 | 0.7 | 0.7 |
| as % of FDI inflows | 16.2 | 22.8 | 14.4 | 21.7 | 23.4 | 21.3 | 19.3 |
| as % of aid flows | 125.0 | 215.2 | 103.8 | 112.8 | 128.8 | 152.9 | n.a. |
| Europe and Central Asia | | | | | | | |
| as % of GDP | 1.4 | 1.3 | 1.4 | 1.1 | 1.0 | 0.9 | 1.0 |
| as % of FDI inflows | 38.0 | 32.6 | 35.4 | 28.6 | 29.8 | 29.6 | 34.5 |
| as % of aid flows | 89.9 | 126.8 | 131.4 | 84.4 | 90.6 | 97.8 | n.a. |
| Latin America and the Caribbean | | | | | | | |
| as % of GDP | 1.3 | 1.2 | 1.1 | 1.1 | 1.2 | 1.3 | 1.4 |
| as % of FDI inflows | 28.8 | 20.6 | 20.2 | 19.2 | 25.3 | 32.6 | 59.5 |
| as % of aid flows | 232.7 | 302.2 | 328.9 | 359.6 | 505.3 | 434.6 | n.a. |
| Middle East and North Africa | | | | | | | |
| as % of GDP | 3.4 | 3.0 | 3.1 | 2.9 | 2.8 | 3.0 | 3.0 |
| as % of FDI inflows | 1,300.0 | 151.6 | 137.3 | 328.1 | 436.0 | 238.2 | 466.7 |
| as % of aid flows | 171.7 | 195.8 | 219.1 | 244.2 | 294.6 | 335.9 | n.a. |
| South Asia | | | | | | | |
| as % of GDP | 3.7 | 3.8 | 3.1 | 3.2 | 2.6 | 2.6 | 2.6 |
| as % of FDI inflows | 351.4 | 298.0 | 380.0 | 487.1 | 435.5 | 363.4 | 320.0 |
| as % of aid flows | 236.5 | 339.5 | 271.4 | 351.2 | 321.4 | 252.5 | n.a. |
| Sub-Saharan Africa | | | | | | | |
| as % of GDP | 1.4 | 1.7 | 1.4 | 1.3 | 0.7 | 0.7 | 1.1 |
| as % of FDI inflows | 62.8 | 46.9 | 55.4 | 43.2 | 32.8 | 17.4 | 57.1 |
| as % of aid flows | 18.0 | 28.6 | 27.1 | 28.7 | 16.4 | 18.9 | n.a. |
| Developing countries | | | | | | | |
| as % of GDP | 1.6 | 1.7 | 1.4 | 1.4 | 1.3 | 1.3 | 1.3 |
| as % of FDI inflows | 41.2 | 37.0 | 34.1 | 36.1 | 40.2 | 42.1 | 55.9 |
| as % of aid flows | 101.3 | 134.5 | 118.3 | 123.5 | 127.9 | 139.0 | n.a. |

Notes:  Remittances are calculated as the sum of workers' remittances and compensation of employees.
FDI is foreign direct investment. Aid flows are official development assistance.
E = estimate. n.a. = not available.

an important source of macroeconomic volatility. Often, private capital flows *lead* macroeconomic cycles. In contrast, remittances can even be counter-cyclical, as emigrants send money home in bad times to provide a source of income support.

At the level of individual countries, remittances are relatively concentrated in a group of 20 developing countries that capture around 80 per cent of total remittances to the developing countries (see Figure 5.2). In turn, the GDP of these 20 countries represents around 60 per cent of the GDP of developing countries.[6] The main recipient of workers' remittances in 2001 was India, which received an annual flow of US$10 billion, followed by Mexico with US$9.9 billion and the Philippines with US$6.4 billion. At the lower end of the top 20 developing-country recipients of remittances are

### Table 5.4 Resource flows to developing countries, 1991–2002
### (current US$ billions and %)

|  | Remittances[a] | | Aid flows[b] | | Other official flows[c] | | FDI | | Other private flows[d] | | Total | |
|---|---|---|---|---|---|---|---|---|---|---|---|---|
|  | US$ | % | US$ | % | US$ | % | US$ | % | US$ | % | US$ | % |
| 1991 | 33.1 | 21 | 49.5 | 32 | 11.4 | 7 | 35.7 | 23 | 26.3 | 17 | 156 | 100 |
| 1992 | 37.2 | 19 | 46.4 | 24 | 10.1 | 5 | 47.1 | 24 | 52.2 | 27 | 193 | 100 |
| 1993 | 38.9 | 15 | 41.7 | 16 | 11.9 | 5 | 66.6 | 26 | 100.2 | 39 | 259.3 | 100 |
| 1994 | 44.1 | 16 | 48.1 | 18 | −0.1 | 0 | 90.0 | 34 | 85.6 | 32 | 267.7 | 100 |
| 1995 | 47.9 | 15 | 61.0 | 19 | 8.9 | 3 | 105.0 | 33 | 99.1 | 31 | 322.3 | 100 |
| 1996 | 52.6 | 14 | 51.9 | 14 | −7.8 | −2 | 128.0 | 34 | 148.44 | 40 | 372.9 | 100 |
| 1997 | 62.7 | 15 | 46.6 | 11 | 7.2 | 2 | 169.0 | 41 | 131.37 | 31 | 417.2 | 100 |
| 1998 | 59.5 | 15 | 50.3 | 12 | 16.2 | 4 | 175.0 | 43 | 108.75 | 27 | 409.3 | 100 |
| 1999 | 64.7 | 19 | 52.4 | 15 | 5.0 | 1 | 179.0 | 52 | 45.09 | 13 | 346.6 | 100 |
| 2000 | 64.6 | 19 | 50.5 | 15 | −3.0 | −1 | 161.0 | 48 | 65.15 | 19 | 338.0 | 100 |
| 2001 | 72.3 | 25 | 52.0 | 18 | n.a. | n.a. | 172.0 | 60 | −11.73 | −4 | 284.3 | 100 |
| 2002E | 80.0 | 36 | n.a. | n.a. | n.a. | n.a. | 143.0 | 64 | n.a. | n.a. | 223.0 | 100 |
| Average 1991–2001 | 52.51 | 18 | 50.04 | 18 | 5.98 | 2 | 120.75 | 38 | 77.32 | 25 | 306.04 | 100 |

Notes:
a  Remittances are calculated as the sum of workers' remittances and compensation of employees.
b  Aid flows are official development assistance and official aid.
c  Other official flows are total official flows (official development finance), net of aid flows.
d  Other private flows are portfolio flows and bank and trade.
n.a. = not available. E = estimate.

Source:  IMF 2003 for remittances. World Bank 2003 for all other flows.

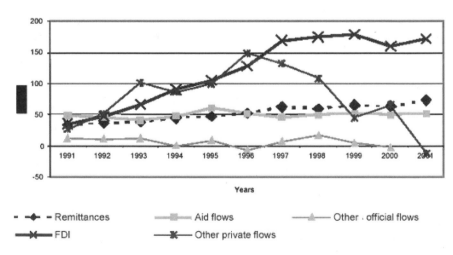

Figure 5.1  Long-term resource flows to developing countries, 1991–2001
Source: IMF 2003 for remittances. World Bank 2003 for all other flows.

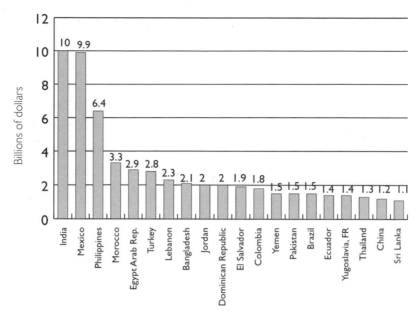

Figure 5.2  Top 20 developing-country recipients of workers' remittances
(US$ billion), 2001

Source: World Bank 2003.

Thailand, China and Sri Lanka. The country ranking changes, however, when remittances are measured as shares of GDP. In this case, the three economies at the top of the ranking are Tonga, Lesotho and Jordan with remittances between 20 and 40 per cent of GDP. At the lower end we find Philippines, Uganda, Ecuador and Sri Lanka, all with shares between 7 and 9 per cent of GDP (see Figure 5.3).

On the other side, the top 20 *source* countries of remittances (in 2001) are headed by the United States with US$28.4 billion, followed by Saudi Arabia (US$15.1 billion) and Germany (US$8.2 billion) (see Figure 5.4). On the lower end of the top 20 senders we find the Czech Republic, Venezuela and Norway (all three with US$0.7 billion in 2001).

Let us turn to the motives for remittances, hoping that these will shed light on the empirical behaviour of remittances highlighted in this section.

## Measurement, micro-motives for remittances and cyclical behaviour

In this section, we will review: (1) measurement issues; (2) the micro-motives to remit; and (3) the stability of remittances during the cycle.[7]

### Definition and measurement issues

The economic significance of remittances often goes beyond what is suggested by the official balance of payments statistics in sending and receiving countries.

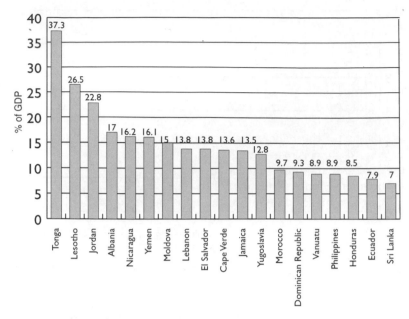

**Figure 5.3  Top 20 developing-country recipients of workers' remittances (% of GDP), 2001**

Source: World Bank 2003

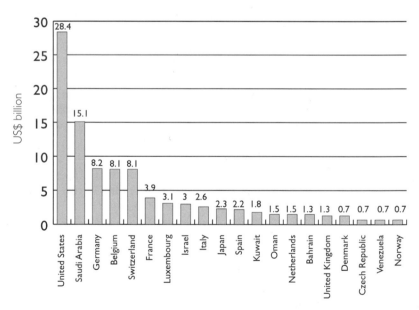

**Figure 5.4  Top 20 sources of remittance payments (US$ billion), 2001**

Source: World Bank 2003

The important concept for measuring the economic impact of remittances is the resource transfer – monetary or in-kind – made by a migrant to his home country. Monetary transfers in dollars directly increase the availability of foreign exchange in the country of origin of the migrant, whereas remittances-in-kind save foreign exchange for the recipient country. These distinctions are important, as there are several modalities for sending remittances. Some of them are recorded while others are not. For example, when remittances are sent through formal channels they are recorded in the receiving country's current account of the balance of payments. Conversely remittances sent informally in cash, for example through couriers, go unrecorded in the official statistics. Remittances can be in–kind, such as goods sent to house-holds in the home country. Only part of the latter will be recorded as imports. Migrants can also make donations in the host country to institutions like the church and charitable organisations formed by co-nationals. They can also make several payments (insurance premiums, school fees, payments for inter-national airfares directly to the airlines) on behalf of relatives or friends from their home country.[8] Although most of these payments should be treated as 'remittances' in an economic sense, they are rarely recorded as such. In sum, all these considerations should be borne in mind when assessing the true magnitude of remittance transfers based on official statistics, which for the reasons mentioned above tend to *underestimate* their full economic impact.

In general, data on remittances are available from three items in balance of payments reports at country level (data for different countries are compiled in the IMF's *Balance of Payments Statistical Yearbook*): (1) 'workers' remit-tances' (money sent by workers abroad for more than one year); (2) 'employee compensations' (gross earnings of foreigners residing abroad for less than a year); and (3) 'migrant transfer' (net worth of migrants moving from one country to another) (see Gammeltoft 2002).

## Microeconomic motivations to remit
The analytical literature[9] on motives for remittances can be summarised in four approaches.

### The altruistic motive
In this view the migrant sends remittances back home out of concern for the well-being of his or her family in the home country. Furthermore, it is an empirical regularity that migrants have a higher education level than other family members who stay at home. As migrants go to countries in which average wages and *per capita* incomes are higher than at home, their income levels after getting a job will be higher than those of comparable workers at home. The main prediction of the altruistic model is that remittances will tend to decrease over time.[10] One reason for this is that family attachment decreases as family members pass more time in different countries. Also the migrant may plan to stay abroad for a long time (and even eventually retire there), bringing his family at some stage. This, of course, reduces remittances.

The converse case would be return migration, in which the migrant brings fresh funds when returning home, raising remittances.

### The self-interest motive

A diametrically opposed explanation assumes that the emigrant is mainly motivated by economic and financial self-interest when sending remittances to the home country. The story goes like this: the successful emigrant in the foreign country saves. Then, the need arises to decide how (in which assets) and where (in which country) to accumulate wealth. An obvious place to invest at least part of the saved assets is in the home country – buying property, land, financial assets, etcetera. These assets may earn a higher rate of return than assets in the host country, although their risk profile can also be greater. In turn, the family can administer them for the migrant during the emigration period, thus acting as a trusted agent. Another motivation to remit is the desire of the emigrant to receive an inheritance from his or her parents. In this case, those family members that have contributed to increasing the wealth of the family (by sending remittances, for example) become obvious candidates for receiving an inheritance in the future.

### Implicit family contract 1: loan repayment

Economic theory has developed explanations of the remittances process that take the family – rather than the individual – as the main unit of analysis.[11] The assumption is that families develop an implicit contract among those who choose to live abroad, the migrants, and those who stay at home. The implicit contract has an inter-temporal dimension, with a stretch of years or even decades as a time horizon. The contract combines elements of investment and repayment. In the loan repayment theory, the family invest in the education of the emigrant and usually finance the cost of migrating (travel and subsistence costs in the host country). This is the loan (investment) element of the theory. Repayment comes after the migrant settles in the foreign country, attains an income profile that rises over time and becomes able to repay the loan (principal and interest) back to the family in the form of remittances. So the family invest in a higher-yield 'asset' (the migrant) who earns a higher income level in the foreign country than other family members who live and work at home. This model predicts various time profiles for remittances, depending upon the time it takes for the migrant to get established in the foreign labour market and also on the duration of the stay abroad. The quicker the insertion of the migrant in the foreign labour market, the faster the remittances flow. The amount to be remitted will depend, among other things, on the income profile of the migrant. In this model remittances do not need to decrease over time, as in the altruistic model.

### Implicit family contract 2: co-insurance

Another variant of the theory of remittances as an implicit family contract between the migrant and those at home relies on the notion of risk diversification. The idea is simple. As insurance markets and capital markets in the real world are incomplete; many risks cannot be diversified by the absence of financial assets that edge risk. In addition, borrowing constraints, particularly serious for poor migrants, limit the ability to smooth consumption or finance investment. Assuming that economic risks between the sending and foreign country are not positively correlated, it becomes a convenient strategy for the family as a whole to send some of its members abroad (often the most educated) to diversify economic risks. The migrant, then, can help to support the family in bad times at home. Conversely, for the migrant, having a family in the home country is insurance against bad times in the foreign country.

In this model, emigration becomes a co-insurance strategy, with remittances playing the role of an insurance claim. As in any contract, there is potentially a problem of enforcement (ensuring that the terms of the contract are respected by the parties, for example). However, we can expect enforcement to be simpler, in principle, because these implicit family contracts are underwritten by considerations of family trust and altruism (a feature often absent in legally sanctioned contracts).

## Stability of remittances in the economic cycle

As mentioned in the previous section, workers' remittances are more stable than portfolio investments and bank credit. Remittances can even be counter-cyclical. The different theories of motivation reviewed above can shed some light on this behaviour. In the model of remittances as altruism migrants can increase their remittances back home when there is an economic downturn in the home country (as the incomes of their families decline). In this case, remittances would be the equivalent of a private 'welfare payment' sent from abroad to help smooth consumption by recipients at home. However, business cycles may be internationally synchronised. The growing economic inter-dependencies of globalisation make this a more plausible case. In this situation, a recession in the receiving country may be positively correlated with a recession in the source country, so the ability of immigrant workers to send remittances may be hampered by economic conditions in the host country. This is a real possibility, although the sender may also draw on existing savings to maintain a steady flow of remittances.

If remittances were driven by the portfolio decisions of the migrants (remittances driven by investment), again the relevant issue would be the correlation between the rate of return on assets in the host country and the rate of return on assets at home. Here the international correlation of business cycles matters as much as the degree of financial integration between source and receiving countries. In the model of remittances as a co-insurance mechanism, risk diversification may call for a steady flow of remittances in the absence of a strong positive correlation in business cycles between source and receiving countries.

## The development impact of remittances

Potentially, remittances can have a positive impact as a development tool for the recipient countries, with effects on savings, investment, growth, consumption, poverty and income distribution. The impact on growth of remittances in receiving economies is likely to act through savings and investment as well as short-run effects on aggregate demand and output through consumption. The indirect effect of migration on output also depends on the productivity level of the emigrant in the home country before departure. The total savings effect of remittances comes from the sum of foreign savings and domestic savings effects. Workers' remittances are a component of foreign savings and they complement national savings by increasing the total pool of resources available to investment.

Part of the savings effects of remittances takes place in the community. In fact, migrant associations, often called home town associations (HTAs) in the United States, organise migrants from various Latin American countries such as El Salvador, Guatemala, Honduras, Mexico and the Dominican Republic. HTAs regularly send donations to finance investment for community projects and local development in the home countries.[12] Migrant associations from El Salvador send home donations of about US$10,000 per year. This modest total is made up of small individual contributions, but in the recipient countries such sums can still have an impact. Mexican migrant associations send home US$5,000–25,000 per year (see Ellerman 2003). In the Mexican state of Zacatecas, the federal and local governments match (at the rate of two to one or three to one) every dollar donated to local projects by HTAs, typically oriented to small infrastructure projects: water treatment, schools, roads, parks, etcetera. Through this programme, more than 400 projects have been completed in eight years in Zacatecas.[13] The total investment made by migrants in those projects amounts to about US$4.5 million (World Bank 2002). In this way, public savings are mobilised along with remittances to finance small community projects.

This chapter has already suggested that the direct effects of remittances on investment are bound to focus on small community projects. Ratha (2003) cites positive effects of remittances on investment in home economies such as Mexico, Egypt, and the countries of sub-Saharan Africa. In these countries, remittances have financed the building of schools, clinics and other infrastructure. In addition, return-migrants bring fresh capital that can help finance investment projects.

Remittances also finance consumption; thus, private savings will increase less than proportionally with an increase in income from external remittances. A study of remittances for Ecuador (Bendixen and Associates 2003) shows that around 60 per cent of remittances in Ecuador are spent on food, medicines, house rents and other basic commodities. The same study shows that less than 5 per cent of remittances are used in the acquisition of residential property.

The combined effects of remittances on investment and consumption can increase output and growth. The sustainability of this effect is an open question. If remittances are a response to recent migration, remittances may be transitory and their effects on investment, consumption and growth likewise. In contrast, if migrants form associations and their commitment to their home country thus becomes institutionalised, then the positive developmental effects of remittances may become more permanent.

The indirect effect of remittances on growth (or output) depends on the type of emigrant that left home, the state of labour markets and the productivity of the emigrant. If the emigrant was an unskilled worker of low productivity, or an unemployed person, reflecting slack and excess supply in the labour market, then the effect of emigration on output in the home country is bound to be small. In contrast, if the emigrant is a highly skilled worker, an information technology expert or an entrepreneur with a high direct and indirect contribution to output, the adverse growth effect of emigration is bound to be considerable (see Solimano 2001, 2002).

A possible negative effect of (large amounts) of remittances is the possibility that they may produce a 'Dutch disease' effect.[14] For countries that receive sizeable sums of remittances, there is a tendency for the real exchange rate to appreciate, penalising non-traditional exports and hampering the development of the tradable goods sector.

Remittances may also have a poverty-reducing and income distribution effect. As mentioned above, the recipients of remittances are often low-income families whose offspring left the country to work abroad. In a way, emigration is a response to escape poverty at home:[15] emigrants attempt to improve their income-earning capacity by seeking to enter foreign labour markets in richer countries. At the same time, remittances serve to alleviate the poverty of the families of migrants in the home country by supporting their income through transfers. The negative side of this is that remittances may also create a certain 'culture of dependence' on remittance incomes. This, in turn, can impair efforts by the recipients of remittances to escape from poverty through education and work.

The distributive effect is another dimension of the development effects of remittances.[16] Stark (1991) studies the effects of remittances on domestic inequality in two Mexican villages near the border with the US in which villagers engage both in internal rural–urban migration and migration to the United States. The study found that remittances from internal migration are more correlated with schooling years than remittances from international migration to the United States, as the latter often go to low-skilled, labour-intensive jobs. Stark concludes that the inequality impact of changes in remittances depends on (1) the location of remittance recipients in the village's income distribution; (2) the share of remittances in villages incomes; and (3) the distribution of remittances themselves. These variables, in turn, depend on the distribution of human capital (education and skills) among villagers and the distribution of migration opportunities in the villages.

Another piece of evidence is provided by Ratha (2003), who reports, for Pakistan, a household data survey showing that the share of income originated by external transfers increases with income levels (the households with the highest incomes receive the largest shares of their income from remittances). So remittances might appear to be increasing local inequality. However, income distribution between countries may eventually improve with remittances, as income *per capita* is redistributed from higher-income source countries to lower-income receiving countries. As we saw in the section on global and regional trends in remittance flows, remittances represent a very significant share of GDP in several low-income countries.

A final remark here: the development effect of remittances depends on the 'life cycle' of the whole migration process at the level of countries. In fact, where receiving countries have growing economies with rising *per capita* incomes, differentials in incomes per head across countries will narrow, reducing the incentives for emigration. Therefore the relative importance of remittances is likely to decline as a country moves up the development ladder. This is valid mainly for remittances from low-skilled migration, however. In the case of high-skilled, well-educated individuals, migration flows are likely to continue at high *per capita* income levels, a feature we observe within the European Union or between Europe and the US. In this case remittances may continue although the economic effects of those remittances are probably quite different than those discussed here for the case in which the recipients of remittances are developing countries.

## The international markets for remittances

Remittances are channelled through financial entities such as money transfer operators (MTOs), post offices or travel agencies; they are hand-delivered by couriers or reach the recipients through informal financial institutions. MTOs owned and run by immigrants (or naturalised citizens of the same ethnic or national group) are denominated as 'ethnic stores'. Commercial banks are also in the remittances business, but they are not, in general, important players. The commonly used financial intermediaries often charge fees for money transfers that are well above the marginal cost of those transfers (see Orozco 2003).

The most important MTO at global level is Western Union, with branches in many countries, followed by MoneyGram and Thomas Cook. The less competitive, more concentrated and more segmented the market for remittances, the higher the cost. There are a number of reasons why the international market for remittances tends to be thin and poorly competitive (a few players dominate the market; costs of intermediation are high). First, the legal status of the migrants who send remittances is not always regularised. Some migrants have resident (working) visas, others are waiting for their visas to be processed and others are simply 'illegal'. Commercial banks are reluctant to enter into the market in financial services for low-income migrants, who often have a non-regularised immigration status.[17] The result is less competition in the market; besides, migrants are not well integrated, as customers, in formal banking circuits.

Second, it is important to note that workers' remittances are small-scale. In Latin America, the typical remittance per migrant person is in the range of US$200–300 per month.[18] As individual transactions are small, service standardisation is needed for the remittance market to be a profitable activity at competitive fees. In this context, high fees may compensate for the cost of small transactions.[19] Finally, other factors that affect the market for remittances are: exchange rate risk, government regulations for foreign exchange transactions in the receiving country, and regulations in the sending country such as licensing costs.

## Costs of remittances

Let us turn now to the efficiency of the market for remittances to the Andean region. If the costs of remittances are above the marginal cost (including a normal return to capital) of sending money, then the amount of remittances is below the socially optimal level. As a consequence of this, there are foregone consumption, investment and output opportunities in the receiving country that could not be realised.

The work by Orozco (2001, 2002) highlights two main cost components in sending remittances:

Total charge for remittance = explicit fee + exchange rate spread.

Companies charge an explicit fee that can be a percentage of the amount remitted or a fixed amount (often in dollars). The fee usually depends on the services offered (speed of delivery, home delivery, etcetera). The exchange rate spread is the difference between the exchange rate applied by the money transmitter company to convert dollars into local currency and the market (inter-bank, for example) exchange rate. Money transfer companies usually offer a less favourable exchange rate to the sender than the market rate. This is an additional source of profits for the MTOs and an additional cost component for the user.

The average cost of sending US$200 of remittances through commercial banks to selected non-Latin American countries is 7 per cent compared to 12 per cent if money is sent through MTOs such as Western Union and Money-Gram (see Table 5.6).[20] Clearly, sending money through banks is less expensive than sending it through MTOs. Banks also offer a variety of money transfer services and charges decline substantially when deposited in accounts of the same bank in the source and destination countries. Foreign exchange spreads represent around 14 per cent of the total costs of remittances for non-Latin American countries. However, country averages mask significant cross-country differences in the cost of sending remittances. According to Orozco (2003), the cost of sending money through banks is lowest for Pakistan and highest for the Philippines. These costs are much more

### Table 5.5 Countries and companies studied

| Receiving country | Remittances sent from | Number of companies reviewed Banks | MTOs[a] | Other | All businesses |
|---|---|---|---|---|---|
| Philippines | United States | 5 | 14 | 5 | 24 |
| Egypt | United States | | 2 | | 2 |
| Greece | Germany and USA | 4 | 2 | | 6 |
| India | Saudi Arabia, USA, UK | 7 | 11 | | 18 |
| Pakistan | Saudia Arabia, USA, UK | 7 | 1 | | 8 |
| Portugal | France, USA | 3 | 2 | | 5 |
| Turkey | Germany, USA | 3 | 2 | | 5 |
| Mozambique | South Africa, USA | 1 | | | 1 |
| Zimbabwe | South Africa, USA | | 7 | | 7 |
| Bangladesh | UK | 1 | 3 | | 4 |
| Ghana | UK | | 7 | | 7 |

[a] Money transfer operators
Source: Orozco 2003.

### Table 5.6 Average cost of sending money to select non-Latin American countries

| Type | For a remittance of US$200 FX % | Fee % | Total% |
|---|---|---|---|
| Bank | 1.0 | 6.5 | 7.0 |
| Major MTO | 1.7 | 10.9 | 12.0 |

Source: Orozco 2003.

### Table 5.7 Charges (%) by type of business for sending US$200 to selected countries

| Type | Type of business Bank | Ethnic store/exchange house | Major MTO |
|---|---|---|---|
| Egypt | | | 13.8 |
| Philippines | 8.0 | 10.1 | 10.3 |
| India | 6.0 | 2.5 | 13.8 |
| Greece | 6.8 | | 9.5 |
| Pakistan | 0.4 | 3.0 | 13.0 |
| Portugal | 3.4 | | 12.3 |
| Turkey | 3.1 | | 9.5 |
| Mozambique | 1.0 | | |
| Mean | 7.0 | 6.0 | 12.0 |

Source: Orozco 2003.

Table 5.8  Average charges for sending US$200 from the United States to Latin America (in US$ dollars, and as %)

| Type | November 2001 | | November 2002 | |
| | US$ | % | US$ | % |
|---|---|---|---|---|
| Total charge | 17.46 | 8.77 | 16.02 | 8.01 |
| FX charges | 4.73 | 2.44 | 2.97 | 1.48 |
| Fee charge | 15.33 | 7.66 | 14.05 | 7.02 |

Source: Orozco 2003.

Table 5.9  Cost of remittances from the US to the Andean countries (in local currency versus US$, averages per country)

| Type Amount | Country | Currency | Fxchange Level | % | Fee charge % | Total charge Level | % |
|---|---|---|---|---|---|---|---|
| US$200 | Colombia | Local | 9.30 | 4.65 | 10.67 5.33 | 19.96 | 9.98 |
| | | Dollar | 0.00 | 0.00 | 12.33 6.17 | 12.33 | 6.17 |
| | Ecuador | Dollar | 0.00 | 0.00 | 11.23 5.62 | 11.23 | 5.62 |
| | Bolivia | Local | 6.50 | 3.25 | 21.00 10.50 | 27.50 | 13.75 |
| | | Dollar | 0.00 | 0.00 | 16.80 8.40 | 16.80 | 8.40 |
| | Peru | Local | −3.54 | −1.77 | 18.50 9.25 | 14.96 | 7.48 |
| | | Dollar | 0.00 | 0.00 | 13.00 6.50 | 13.00 | 6.50 |
| | Venezuela | Local | 12.04 | 6.02 | 15.00 7.50 | 27.04 | 13.52 |
| | | Dollar | 0.00 | 0.00 | 21.00 10.50 | 21.00 | 10.50 |
| U5$250 | Colombia | Local | 11.62 | 4.65 | 13.25 5.30 | 24.87 | 9.95 |
| | | Dollar | 0.00 | 0.00 | 15.39 6.16 | 15.39 | 6.16 |
| | Ecuador | Dollar | 0.00 | 0.00 | 13.96 5.58 | 13.96 | 5.58 |
| | Bolivia | Local | 8.12 | 3.25 | 27.00 10.80 | 35.12 | 14.05 |
| | | Dollar | 0.00 | 0.00 | 20.80 8.32 | 20.80 | 8.32 |
| | Peru | Local | −4.42 | −1.77 | 22.50 9.00 | 18.08 | 7.23 |
| | | Dollar | 0.00 | 0.00 | 16.25 6.50 | 16.25 | 6.50 |
| | Venezuela | Local | 15.05 | 6.02 | 18.75 7.50 | 33.80 | 13.52 |
| | | Dollar | 0.00 | 0.00 | 25.00 10.00 | 25.00 | 10.00 |
| US$300 | Colombia | Local | 13.95 | 4.65 | 14.88 4.96 | 28.82 | 9.61 |
| | | Dollar | 0.00 | 0.00 | 17.22 5.74 | 17.22 | 5.74 |
| | Ecuador | Dollar | 0.00 | 0.00 | 15.38 5.13 | 15.38 | 5.13 |
| | Bolivia | Local | 9.75 | 3.25 | 27.00 9.00 | 36.75 | 12.25 |
| | | Dollar | 0.00 | 0.00 | 22.40 7.47 | 22.40 | 7.47 |
| | Peru | Local | −5.31 | −1.77 | 24.00 8.00 | 18.69 | 6.23 |
| | | Dollar | 0.00 | 0.00 | 17.83 5.94 | 17.83 | 5.94 |
| | Venezuela | Local | 18.05 | 6.02 | 20.00 6.67 | 38.05 | 12.68 |
| | | Dollar | 0.00 | 0.00 | 29.00 9.67 | 29.00 | 9.67 |

Source: Solimano 2003.

uniform, but also higher, when money is sent through major MTOs (in the range of 9.5 per cent and 13.5 per cent).

Rates for sending money from the United States to Latin America are in the 8–9 per cent range. Interestingly, the component of exchange rate spreads, as a share of the total cost of sending remittances, is twice as high to Latin American as to non-Latin American countries. In fact, the exchange rate spread component is about 14 per cent of the total cost of sending remittances to non-Latin American countries, and nearly 28 per cent in the case of Latin American recipient countries. Finally, let us look at the cost of remittances to the Andean countries of Latin America (Bolivia, Colombia, Ecuador, Peru and Venezuela). Table 5.9 provides the average cost of sending remittances to the five Andean countries for sums of US$200, US$250 and US$300.

The data are based on a survey of MTOs and ethnic stores in the United States that are engaged in the remittances industry with the Andean countries. The survey was conducted in January of 2003.[21] Table 5.9 sets out the comparative cost of sending money to be delivered in dollars and in local currency. The percentage charges are systematically lower across countries for remittances to be sent in dollars, a difference that can range from 3 to 5 percentage points. There is a wide range of costs in a range of 5.6 per cent to 13.8 per cent (for remittances in the range US$200–250) and 5.1 per cent to 12.7 per cent for remittances of US$300. In general, charges decline with the amount remitted. We find significant differences among individual countries. The lowest charges are for Ecuador and the highest for Venezuela. An important factor explaining the lower cost for money remitted to Ecuador is that the exchange rate spread component of the total cost (for the sender) disappears, since Ecuador uses the US dollar as its official currency. This is an important result: an Andean economy that adopts the US dollar faces a lower remittance cost than an economy with a national currency.[22]

## Policies to reduce the cost of remittances and enhance their development impact

As we have demonstrated in this chapter, the cost of sending money transfers to developing countries is high, leading to an inefficient level of transfers. How can the cost of sending money abroad be reduced? How can competition in the international market for transfers be increased? How can the development impact of remittances in receiving countries be enhanced? Measures are needed at both ends of the transfer.

### The sending side
The formalisation of the legal status of the migrant would certainly encourage greater migrant access to a variety of bank services, including remittance services. This should lower the costs of remittances. For example, the use of

ATM cards for making transfers rather than the more costly methods currently used can be an effective mechanism for reducing remittance costs.

Another factor that appears to be hindering competition in the remittance business in the US is the cost of getting an MTO licence: about $100,000 per state. Prospective operators find this cost high.

It is also important to avert an adverse impact on the workers' remittances industry of increases in transaction costs and remittance regulation resulting from mounting controls on financial intermediaries to prevent money laundering activities and the financing of terrorism.

In sum, we believe that increasing the efficiency of the market for remittances requires:

1 Containing or reducing the costs of licensing for new operators, making less costly, and quicker, the process of certification of new financial intermediaries in the remittance business.

2 Expediting the process of granting residence visas and/or citizenship and avoiding long visa processing periods for migrants (they currently take several years, at least in the US). This would help to regularise the immigrant sector, inviting commercial banks to target the financial needs of the migrants.

3 Encouraging domestic banks (particularly those with an international scope) to develop new product lines for migrants, such as cheque or savings accounts, remittance services, etcetera. The creation of 'banks for migrants' is an idea worth exploring.

The remittance-receiving nations would benefit from a more efficient and less costly market for remittances. Currently, a significant slice of remittances goes to profit the operators rather than to the families of the migrants in developing countries. This has adverse efficiency and social effects.

## The recipient countries side

From the viewpoint of recipient countries, leveraging remittances and enhancing their productive use for development are two important issues. There are various mechanisms for leveraging remittances in receiving countries. Governments and local financial institutions can issue bonds to emigrants, who would earn an interest rate, creating a more attractive instrument for channelling remittances.

Another possibility is for domestic banks to offer foreign currency accounts to migrants free of exchange rate taxes and other regulations. In addition, housing and education accounts can be created to channel remittances to various productive uses in the home country.

The development of alliances between domestic banks in receiving countries and banks, credit unions and MTOs in sending nations can help to increase efficiency and reduce costs in the remittances market. Mechanisms to ensure a productive use of remittances include the mobilisation of home town associations that have spread through the United States in recent years (Mexican migrants have been very active in creating HTAs and these efforts are being aided by their government).

Finally, taxing remittances (mainly workers' remittances) in sending or receiving countries does not seem to be a good idea.[23] These are transfers, sent in general by and to low-income groups. So it is doubly inequitable that such flows, based on income that has already been subject to the income-tax system of the sending country, should be taxed. In receiving countries, remittances are a source of foreign exchange, a complement of national savings and a transfer to low-to-medium-income groups. It is unclear the social gain for governments in interfering directly with these income flows in any way likely to diminish them.

## Conclusions

This chapter has examined several developmental and financial dimensions of remittances from international migrants. Remittances are currently the second most important source of development finance at global level after foreign direct investment. They are also more stable than private capital flows such as portfolio investment and bank credit. The sustainability over time of remittances as a source of income for developing countries will also depend on the cycle of migration (recent versus older) and its expected flow. Remittances have become a very significant source of development finance for several developing countries: they are a source of foreign exchange; they support consumption levels of low-to-middle-income families; and they con-stitute a direct source of funding for small, community-oriented investment projects. Migrant associations send home donations to fund projects of this type (so-called 'community remittances'). From a social point of view, remit-tances can have a positive poverty-reducing effect, as many of the families who receive remittances are low-income people, although the syndrome of dependence on remittance income should be avoided. Properly mobilised, remittances can contribute to increased investment in basic infrastructure such as water, roads, low-income housing and school buildings; by funding education they can increase investment in human capital; and with their help micro and small-scale firms can be financed. For remittance-sending countries, remittances represent a market-based international transfer to developing countries that, indirectly, reduces the demand for official develop-ment assistance. In considering these positive effects, however, we should not overlook the implicit trade-off between earning foreign exchange through remittances and the outflow of skilled nationals and manpower from sending countries.

Currently, the potential development impact of remittances is impaired by the existence of a costly, concentrated and poorly competitive international market for remittances. The empirical evidence shows that the cost of remittances is above the marginal cost of (electronically) transferring funds, provided such transfers can be made. Although the involvement of commercial banks in the remittances business is still slight, the evidence shows that the cost of sending remittances tends to be lower through banks than through MTOs. In addition, there are differences in the cost of sending remittances to non-Latin American as compared to Latin American countries: the exchange rate spread component of the remittance cost is higher for the latter than the former. Our empirical analysis, based on a detailed survey of MTOs based in the US and remitting to the Andean region of South America, shows that the total cost of sending remittances to these countries varies in a wide range (5–12 per cent of the value remitted), depending on the type of currency that is delivered, the destination country, the type of financial operator involved and other factors. Reducing this cost by, say, 5 per cent could increase by a few billions the amount of remittances received by the developing countries.

What can be done to increase competition and reduce costs in the remittances market? In sending countries, facilitating the process of opening bank accounts for immigrants would be an important step towards incorporating the migrant community into the financial system of the host country. This should increase competition in the remittance market and reduce the cost of sending remittances. On the other hand, the cost of licensing for new operators and other regulations for bank and non-bank financial intermediaries should be minimal to avoid creating barriers to entry in this market. Nor should the control of money laundering and the financing of terrorism unnecessarily increase the cost of sending remittances home. On the recipient side, the issuance of remittance bonds, the opening of foreign currency accounts for migrant workers in the home country, and the creation of facilities for voluntary donations to projects are all measures to leverage remittances for development. In turn, the creation of education and housing accounts at home for migrants could help to encourage the productive and social use of remittance proceeds, while attracting the return of emigrants, whose fresh capital, new ideas and international contacts can be a promising source of growth and development in receiving countries.

## Notes

1 This paper is reproduced with the kind permission of the author and the United Nations University World Institute for Development Economics Research (UNU–WIDER), and was originally prepared within the UNU–WIDER research project on 'Innovative Sources for Development Finance', directed by A. B. Atkinson and supported by the United Nations Department of Economic and Social Affairs (UN–DESA). A collection of papers from the project edited by A. B. Atkinson is published as *New Sources of Development Finance* (Oxford: Oxford University Press, 2004). Very useful comments by Anthony B. Atkinson were greatly appreciated. Likewise, I express warm

thanks for comments by participants at the workshop of the WIDER project 'Innovative Sources for Development Finance', held in Helsinki, Finland, 17–18 May 2003. Finally, I am indebted to Claudio Aravena for efficient assistance.

2 New immigrants may initially come alone to the foreign country, leaving their families at home. Later on, when their employment situation in the host country is consolidated, they bring their families. This may have implications for the flow of remittances and their persistence over time, as families are often the main recipients.

3 See Ellerman (2003) and Solimano (2002a) for a discussion of these issues.

4 See the third section for statistical issues and definitions on how remittances are measured.

5 Since remittances are also sent through informal and unrecorded channels, official data may underestimate actual remittances (see third section).

6 World Bank 2003.

7 This section draws mainly on Solimano 2003.

8 See Brown 1997.

9 See Stark 1991, Brown 1997, Poirine 1997 and Smith 2003.

10 See Stark 1991, Chapter 16.

11 See Poirine 1997 and Brown 1997 for elaborations on this specification of remittances.

12 See Micklewright and Wright 2003 on the role of private donations, mainly from foundations and other vehicles, as a source of development finance.

13 It would also be relevant to know how many of those projects are maintained.

14 This effect afflicts all kinds of transfers, not only remittances.

15 However, extreme poverty may also impede emigration, as the very poor may not be able to finance the costs of migrating to a foreign country.

16 The distributive effects of remittances in the home country are more ambiguous. The issue is investigated in Barham and Boucher 1998.

17 In the United States, migrants must produce a Tax Identification Number (TIN) when opening a bank account. Recently, some banks have begun to accept consular identification cards for opening bank accounts. Many migrants are fully compliant with tax payments, even though their immigration status is not fully regular.

18 See Orozco 2002, Solimano 2003.

19 In the aggregate, however, this is a sector that mobilises a large volume of resources: for the main 12 recipient countries in Latin America, aggregate remittances were of the order of US$32 billion dollars in 2002 (see Orozco 2003).

20 Table 5.7 draws on the countries and companies studied to determine the cost of remittances according to major source/destination countries and type of financial operator.

21 See Solimano 2003.

22 See Beckerman and Solimano 2002 for an analysis of the macroeconomic and social impact of official dollarisation in Ecuador.

23 Another possibility is to make remittances tax-deductible.

# References

Atkinson, A. B. 2003. 'Innovative Sources of Development Finance. Global Public Economics'. Paper prepared for ABCDE World Bank Conference on Development Economics-Europe, Paris.

Barham, B. and S. Boucher. 1998. 'Migration, Remittances and Inequality: Estimating the Net Effects of Migration on Income Distribution'. *Journal of Development Economics*, 55: 307–31.

Beckerman, P. and A. Solimano (eds.). 2002. *Crisis and Dollarisation in Ecuador. Directions in Development*. Washington, DC: World Bank.

Bendixen and Associates. 2003. 'Receptores de Remesa en Ecuador; Una investigacion del mercado'. Presentation at Multilateral Investment Fund–Pew Hispanic Center Conference on Remittances and Development, Quito, Ecuador (May).

Brown, R. 1997. 'Estimating Remittances Functions for Pacific Island Migrants'. *World Development*, 25, 4: 613–26.

ECLAC. 2002. 'International Migration and Globalisation', Chapter 8 in *Globalisation and Development*. Report for the 29th session of the United Nations Economic Commission for Latin America (UN–ECLAC), Brazilia.

El-Sakka, M. and R. McNabb. 1999. 'The Macroeconomic Determinants of Emigrant Remittances'. *World Development*, 27, 8: 1493–1502.

Ellerman, D. 2003. 'Policy Research on Migration and Development'. World Bank Policy Research Working Paper No. 3117, August.

Faini, R. 2002. 'Migration, Remittances and Growth'. Paper presented at UNU–WIDER conference on International Migration, September 2002.

Gammeltoft, P. 2002. 'Remittances and other Financial Flows to Developing Countries'. Working Paper 02.11 (August), Centre for Development Research, Copenhagen.

Ilahi, N. and S. Jafrey. 1999. 'Guest-worker Migration, Remittances and the Extended Family: Evidence for Pakistan'. *Journal of Development Economics*, 58: 485–512.

IMF. 2003. 'Balance of Payments Statistic Yearbook', Washington, DC: IMF.

Micklewright, J. and A. Wright. 2003. 'Private Donations for International Development'. Paper contributed to WIDER Project on Sources of Development Finance.

MIF. 2001. 'Survey of Remittance Senders: US to Latin America'. Multilateral Investment Fund of the Inter-American Development Bank.

Orozco, M. 2001. 'Globalisation and Migration: the Impact of Family Remittances in Latin America'. Report for the Multilateral Investment Fund of the Inter-American Development Bank.

—— 2002. 'Attracting Remittances: Markets, Money and Reduced Costs'. Report for the Multilateral Investment Fund of the IADB.

—— 2003. 'Workers Remittances: the Human Face of Globalisation'. Report for the Multilateral Investment Fund of the Inter-American Development Bank.

Poirine, B. 1997. 'A Theory of Remittances as an Implicit Family Loan Arrangement'. *World Development*, 25, 4: 589–611.

Ratha, D. 2003. 'Workers' Remittances: an Important and Stable Source of External Development Finance', in Chapter 7, *Global Development Finance*. Washington, DC: World Bank.

Smith, A. 2003. 'Leveraging "Mobile" Human Capital for Development. Migration and Development Finance'. Mimeo.

Solimano, A. 2001. 'International Migration and the Global Economic Order: an Overview'. World Bank Policy Research Working Paper No. 2720.

—— 2002a. 'Globalising Talent and Human Capital: Implications for Developing Countries'. Macroeconomics of Development Series, No. 15, United Nations Economic Commission for Latin America (UN–ECLAC).

—— 2002b. 'Development Cycles, Political Regimes and International Migration: Argentina in the Twentieth Century'. Paper presented at WIDER–UNU conference on International Migration, September 2002.

—— 2002c. 'Globalisation, History and International Migration: a View From Latin America'. Paper presented at workshop, World Commission on the Social Dimensions of Globalisation, Geneva, 16–17 December 2002.

—— 2003. 'Workers' Remittances to the Andean Region: Mechanisms, Costs and Development Impact'. Mimeo, United Nations Economic Commission for Latin America (UN–ECLAC).

Stark, O. 1991. *The Migration of Labour*. Oxford: Basil Blackwell.

World Bank. 2002. *Migrants' Capital for Small-Scale Infrastructure and Small Enterprise Development in Mexico*. Washington, DC: World Bank, January.

—— 2003. *Global Development Finance. Striving for Stability in Development Finance*. Washington, DC: World Bank.

# 6

## The Commodities Crisis and the Global Trade in Agriculture: Present Problems and Some Proposals

### MARTIN KHOR

## Background and rationale

Two of the world's most urgent problems are the global commodities crisis, and the distorting nature of global agricultural trade. The two issues are of course interconnected, as agricultural products form a major part of commodities exported by developing countries. For many of these Third World commodities, a large part of the problem lies in the effects of distortions caused by continued high protection through subsidies and tariff peaks and escalation in the North. Thus, the two issues of commodities and agricultural trade can fruitfully be examined together.

These two issues have to be tackled in any process aimed at eradicating poverty, establishing greater equity, and bridging North–South divides. They have been recognised as important issues to resolve by such landmark international processes as the Millennium Development Goals.

### Commodities crisis

The commodities crisis has been a long-standing problem since developing countries attained their independence, and even before that. It used to be the major economic issue on the international agenda, and was a major impetus for the establishment and initial work of the United Nations Conference on Trade and Development (UNCTAD) when negotiations on commodities were the main item on the international trade agenda. However, from the mid-1980s there has been a steady decline in the priority accorded to this issue. This has been unfortunate, as the decline in commodity prices in general has continued, with devastating effects on many developing countries. The commodities crisis has been a major cause of the persistence of or increase in poverty in the developing world. The tenacity of low levels and decline in commodity prices reduces the incomes of rural producers, places a constraint on export earnings, increases trade deficits and keeps many countries trapped in external debt.

In 2003 President Jacques Chirac spoke of a 'conspiracy of silence' on the commodities crisis and launched an initiative to address the issue at the Group of Eight Summit in Evian. His proposal was not accepted, blocked by objections from some major countries. However, there have been other recent initiatives to revive the commodities issue, including the Eminent Persons' Report commissioned by the UN General Assembly and the decision at the UNCTAD XI meeting in June 2004 to establish a task force on commodities.

## Global agricultural trade

Global agricultural trade is clearly an issue that is presently dividing the countries of North and South, particularly in the area of global trade negotiations. Indeed the collapse of the World Trade Organisation's Cancun Ministerial Conference in September 2003 was significantly due to the North–South impasse on agriculture. In July 2004 the WTO adopted a 'framework agreement' on agriculture as part of a larger 'July package' of decisions. The framework is to guide further discussions on the modalities for negotiating revisions to the WTO's Agreement on Agriculture (AoA). Although the Cancun impasse has been broken, there are many ambiguities in the July 2004 framework, and much negotiation remains to be undertaken.

Problems with agricultural trade affect the largest number of developing countries and of poor communities worldwide, as agriculture is the economic sector providing livelihoods to most people in a majority of developing countries. This issue is crucial to resolve if there is to be progress in achieving many of the Millennium Development Goals, in particular Goal 1 (eradicate poverty and hunger), and Goal 8 (develop a global partnership for development). The distortions and imbalances in agricultural trade have affected the prices, incomes and livelihoods of small farmers in developing countries; removal of these imbalances is a necessary step if the goals of eradicating poverty and of Target 12 of Goal 8 (to develop an open, rule-based, predictable and non-discriminatory trading and financial system) are to be seriously tackled. The imbalance in agriculture is the most glaring adverse aspect of the trading system.

The general problems facing many developing countries over global agricultural commodity trade have several interrelated aspects:

1   The decline in export prices in many of the developing countries' agricultural commodities, instability in the markets, and also, in some cases, the falling share of developing countries in total exports.

2   Continued protection by the developed countries of their agricultural sectors, including the maintenance of domestic support measures and export subsidies. This denies developing countries access to the agricultural

markets of the North, and also facilitates the dumping of Northern exports on the South.

3   The limited capacity of many developing countries to export or to derive adequate benefits from export, including a higher position in the 'value chain' of the commodities they produce. This constrains the ability of these countries to benefit from agricultural trade.

4   The rapid liberalisation of imports in developing countries and the effects of this on the prices, incomes and livelihoods of farmers.

5   The global framework governing agricultural trade, which is presently imbalanced and creates disadvantages for developing countries.

This chapter describes the major problems in these areas, reviews some recent developments, and makes some suggestions on measures to improve the situation.

## The developing countries' commodities problem

Agricultural products form a large portion of the export commodities of many developing countries, especially the poorer ones. They face steep and in some cases catastrophic declines in the prices of these commodities. From 1980 to 2000, world prices for 18 major export commodities fell by 25 per cent in real terms. The decline was especially steep for cotton (47 per cent), coffee (64 per cent), rice (61 per cent), cocoa (71 per cent) and sugar (77 per cent) (World Commission 2004: 83).

The effects of falling commodity prices have been devastating for many countries. According to UN data, in sub-Saharan Africa a 28 per cent fall in the terms of trade between 1980 and 1989 led to an income loss of US$16 billion in 1989 alone. In the four years 1986–9, sub-Saharan Africa suffered a $56 billion income loss, or 15–16 per cent of GDP in 1987–9. For 15 middle-income highly indebted countries, there was a combined terms-of-trade decline of 28 per cent between 1980 and 1989, causing an average loss per year of US$45 billion in the 1986–9 period, or 5–6 per cent of GDP (Khor 1993).

In the 1990s, the losses were higher. Non-oil primary commodity prices fell by 33.8 per cent from the end of 1996 to February 1999, resulting in a cumulative terms-of-trade loss of more than 4.5 per cent of income during 1997–8 for developing countries. Income losses were greater in the 1990s than in the 1980s (UNCTAD 1999: 85).

Among agricultural commodities exported by developing countries, some are and some are not in competition with the same commodities produced by developed countries.

*Developing-country commodities that compete with developed countries.* In these cases, such as cotton and sugar, world prices are lower largely because of the high domestic and export subsidies attached to the developed countries' commodity exports. The share of global export revenue accruing to developing countries has dropped in many cases, with the developed countries having an increased share. A large part of the problem facing developing countries is related to subsidies in the rich countries, which give the latter an unfair advantage (see the example of cotton in the next main section of this chapter).

*Developing-country commodities that do not compete with developed countries.* In these cases, developing countries face a range of problems, including their products being at the lower end of the value chain and a lack of capacity (or of market access) to climb the chain through processing and manufacturing. Another problem is a situation of global oversupply in the case of some commodities, which exerts a downward pressure on prices. This is partly the result of too many countries being advised by international agencies to expand the export of the same commodities. Yet another problem is that the developing countries have little bargaining power when selling their products to monopolist buyers (usually transnational companies), and thus get lower prices. The case of coffee within this category of commodities is reviewed below.

## The case of coffee

The price of coffee beans has dropped sharply, and the share of the coffee market revenue accruing to producer countries has declined accordingly. The price of coffee fell from 127 US cents per pound in 1980 to 46 cents in 2001. In 1992, producer countries earned US$10 billion from a global coffee market worth around US$30 billion; in 2002 they received less than US$6 billion in export earnings from a market that has doubled in size. Their share of revenue fell from 33 per cent to less than 10 per cent (Oxfam 2002).

The effect of the fall in the coffee price has been very serious for many countries and the 25 million coffee growers around the world. Coffee accounts for over 50 per cent of Ethiopia's export revenue and 80 per cent of Burundi's. Coffee is linked to the livelihoods of a quarter of the population in Uganda, 10 per cent in Honduras and 8 per cent in Guatemala. In Brazil there are 230,000–300,000 coffee farmers and another three million are employed in the coffee industry, the same number similarly employed in India (Oxfam 2002: 8). The price fall has had a devastating effect on national export revenues and communities alike. There has been a steep increase in unemployment, reduced income and hunger among the coffee-growing communities in the developing countries (Oxfam 2002).

The main reason for the fall in price is increasing oversupply. Supply has grown by over 2 per cent per year, whilst demand growth has been lower at 1–1.5 per cent per year, leading to stocks being built up to the level of 40 million bags. Up to 1989, the coffee market was regulated by the International Coffee Agreement (ICA), made up of producer and consumer countries, and managed by the International Coffee Organisation (ICO). The ICA broke down in 1989, with opposition from the US (which withdrew its member-ship) a major factor. The Agreement remains but no longer has the power to regulate supply through quotas and the price band. Coffee prices are now determined by futures markets. After the ICA broke down, prices dived. Pro-posals to revive the Agreement have been impeded by lack of political will, with consumer countries unwilling to resume participation (Oxfam 2002).

Another reason for the low prices is the expansion of production by some countries, including Vietnam (a relatively new major coffee producer) and Brazil, the largest producer. The increased overall supply has not been matched by a similar rate of increase in demand, resulting in an imbalance in demand and supply that is depressing price levels. Moreover, there is a great imbalance in the global coffee supply chain, with small farmers at the lowest end being paid very low prices by their traders, the exporting traders in developing countries being paid little by the large roaster companies in the US and Europe that buy the coffee beans, and these latter companies reaping much of the overall benefit through their link in the chain, the retail coffee business. In a study of the stages and prices along the value chain, Oxfam found that the coffee farmer in Uganda received 14 US cents for his kilo of green beans, which pass through various traders to the roaster factory at a price of US$1.64 per kilo. It ends up on a UK supermarket shelf as soluble coffee at US$26.40 a kilo, 7,000 per cent higher than the price paid to the farmer. A similar journey into a pack of roast and ground coffee sold in the US involves a price rise of nearly 4,000 per cent (Oxfam 2002).

## Global agricultural trade and continued protection in developed countries

### Continuation of protection in developed countries

Despite the establishment of the Agreement on Agriculture in the WTO, aimed at reducing subsidies and protection, the developed countries have continued high protection of their agriculture. This is largely due to the weaknesses of the AoA and its implementation.

First, the high tariffs on selected items of potential interest to the South have had to be reduced only slightly. In the first year of the agreement, there were tariff peaks at very high rates in the United States, the EU, Japan and Canada. The AoA mandates the developed countries to reduce their tariffs by only 36 per cent on average to the end of 2000, and thus the rates for some products remain prohibitively high.

Second, domestic support has increased rather than decreased. Although developed countries reduced their Amber Box subsidies (as the AoA has obliged them to), they also increased the exempted subsidies (under the Blue and Green boxes), resulting in an increase in total domestic support. OECD data show that the Total Support Estimate, a measure of domestic support, in the 24 OECD countries rose from US$275.6 billion (annual average for the base period 1986–8) to US$326 billion in 1999 (OECD 2000).

Third, export subsidies are still high, as the AoA only obliges the developed countries to reduce the budget outlay by 36 per cent and the total quantity of subsidised exports by 21 per cent. Thus, even in 2000 export subsidies are allowed to be as high as 64 per cent of the base level in 1986–90.

Of the three aspects above, worldwide public criticism has focused most on the expansion of Northern domestic subsidies. The AoA has a loophole allowing developed countries to increase their total domestic support by shifting from one type of subsidy (price-based, which distorts trade directly) to two other types (direct payments to farmers, and other 'indirect' subsidies) that are exempted from the reduction discipline. In reality, the Blue and Green Box subsidies also have significant effects on the market and trade. For the farmer, what is important is whether he can obtain sufficient revenue and make a profit. If a subsidy, in whatever form, is assisting the farmer to obtain revenue and be economically viable, then that subsidy is having a significant effect on production and on the market.

### Effects of Northern subsidies and protection on import surges and lost opportunities in developing countries

The effect of agricultural subsidies in developed countries is that their farm production levels are kept artificially high and their producers dispose of their surplus in other countries, often by dumping on world markets at less than the production cost. Farmers in developing countries incur losses in three ways:

1   They lose export opportunities and revenues from having their market access blocked in the developed countries using the subsidies;

2   They lose export opportunities in third countries, because the subsidising country is exporting to these countries at artificially low prices;

3   They lose their market share in their own domestic market, or even lose their livelihoods, due to the inflow of artificially cheap subsidised imports.

High protection in developed countries and further liberalisation in developing countries (under AoA and structural adjustment loan conditionalities) have resulted in surges of imports to many developing countries across the world. In many cases these imports were artificially cheapened by domestic or/and export subsidies. There are many cases of dumping in which the export price of developed-country products is below the cost of production, and where the farms or companies in developed countries are still able to make a profit because their revenues are pumped up by subsidies.

As long as the subsidies continue, so will the dumping of artificially cheapened agricultural products on developing countries. This has serious effects on rural livelihoods and food security in developing countries. Artificially cheapened products are being imported into developing countries. Often, the poorer countries may have more efficient farmers, but their livelihoods are threatened by inefficient farmers in rich countries because of subsidies.

### The case of cotton subsidies

The case of cotton illustrates the effect of Northern subsidies on developing countries. The President of Burkina Faso, Blaise Compaoré, addressing the WTO in June 2003, called for a decision at the WTO's Cancun Ministerial Conference to adopt measures to eliminate cotton subsidies, and until then, to pay financial compensation to the least developed countries that suffer losses due to the subsidies (Compaoré 2003). He highlighted the plight of West and Central African cotton-exporting countries resulting from the developed countries' agricultural subsidies and the hypocrisy of trade rules and structural adjustment reforms that influenced West and Central African states to eliminate their agricultural subsidies, only to have any positive benefits from these reforms nullified by the 'multiform subsidies' of some WTO members 'in total contradiction of WTO basic principles'. In 2001, the rich countries' farm subsidies (US$311 billion) were six times the amount they dispensed as aid (US$55 billion). Mali received US$37 million in aid but lost US$43 million from lower export revenues caused by other producer countries' cotton subsidies.

African farmers produce cotton 50 per cent cheaper than their competitors from developed countries, ranking them among the most competitive in the world. But cotton subsidies have caused a crisis, with Burkina Faso losing 1 per cent of its GDP and 12 per cent of its export income, Mali 1.7 per cent and 8 per cent, and Benin 1.4 per cent and 9 per cent respectively. Over 10 million people in West and Central Africa depend on cotton production and several other millions are indirectly affected by the distortion of world prices due to subsidies.

Referring to the proposal by Benin, Burkina Faso, Chad and Mali (issued on 16 May 2003), Compaoré suggested that the Cancun Ministerial 'set up a mechanism to progressively reduce support to cotton production and export, with a view to fully suppressing all cotton subsidies at a defined deadline'. Also, as an immediate and transitory measure in favour of least-developed countries, he suggested that a mechanism be adopted to compensate their farmers for revenue losses incurred because of cotton subsidies.

The cotton issue received priority status in the WTO's Cancun Ministerial in September 2003. However, support for the case of developing-country producers was not forthcoming, especially not from the United States. The draft Cancun Ministerial text of 13 September 2003 was seen by developing countries as very unsatisfactory. It ignored the two demands of the West African countries – for developed countries to eliminate subsidies; and for financial compensation for losses due to the subsidies. Instead, the paragraph disperses the cotton issue, leaving it to be addressed by various negotiating bodies – on agriculture, non-agricultural market access, and rules – and instructs the WTO Director General to consult with bodies like the World Bank and the Food and Agriculture Organisation (FAO) to direct existing programmes and resources towards diversification of the economies from cotton dependency, thus sidestepping the main issue of eliminating subsidies.

## Lack of capacity of developing countries

A major reason why developing countries are unable to benefit from trade is their lack of capacity to produce and market. Thus, even if there is market access for these countries, especially the LDCs, this 'supply constraint' prevents them from being able to take advantage of the access. The supply and marketing constraints on trade span the range of stages, including formulating appropriate export strategies (including choice of products and markets), providing incentives, training, credit and technology assistance to enterprises, product design and production techniques, and marketing, as well as the government's role in providing general health, housing and education facilities to citizens in order to generate a skilled labour capacity.

For large numbers of small farmers, the main problems remain the domestic structural factors such as lack of access to land, security of land, terms of tenancy, lack of credit, and storage and transportation infrastructure. Resolving these basic problems is thus also important.

## Effects of import liberalisation on developing countries

Perhaps the most serious problem facing developing-country farmers is that they are exposed to excessive and rapid import liberalisation. This has taken place mainly under the loan conditionalities of the World Bank and IMF, as well as the WTO's agriculture agreement. There are now many case studies of the incidence and damaging effects of import liberalisation on local communities and rural producers in developing countries. These studies show how farmers in many sectors (staple crops like rice and wheat; milk and other dairy products; vegetables and fruits; poultry; sugar) have had their incomes reduced and their livelihoods threatened by the influx of imports.

A recent FAO paper on trade policy, agricultural imports and food security (FAO 2003) shows a very high incidence of import surges in 1984–2000 (the incidence rises markedly after 1994) for eight key products in 28 developing countries. For example, Kenya experienced 45 import surges, the Philippines 72 cases, Bangladesh 43, Benin 43, Botswana 43, Burkina Faso 50, Côte d'Ivoire 41, Dominican Republic 28, Haiti 40, Honduras 49, Jamaica 32, Malawi 50, Mauritius 27, Morocco 38, Peru 43, Uganda 41, Tanzania 50 and Zambia 41.

The import surges documented by the FAO were also accompanied in some cases by production shortfalls in some of the same products where there were import surges. For example, in Kenya, in wheat there were 11 cases of import surge and seven cases of production shortfall; and in maize there were five cases of import surge and four cases of production shortfall. This indicates that the import surges were sometimes linked to declines in output by the farmers in the importing countries. The rise in imports led to decline in the output and incomes of the farmers, affecting their livelihoods. As the FAO report concluded, 'Given the large number of cases of import surges and increasing reports of the phenomenon from around the world, this could be potentially a serious problem'.

A major imbalance of the AoA is that its special safeguard mechanism only applies if a country has tariffied a product in the Uruguay Round. Only 20 developing countries are eligible. Thus most developing countries have no proper instrument to counter import surges. The FAO study also cites several recent studies on import surges that trace the problem to unfair trade practices (dumping, for example), export subsidies and domestic production subsidies. Import surges are more common for products where there are high subsidies: examples include dairy/livestock products such as milk powder and poultry parts, certain fruit and vegetable preparations, and sugar.

## The global framework regulating agricultural trade

Many of the problems raised above are linked to the global framework that regulates or influences agricultural trade, which in turn also affects domestic production. This global framework in turn has two major aspects:

1  The WTO's Agreement on Agriculture, which at the moment is tilted in favour of the developed countries; they are able to maintain high protection (mainly because they are able to pay for high subsidies) whilst exerting pressure on developing countries (which lack the funds to protect their producers through subsidies) to liberalise.

2  The loan conditionalities of the World Bank and IMF that relate to trade. These conditionalities have led many developing countries to slash their applied tariff rates for agricultural products. Many countries have not been allowed to raise their rates when cheaper imports threaten to ruin local farmers, not even when the WTO rules allow these countries to increase their applied rates to the bound rates level.

There are concerns that during current WTO negotiations the developed countries have not yet offered a significant reduction of their subsidies. Yet there are strong pressures to get the developing countries to reduce their bound tariffs significantly. This is an unhealthy combination, since tariff reductions in the South in the face of continued protection and subsidies in the North can result in the influx of artificially cheapened imports into the developing countries, threatening the livelihoods and incomes of their farmers.

## Previous and recent efforts to improve the commodities situation

### Previous attempts to deal with commodities
In the 1960s, 1970s and part of the 1980s the need to resolve troughs and volatility in prices and the demand for commodities was a major part of international economic discussions and initiatives. The 'unequal exchange' suffered by developing countries, of having their commodities sold at low

prices to the world market whilst having to import manufactured goods at high prices, and the declining terms of trade, were major factors that led to the formation of UNCTAD in the 1960s. Much of UNCTAD's work in its first two decades had focused on hosting negotiations between commodity-producing and -consuming countries, giving rise to several producer–consumer commodity agreements, and the establishment of the Common Fund for Commodities. In fact, a great deal of international trade negotiation had taken place within UNCTAD (not GATT), and the major issues discussed related to commodities.

The establishment of commodity agreements for products such as coffee, cocoa, rubber and sugar helped to stabilise the prices of the commodity concerned, as these prices were maintained within price bands agreed to by the producer and consumer countries. The agreements were managed by organisations set up for the purpose, and also involved the purchase of surplus stocks, aimed at smoothing the relation between supply and demand. In the 1980s, however, major developed countries led by the US and the UK decided that these commodity agreements clashed with their new free-market philosophy, and withdrew their interest and support from these agreements. As a result, by the end of the 1980s the organisations running these agreements were unable to carry out their most important functions, relating to the purchase and maintenance of stocks, and the management of prices (which were to remain within an agreed band). The removal of these functions left the prices of the commodities to be determined by the market. And with supply growth outstripping demand growth, most commodities have since then suffered a general decline in their price levels. The case of coffee, outlined earlier in this chapter, illustrates the general situation.

Following the collapse of the commodity agreements, there has been a big vacuum in the international arena, centred on the absence of international institutions or mechanisms to tackle the key concerns of low level and volatility in commodity prices and the mismatch between supply and demand. In the absence of a coordinated framework of international cooperation, individual agencies such as the international financial institutions and UN organisations have suggested measures that individual producer countries can take to counter the fall in prices and to increase their export earnings. These include 'niche marketing, risk management, quality improvement, fair trade, sales promotion, and so on' (Robbins 2003). However, as Robbins points out, most of these suggested schemes have not worked, as they did not tackle the root problem of excess supply and the absence of a regulated framework. Moreover, 'these strategies have often only intensified competition between producers' ( Robbins 2003). Robbins also provides a detailed critique of most of the suggested but inadequate strategies, including technical fixes (such as achieving higher yields, cost cutting, diversification, increasing quality and introducing genetic engineering) and market-linked schemes (such as organic products, fair trade, niche marketing and risk management via hedging and derivatives trading).

The disappearance of commodities from the agenda of international cooperation, action or even discussion has been a major setback, especially for the commodity-dependent developing countries. The problems they face remain and have actually worsened significantly, yet these problems are no longer recognised as worthy of priority or action at the international level. Implicitly, each country has been asked to deal with its commodity problem by itself. As this has not worked, the crisis has deepened. We have seen that President Chirac's attempt to intervene in 2003 failed to receive a favourable response from influential G-8 leaders: there was no follow-up.

### UN Eminent Persons' Report on Commodities (October 2003)

In December 2002 the United Nations General Assembly adopted a resolution that, among other measures, asked UNCTAD to convene independent eminent persons to examine and report on commodity issues, including the volatility in commodity prices, declining terms of trade and the impact these factors have on the development efforts of commodity-dependent developing countries.

The eminent persons met in September 2003 and their report was presented to the UN General Assembly the following month. The report came up with several proposals: short-term ones (involving urgent action in response to severe crises); medium-term ones (involving policy reorientation and proposals that are eminently feasible); and long-term ones (where discussions should start now but implementation could take time).

1 *Trade and WTO-related issues.* Developing countries are the victims of subsidy policies in the developed countries which harm producers of many agricultural commodities, who are facing unfair competition from developed-country farmers. The report called for a speedy resumption of negotiations leading to agricultural liberalisation in the North. It also called for action to compensate developing-country farmers for the losses that they suffer as a result of current developed-country policies. In line with the proposal by four African countries at the WTO Ministerial Meeting at Cancun, the report called for an early elimination of subsidies provided in developed countries to cotton and for the compensation of the loss of earnings due to the supplies of cotton subject to subsidies. Research should be done on modalities for such a compensation mechanism. The report also called for further work on the appropriateness of extending the model of the 'cotton initiative' to other relevant commodities. It called for a special mechanism for developing countries to safeguard against the import of cheap subsidised commodities that could affect the output of their farmers.

2 *Coffee.* Given the crisis situation in coffee, the report suggested that the International Coffee Organisation consider imposing an export fee, using the proceeds of the fee to help alleviate poverty arising from low coffee prices. Producing and consuming countries and international organisations should support such a programme and associated actions by the ICO.

3  *Debt relief.* Debt-servicing and repayment expenditures of many developing countries are financed by revenues from commodity exports. Because of low export prices, many countries cannot service their debts. The report called for mechanisms to be introduced as soon as possible to better tailor debt-relief efforts to the needs of commodity-exporting developing countries, in particular LDCs and HIPCs.

4  *Oversupply.* Several sections of the report dealt with oversupply as a major problem. For several commodities there is a global situation of excess supply as output has increased at a faster rate than demand, and this has contributed to the decline in prices. In the case of some commodities, a significant factor has been the high subsidisation of production, mainly in industrialised countries. In other cases, global oversupply may be due to a number of factors: several countries deciding to increase output at the same time; advice provided by international agencies and by financial assistance programmes; and over-optimistic projections of demand and prices (United Nations 2003). For commodities facing structural oversupply, a concerted effort is necessary to bring demand and supply into balance at a point where prices are sufficiently remunerative for the average producer. Action on both demand and supply sides can be envisaged. On the supply side, the report suggested medium-term measures such as diversification into other productive activities, and research and development into new end-uses of commodities (United Nations 2003).

In the short term, however, measures to reduce the supplies put on the market may be necessary. Producer countries that face a situation of over-supply are also encouraged to take national measures. Relevant institutions could be approached for organising meetings to examine experiences in this area. Countries that are not party to such schemes should agree to apply a favourable interpretation of Article XXXVI and other relevant articles of GATT and WTO and to forego using competition policy measures against such schemes. Developed countries should eliminate subsidies, where feasible, to contribute to reducing oversupply (United Nations 2003). Another part of the report (United Nations 2003: para 49) stated that:

> It was agreed that, ideally, measures to limit supply should be undertaken in cooperation between producers and consumers. If that were not possible, however, producers would have to agree on methods among themselves. This would be facilitated if consumers were prepared to abstain from actions to block any such plans. If coordinated action by producers was not possible, production and/or export cuts would have to be implemented on an individual country basis.

The report mentions the recent cooperation between Indonesia, Malaysia and Thailand in relation to natural rubber as an example of successful cooperation among producing countries with regard to a particular commodity.

5 *Compensatory finance.* The report proposed that compensatory financing schemes should be used to reduce price volatility and to insulate developing countries from the worst effects of such volatility. Existing schemes should be adapted and made operational. To be effective, such financing schemes should operate on the basis of *ex-ante* rather than *ex-post* mechanisms (in other words, clearly link automatic pay-outs to specific occurrences); they should be easy to access in terms of technical requirements and the recipient should not be burdened with conditionalities for receiving the finance.

6 *Capacity building for improving supply capacities and market entry.* There should be international assistance to strengthen supply capacity in the commodity sector of commodity-dependent countries. This should include support to design and implement strategies, policies and measures for commodity-based development and diversification, the improvement of domestic research and development, and support to the organisation of small-scale producers, processers and traders to enhance their capacity for technology absorption and marketing. We emphasise the importance of assistance aimed at enabling small producers to meet quality and traceability requirements, as well as market exigencies reflected in the specifications of importing firms.

7 *Information and analysis.* Developing country governments, firms and farmers suffer from a lack of access to timely, comprehensive, accurate and user-friendly information and analysis, as well as the capacity to utilise it in decision making at the government, firm and farm levels. Better decision making requires strategic and organised information at the international level (including the early recognition of trends and real income losses resulting from deterioration in the terms of trade); at the local level it is important to give farmers the information they need, if possible on a real-time basis. The report notes with concern the decline in resources devoted to the analysis of commodity issues in some international agencies. It calls for the strengthening of the capacities of UNCTAD and other competent international organisations to regularly disseminate specialised information and analysis covering a broad range of commodities and commodity issues, to establish networks that contribute to market transparency, and to develop collaborative tools to facilitate the use of this information, particularly by producers.

8 *Exchange of experiences on commodity policies.* The report notes the interesting experiences of developing countries in devising innovative approaches to strengthen their commodity sector and cope with negative aspects (such as volatility). There is a need for more exchange of experience on

commodity-related policy options, and scope for greater South–South cooperation, and the report urges UNCTAD to develop a suitable forum.

9 *International export diversification fund.* A long-term measure proposed by the report is the establishment of an 'International Diversification Fund' linked to an existing institution, such as the Common Fund for Commodities. The Fund is aimed at enabling countries to diversify their productive capacity (within the commodity sector, through means such as adding value, and outside the sector). In addition to strengthening the institution-building and other relevant activities mentioned earlier, it would develop strong producer associations, with a proper role for the majority of producers (women); develop key infrastructure; and stimulate investments (for example, by providing risk capital, or temporary compensation for certain infrastructural weaknesses). The report urged the international community to have a new look at such a Fund, and, in particular, to consider a new mode of financing it. This would be justified given the long-term decline in the terms of trade for commodity exports from developing countries, which implies a real resources transfer to consuming countries.

Besides the above, the report also proposed measures relating to coffee, policy design and implementation, corporate social responsibility, institution building, preferential schemes and South–South trade, fiscal management and revenue utilisation, and risk management. The eminent persons also made four concluding requests addressed to the UN system:

1 That the UN Secretary-General distribute the report to the relevant UN organisations, international financial institutions and bilateral donors, suggesting that, in the light of the Millennium Development Goals and the importance of commodities for most of the world's poor, they should upgrade the priority that they accord to commodity issues; and informing them that he will contact them again in one year's time with a view to reporting to the General Assembly how they have adapted their policies and programmes to the needs of the commodities sector.

2 That UNCTAD explore the possibilities for a new partnership between governments, private business, producers' and traders' associations, civil society and international organisations in the commodity area, and announce such a partnership and concrete steps to implement it at the UNCTAD XI meeting.

3 That the UNCTAD Secretary-General convey to the heads of the European Commission and the IMF the importance of a properly functioning system of compensatory finance and invite them to work with UNCTAD to design a system that meets the criteria set out.

4 That the General Assembly assign to a competent organisation the responsibility to lead discussions with stakeholders on the creation of a new International Export Diversification Fund.

## *Establishment of international task force on commodities at UNCTAD XI (June 2004)*

At least one of the above 'concluding requests' has been implemented: UNCTAD has explored the possibilities of a new partnership in the commodity area. At the eleventh session of UNCTAD (UNCTAD XI), held in June 2004 in São Paulo, the commodities crisis was one of the main themes. It was highlighted by the President of the UN General Assembly (the Foreign Minister of St Lucia, Julian Hunte), other leaders, the UNCTAD Secretary-General Rubens Ricupero, and a well-attended UNCTAD–Common Fund for Commodities side event on commodities.

UNCTAD XI adopted a decision to establish an international task force on commodities. The decision is contained in an Annex to the São Paulo Consensus, entitled UNCTAD XI Multi-Stakeholder Partnerships. The section on commodities states that there is at present no comprehensive and systematic consultative framework to share information and use expertise among key actors in reviewing the commodity situation, and that therefore efforts of all interested stakeholders should be pooled, with a focus on breaking the cycle of poverty in which commodity producers are now locked.

The decision in the Annex stated that 'an independent task force on commodities will be established in consultation with interested stakeholders to address the above set of issues. The task force will function in an informal and flexible manner, with partners cooperating in a spirit of voluntary enterprise'. Partners will include member states, international organisations (the FAO, the IMF, the International Trade Centre, UNDP, the Common Fund for Commodities, the World Bank), commodity-specific bodies (international commodity organisations and study groups), the private sector (in particular major corporations engaged in production, marketing and distribution of commodities), NGOs promoting action on commodity issues, and the academic community researching into commodity problems and solutions.

The issues mentioned for the task force to address include: facilitating collaboration among stakeholders and achieving greater coherence in integrating commodity issues in development portfolios; collecting and sharing best practices and lessons learnt and maximising the mobilisation of resource flows; commodity sector vulnerability and risks; facilitating participation of developing-country farmers in international markets; distribution of value added in the commodity value chain; promotion of economically, socially and environmentally sustainable approaches to production and trade of individual commodities of interest to developing countries; mining and sustainable economic development; promoting business networks; and commodity information and knowledge management.

The establishment of the task force and the cautious list of issues it is to cover are very limited when compared with the work done by UNCTAD in the 1960s to 1980s, when initiatives to attain fair prices for commodities and negotiations for establishing and maintaining commodity agreements were the bread and butter of UNCTAD's work. Nevertheless, despite its mild and limited agenda, the decision to set up the task force on commodities at UNCTAD XI is a major positive step forward, given the severity of the commodities crisis and the absence of a venue or mechanism in the international system to discuss the crisis, let alone address it. The work of this new task force, therefore, should be supported fully by governments, international agencies and civil society.

## Suggestions for measures and action

This section provides a summary of the suggestions that are contained in the previous sections on various issues.

### *Commodities*

- National governments and international institutions such as the UN General Assembly and UNCTAD should give priority to seeking solutions to the crisis of commodities. The high global priority once given to attaining reasonable and stable prices should be restored. The commodities issue should be included as a priority issue on the agenda of meetings and organisations of the South (the G-77 countries, the Non-Aligned Movement, the African Union, etcetera), of the North (the G-8 process, the European Commission), and the international agencies (the Millennium Development Goals process, the high-profile meetings of the UN in 2005, etcetera).

- A good start was made with the commissioning in 2003 of the Eminent Persons' Report on commodities by the UN General Assembly. This report and its recommendations (United Nations 2003), the key points of which have been summarised above, should be followed up by the UN system, other international agencies and the Helsinki Process.

- A recent major development has been the establishment of an international task force on commodities through the UNCTAD XI meeting. The work of this task force should be actively supported by governments, organisations of the South and North, international agencies, and the Helsinki Process.

- To raise the profile of the commodities problem, there could be an international UN conference or convention on commodities, which would discuss a whole range of aspects of the problem, with institutional mechanisms to provide follow-up. The Helsinki Process could initiate such a conference by creating the political conditions for it. The issues below could be part of the agenda of such a conference.

- A review of the previous experience of joint producer–consumer commodity agreements should be conducted (for example by UNCTAD and the Common Fund for Commodities), including examining the possibility and desirability of reviving such agreements. The experience of the International Coffee Agreement showed positive results in price stabilisation, and its later failure was due to a political decision by some developed countries to withdraw from its fund: the institutional vacuum (with no mechanism to align supply with demand) resulted in the subsequent collapse in prices. A revival of political will among the developed countries that are also major consumers could provide an opportunity for a new round of commodity agreements aimed at rationalising the supply of raw materials, while ensuring fair and sufficiently high prices. The Helsinki Process could explore the possibility and feasibility of such a revival of political will among consumer and producer countries.

- Although international cooperation is the preferred method of tackling the commodity crisis, and attempts should be made to revive it, this may not be feasible at present. In the absence of joint producer–consumer cooperation, producers of export commodities could take their own initiative to trim global supply to global demand. Such initiatives by developing-country supplier countries should be encouraged, rather than frowned upon. Studies should be carried out on emerging producer-only supply arrangements like the one in the rubber market to see whether and how they work, and whether the same principles and operations can be applied in other markets.

- The oversupply problem can also be addressed by regional groupings of developing countries, as well as by countries on an individual basis. Production levels can be reduced during periods of glut. Arrangements such as compensatory finance to affected producers and crop substitution should be examined, and good practices compiled.

- UNCTAD, the UN Industrial Development Organisation (UNIDO) and other agencies can assist commodity-producing developing countries to improve their capacity to profit from their commodities by moving up the value chain and becoming involved in processing and manufacturing as well as marketing. At the same time, developed countries should reduce tariff escalation and allow better market access for developing countries' processed and commodity-based manufactured products, and thus help commodity producers reap better benefits from the trading system.

- In the case of developing-country commodities where developed countries are also producing and exporting, unfair competition from the latter in the form of export and domestic subsidies should be phased out as soon as possible (see more details below).

- Debt relief measures (and measures of debt sustainability) should be expanded to address the financial problems faced by commodity-producing countries. Shortfalls faced by developing countries as a result of declines in commodity prices and earnings should be offset through debt relief.

- Compensatory finance schemes to insulate developing countries from effects of price volatility should be examined and their feasibility and implementation should be addressed.

- A review can be made of the policy advice of the international financial institutions and donor agencies in encouraging developing countries to produce export commodities simultaneously, which could contribute to the oversupply situation and the resulting weakening of prices. More realistic projections of demand and prices, and better planning of supply, should be instituted.

- The abolition of marketing boards and institutions and other support mechanisms in many developing countries (in many cases as a result of loan conditionalities) led to an institutional vacuum and weakened the bargaining power of developing-country producers. This institutional vacuum should be filled. Methods to do this should be examined and implemented (United Nations 2003).

- An international export diversification fund could be established to assist developing countries to move from excessive dependence on a few commodities, and to add value to their commodities through processing and manufacturing (United Nations 2003).

## Review of global framework

The global framework within which agricultural trade is conducted should be reviewed in a comprehensive manner. The review should incorporate the loan conditionalities of the international financial institutions, as they relate to and have an effect on trade, the rules of the WTO and the new proposals, and the workings of commodity markets. A system of monitoring trends and developments in these areas could be set up.

## WTO negotiations and the issues of Northern subsidies and import liberalisation in the South

The problem of continued high subsidies and protection in developed-country agriculture, and the problems caused by excessive import liberalisation in developing countries, can and should be addressed in the WTO negotiations on agriculture. The capacity of policy makers and negotiators of the South should be strengthened. Moreover, there should be regular monitoring and analysis of the ongoing negotiations on agriculture in the WTO. This can be done by or arranged by international agencies with an interest in the conditions of rural producers, and by independent organisations as well as by the producer organisations themselves. Information should be provided to the farmer organisations and ways found to enable them to participate, at least in having their voices heard and their inputs considered. Information should also be provided to policy makers in developing countries, especially in the agriculture ministries and agencies dealing with agriculture and farmers.

In the negotiations on agriculture in the WTO, modalities should be developed which give the utmost priority to the interests of the small farmers in developing countries. The main principles for the modalities should be the reduction and removal of protection in the developed countries as soon as possible, and special and differential treatment for developing countries, especially for ensuring the maintenance or revival of conditions enabling the viability of small-farmer livelihoods. A more detailed proposal would be that:

1   The export subsidies (and concessional export credits) of the developed countries should be eliminated within a specific timeframe.

2   On domestic support for the developed countries, the Amber Box subsidies should be reduced substantially; the Blue Box subsidies should be re-categorised as Amber Box subsidies and subjected to reduction disciplines; and the Green Box subsidies can be re-examined to tighten the criteria, cap the relevant subsidies and reduce them.

3   Developed countries should significantly reduce their high agricultural tariffs and tariff peaks, and a clear policy on market access should be adopted to ensure this.

4   The imbalances in the WTO Agreement on Agriculture that presently curb or limit the ability of developing countries to provide subsidies to their farmers should be corrected. For food products and the products of small farmers, domestic subsidies should not be limited, to take into account the food security and rural development needs of developing countries.

5   Special and differential treatment should be devised and applied to developing counties in the area of market access commitments. Developing countries should not be subjected to further tariff reductions for food products and products of small farmers, at least as long as the high subsidies in developed countries continue. For other products, an average tariff cut (on the lines of the Uruguay Round) may be considered.

6   A special safeguard mechanism (SSM) and the designation of special products (SPs) should be established for developing countries, to enable them to deal effectively with import surges. The SSM and SP mechanisms should be devised in such a way that they are simple and effective to operationalise.

Many of the above points are relevant to the discussions in the WTO in the post-July 2004 process. Besides the above negotiating modalities, there could be established, within the WTO negotiations and elsewhere, a transitional compensation mechanism whereby countries that provide subsidies to their producers compensate developing countries for losses to their income and export revenues. This scheme has been proposed by Burkina Faso's president to offset the losses of African cotton producers (Compaoré 2003). It could be adopted generally for developing-country export commodities which have been affected by subsidies in developed countries. This proposal was contained in the Eminent Persons' Report on Commodities (United Nations 2003) and in a recent UNCTAD report on Africa (UNCTAD 2004).

## Review of loan conditionality relating to trade issues

An ongoing review can be made of the appropriateness of the policies attached to IMF and World Bank loans in the structural adjustment programmes and other recent forms such as the poverty reduction strategy papers (PRSPs). The recommendations of the Structural Adjustment Participatory Review Initiative (SAPRI) report as it pertains to the agriculture sector (SAPRIN 2004) can be considered. For example: (1) policy should be reoriented to give priority to production for the domestic market and ensure food security; (2) trade policy in the sector should be nuanced, allowing countries to pursue some degree of self-reliance while stimulating production by marginalised farmers in order to support the rural poor in accessing affordable food; and (3) the implementation of effective steps to support small producers and achieve food security should precede, and then be integrated with, the opening of the sector and promotion of exports.

In addition, there should also be an independent ongoing review of the trade aspects of the present and proposed conditionalities of present and future loans. Developing countries presently have flexibilities within the WTO rules to adjust their applied tariffs up to their bound rates, and even beyond the bound rates in certain circumstances. Loan conditionality should not prevent or constrain the developing countries from making use of these flexibilities. Moreover, these conditionalities should not oblige developing countries to undertake a rate and scope of liberalisation that is beyond their capacity, or will be damaging to the livelihoods and incomes of rural producers. The approach to liberalisation in developing countries should be reoriented so as to be more realistic, especially since the developed countries are still maintaining high subsidies.

## Improving supply capacity in developing countries

Several international and regional agencies already have programmes to assist developing countries to improve their productive and trade capacity, including the International Trade Centre (ITC), UNCTAD, UNIDO and the multilateral and regional development banks. However, given the continuing weaknesses and deficiencies of many developing countries, these efforts are insufficient. It would be useful for developing countries to identify and assess the impact of programmes being conducted by the various agencies. These should include schemes that assist poor and small producers to increase their production, storage and marketing capacity, and diversification schemes to upgrade from production of primary commodities to enhancing the value-added content through processing and manufacturing based on commodities.

# References

Action Aid, CAFOD and Canadian Food Grains Bank. 2003. *Agriculture Negotiations in the WTO: Six Ways to Make a New Agreement on Agriculture Work for Development.* Mimeo.

Compaoré, Blaise. 2003. 'Address by President Blaise Compaoré of Burkina Faso on the Cotton Submission by West and Central African Countries to the WTO Trade Negotiations Committee'. Reprinted in *The New York Times,* 11 July.

Das, Bhagirath Lal. 1998. *The WTO Agreements: Deficiencies, Imbalances and Required Changes.* Penang, Malaysia: Third World Network.

—— 2003. *Some Suggestions for Modalities in Agriculture Negotiations.* Trade and Development Series, No. 18. Malaysia: Third World Network.

FAO. 2003. *Some Trade Policy Issues Relating to Trends in Agricultural Imports in the Context of Food Security.* Committee on Commodity Problems, Food and Agriculture Organisation, Sixty-fourth Session, Rome, 18–21 March.

Khor, Martin. 1993. *South–North Resource Flows.* Penang, Malaysia: Third World Network.

—— 2003. *Comment on and Implications of Agriculture Part of the Derbez Text.* Penang, Malaysia: Third World Network.

—— 2003a. *Perspective on Elements in Agriculture Modalities.* Penang, Malaysia: Third World Network.

—— 2003b. 'Eliminate Cotton Subsidies at Cancun, TNC Told'. *South North Development Monitor* (SUNS), 11 June.

OECD. 2000. *Agricultural Policies in OECD Countries: Monitoring and Evaluation 2000.* Paris: OECD Secretariat.

Oxfam. 2002. *Mugged: Poverty in Your Coffee Cup.* Research Paper, Oxfam International, pp. 9–12, 17–18, 22.

—— 2002a. *Report on Cotton Subsidies.* London: Oxfam.

Robbins, Peter. 2003. *Stolen Fruit: The Tropical Commodities Disaster.* London: Zed Books, pp. 22–3, 38–60.

SAPRIN (Structural Adjustment Participatory Review International Network). 2004. *Structural Adjustment: The SAPRIN Report. The Policy Roots of Economic Crisis, Poverty and Inequality.* London: Zed Books, p. 151.

Third World Network. 2001. *The Multilateral Trading System: a Development Perspective.* Report prepared for the UNDP. New York: United Nations Development Programme.

United Nations. 2003. *Report of the Meeting of Eminent Persons on Commodity Issues.* United Nations, Document A/58/401 (2 October 2003), paras 16, 17, 27–29, 36, 47.

UNCTAD. 1999. *Trade and Development Report.* New York and Geneva: United Nations.

—— 2004. *Economic Development in Africa: Trade Performance and Commodity Dependence.* Geneva: United Nations Conference on Trade and Development (March), pp. 58–9.

World Commission on the Social Dimensions on Globalisation. 2004. *A Fair Globalisation.* Geneva: ILO.

WTO. 2003. 'Poverty Reduction: Sectoral Initiative in Favour of Cotton. Joint Proposal by Benin, Burkina Faso, Chad and Mali'. World Trade Organisation, Document TN/AG/GEN/4 (16 May 2003).

# 7

## Globalisation, Debt and the 'Hoover Effect': International Structural Changes that Have Led to the Poor Financing the Rich

### ANN PETTIFOR

*Since 2000, the developing world has been a net exporter of capital to the advanced economies.*

World Bank, *Global Development Finance* (2004), p. 7.

### Today's context

Bill Gross manages US$400 billion of assets for Pimco, a US investment fund. According to the *Financial Times* he is known to 'move markets'. When he says there is 'too much debt, geopolitical risk and several bubbles' in the global economy, and that these have 'created a very unstable environment which can turn any minute' (*Financial Times* 19 June 2004) – he is echoing the analysis of the new economics foundation's (nef's) current annual report on the global economy (Pettifor 2003).

In that report, we argue that the global economy is at a tipping point; that the trade and financial imbalances caused by what is celebrated as 'globalisation' have rendered our world dangerously unstable, both economically and environmentally. That instability is reflected in the defaults, or restructurings of distressed public debt in Argentina, Ecuador, Pakistan, the Russian Federation, Ukraine and Uruguay (World Bank 2004a); by booms and bubbles in telecoms, dotcoms, stocks and property markets, and in currencies like the dollar; and by busts in the telecoms and dotcoms markets and in the dollar – with a threatened bust to Western stock and property markets. The costs of these busts is large. The IMF estimates that over the past three decades equity price busts have resulted in a cumulative loss to GDP of about 4 per cent; while housing busts have been twice as severe (IMF 2004).

Instability is caused in part by the historically unprecedented foreign deficit built up by the US, by its excessively high levels of consumption and by its growing fiscal profligacy. But perhaps the most threatening aspect of the unsustainable but exceptionally sustained US boom is the fact that it is financed, in very large part, by the poor, particularly those in Asian economies. As the World Bank notes:

> Financing the US current account deficit has been shouldered by official institutions (i.e. Central Banks using taxpayer resources) in *developing countries* that have invested reserves (i.e. made cheap loans to the US by purchasing US bonds or Treasury bills) accumulated through good trade performance, effective exchange-rate management, and the strengthening in capital flows. Inflows of foreign official assets to the US amounted to $208 billion during 2003, compared with $95 billion for 2002, financing almost 40 per cent of the US current account deficit. (World Bank 2004a: 18, italics added).

Textbooks assure us that capital flows from where it is plentiful to where it is scarce. But today the very reverse is happening. Capital is being 'hoovered up' or sucked out of low-income countries with large numbers of poor people, into high-income countries with large numbers of the very rich. The injustice of transfers from the poor to the rich through unfair terms of trade and through excessive consumption of natural resources by the rich has been widely explored in development literature. However, we do not believe that sufficient attention has been paid to financial transfers that enable rich countries to live off poor countries.

We will discuss in greater detail below the structural changes central to globalisation that have led to poor taxpayers in low-income countries financing rich taxpayers in high-income countries. They are, in part, to do with a system that requires low-income countries to offer low-cost loans to the US, and to hold these loans (or Treasury Bills) as 'reserves'. This system is a major cause of today's imbalances and instability.

Asian and African countries are obliged (because loans to the US have replaced gold as reserves), to maintain dollar reserves, at 14 and 7 per cent of GDP respectively. The US, in contrast, holds only about 1.3 per cent of its GDP in reserves. The cumulative cost for developing countries of holding such high dollar reserves may be as much as 24 per cent of GDP over ten years, which represents a significant drag on growth rates.

Inflows of capital into the US and the UK help to lower interest rates and therefore borrowing costs for the people of these countries, and inflate the value of their currencies by about 20 per cent. This enables rich countries to purchase imports from the rest of the world 20 per cent cheaper than they would have been able to otherwise.

In 2001 developing countries paid US$122 billion in interest payments on their debt – monies that could have been diverted to development. US$55 billion returned to the West in the form of profits made in low-income countries but sent back by multinational corporations. Finally, poor countries transferred US$260 billion in loan principal paid back to creditors in much richer countries. These figures do not include the illegal and thus unrecorded capital flight from poor countries, a function of capital liberalisation. If it were not for capital flight at least 25 African countries would be net creditors, not debtors (Pettifor and Greenhill 2002).

Countries like Argentina find that their governments are borrowing hard currency, only for it promptly to leave the country (in the form of capital flight) for Wall Street, London, Zurich or Madrid – a legitimate process under capital liberalisation. However the poor in these countries are then saddled with huge public debts. Argentina's total external debt of US$150 billion is almost exactly equal to its unrecorded capital flight of US$130 billion.

The instability is, for some, a result of the lack of G7 or other international coordination and cooperation in the management of trade imbalances, exchange rate volatility and climate change. Even IMF staff, the most 'hands-off' of economists, recognise the 'need for a credible and cooperative strategy that both facilitates the necessary medium-term rebalancing of demand across countries and regions and supports global growth' ( IMF 2004: 15). This failure of world leaders to cooperate and coordinate is leading to rising political tensions, to a collapse of multilateralism, and to growing calls for higher subsidies and for protection from unfair competition.

The instability is further exacerbated by the decision of the US Central Bank and government to do nothing to arrest the decline in the value of the dollar. The dollar has depreciated by 30 per cent since 2002, exacerbating trade tensions, causing the Japanese Central Bank to borrow massively to manage the dollar/yen relationship (in effect, Japanese central bankers are managing trading relationships); and has provoked oil producers to raise oil prices, further exacerbating existing imbalances. (Oil is denominated in international markets in dollars, and as a result revenues from oil have fallen along with the dollar.) (World Bank 2004a: 23)

The instability has been fuelled by reckless credit creation – overseen by austere central bankers and finance ministers whose role is to act as guardians of their nation's finances. Instead they encouraged reckless sovereign lending in the 1970s and 1980s; and, more recently, reckless mortgage lending in the Anglo-American economies, including the 'refinancing' boom in the US, and credit card booms in many countries around the world. The result, of course, is high levels of individual, household, corporate, local and central government debt.

This 'easy money' has boosted and inflated markets for assets (housing, stocks, bonds, racehorses etcetera), causing massive booms in these assets. The rich, on the whole, own assets. The poor live on wages, which have declined as a share of GDP in all the major economies over the last thirty years (Greenhill 2003: 39). This fall in wages as a share of GDP has been accompanied by high levels of unemployment – a major cause of social and political instability. Today levels of unemployment in some parts of the rich world are as high, if not higher, than they were in the period leading up to the Great Depression of the 1930s. In many low-income countries, unemployment is much higher than it was during those times. In the US unemployment is at 6 per cent; in the Euro area it is 8.8 per cent; Japan 5.3 per cent; Canada 7.6 per cent; Hong Kong 7.9 per cent. Unemployment in low-income countries is often in double-digit numbers (IMF 2004).

At the same time commodity prices have been at historically low levels. Between 1995 and 2001, the World Bank's index of dollar-denominated commodity prices fell by more than 35 per cent, before rebounding by 14 per cent over the next two years. In real terms (deflated by the US GDP deflater), the downturn was an even steeper 42 per cent (World Bank 2004: 23). As low-income, heavily indebted nations are highly dependent on revenues from commodities to pay for debts and for development, this collapse in income has often been catastrophic. For rich countries, lower commodity prices have helped suppress inflation, lowered input costs and improved profitability.

ODA flows, which while increasing marginally in 2002 remain at US$58 billion, are 'well below historical levels and what is required to meet the Millennium Development Goals', according to the Bank (World Bank 2004a). While their exports of goods and commodities have failed to generate the resources needed for development, low-income countries have discovered one export category that provides a major source of external development finance, but may also be a source of instability: the export of people – in particular young, educated, highly skilled people. Remittances back to the home country from this export category increased by a remarkable 20 per cent during 2001–3, reaching an estimated US$93 billion in 2003. The World Bank invites 'the development community (to) view remittances as a welcome source of external finance'.

Another source of instability in the world is high real interest rates – for governments, corporations and households. Interest rates, which today are effectively determined by international financial markets, are higher than the rates of return on investment (3 per cent on average), making profitability difficult to achieve. They are much higher than during the period 1945–70, when governments managed interest and exchange rates. They are higher even than they were during a period of excessive government expenditure, 1939–45.

They are due to rise even higher. International financial markets are worried by clear signals from central bankers that interest rates are about to be ratcheted upwards. Many economists expect that these interest rate rises may be the 'tipping point' that bursts asset bubbles in Anglo-American economies, causing housing and stock markets to crash – and impacting most damagingly on low-income countries.

At the same time, the poorest countries continue to languish under burdens of unsustainable debt, plagues of disease and climate change. The crisis of sovereign indebtedness has not gone away in Turkey or Indonesia, Uganda or Iraq, Zambia or Tanzania.

By 2001 total long-term public and publicly guaranteed debt (that is, excluding the foreign debts of private companies) owed by developing countries was almost US$1.5 trillion – or one quarter of their total gross national income. Many developing countries are paying sky-high interest rates on their government debt. Moreover, as the World Bank's *Global Economic Prospects* has made clear, foreign capital flows to developing countries are still 'supply driven' – they flow according to the priorities of Western finance holders rather than locally generated needs. (World Bank 2004b).

Many low-income countries are effectively insolvent but, unlike corporate debtors, have no protection against insolvency, and no recourse to a legal framework that could help them return to sustainability. At the same time they are ecological creditors, owed vast sums by Northern countries that have effectively purloined global assets like the atmosphere, recklessly depleted the earth's valuable and scarce resources, and built up unsustainable ecological debts.

A small proportion of the most indebted nations have sought to emerge from long periods of economic stagnation by participating in a creditor framework – the heavily indebted poor country (HIPC) initiative – for cancelling debts. Predictably this framework has proved painfully slow, is subject to excessive conditionality, and is remarkably mean and short-sighted. Most damningly, it fails to address the interests of creditor countries and institutions themselves – which would benefit enormously if debtor nations were restored to economic health and political and social stability. Nef (new economics foundation) has described the HIPC initiative as

> Like a game of snakes and ladders ... countries have climbed the ladder of 'Decision Point' – where debt relief is committed – only to slide back down the snake of suspended debt relief and yet more International Monetary Fund (IMF) conditionalities.
>
> Moreover, civil society organisations in both North and South have often been kept in the dark about why the HIPC initiative is failing so badly. Countries are being forced 'off-track' by IMF programmes – which inevitably delays debt relief and can also result in the suspension of interim debt service relief. However, apart from a selected few finance ministry officials in debtor countries, and, of course, IMF staff, no one quite knows why. Official World Bank and IMF documents on HIPCs – the now yearly *Status of Implementation Reports* – state only that countries have been delayed 'because they have been delayed'. Yet these are the self-same organisations that insist on transparency and 'good governance' in the countries to which they lend. (Greenhill and Sisti 2003)

In July 2004 Ghana jumped the final hurdle and reached 'completion point' under the HIPC initiative – which is now eight years old! It is one of only 14 countries (out of 42) to have completed the marathon game of 'snakes and ladders'. (The others are Benin, Bolivia, Burkina Faso, Ethiopia, Guyana, Mali, Mauritania, Mozambique, Nicaragua, Niger, Senegal, Tanzania and Uganda.) Another 28 countries will receive too little too late, while many more suffer from the economic degradation of unpayable debts which leads in turn to stagnation, unemployment, civil war and environmental instability.

In the absence of any framework of justice for the resolution of sovereign debt crises it is not possible to define objectively how many countries are in need of complete cancellation of debts to return them to sustainability and to allow them to participate in the global economy. As things stand, decisions about debt sustainability are made by a cartel of creditors whose only short-sighted interest is in an 'asset grab' to ensure they do not suffer losses on what may have been unwise loans, but instead make gains; to guarantee future access to Southern markets; and to repress competition from the competitive sectors (in particular agriculture) in poor, debtor nations.

To summarise, since the launch of globalisation, with the removal of controls over capital in the late 1970s, the rich in rich countries, who own capital and assets, have watched as their assets have been inflated by a credit bubble and by the sympathetic policies of central bankers and governments. They have benefited further from the transfer of resources from poor countries to rich countries. In contrast, those whose livelihoods depend on wages and commodity prices have watched as *their* assets have been deflated by structural adjustment and so-called 'growth and stability' policies, and by rising levels of debt. This is why, under globalisation, the rich have become richer and the poor poorer.

How did the leading economists and politicians of the day create a world that has become so divided, so unjust, so threatening and unsustainable? What can be done to restore economic balance and stability, or have things gone too far? And what is the link between financial instability, the current international financial architecture and the indebtedness of low-income countries?

## Historical background to the current debt problem of poor countries

The three decades following the Second World War were a period in which sovereign defaults and liquidity crises were relatively rare (Fichengreen and Lindert 1991). Not so for the period following the abandonment of the Bretton Woods System, so carefully set up in 1944 but dismantled in 1971. The consequences of the fateful decision taken by President Nixon to end the dollar's link to gold, and to create a new currency standard based on US debt (the US Treasury Bill standard) continue to be played out in the international financial system, and to impact on the world's most indebted nations (Hudson 2003). Above all the international financial system established after the collapse of Bretton Woods has transformed two of the world's most powerful economies – the US and Britain – from major exporters of capital into major importers of capital. The effect of this transformation is the 'hoovering up' of savings and resources from developing countries into rich countries.

There are striking parallels and differences between the events dominating today's headlines and those that led to the debt crisis that exploded with Mexico's default on its debts in August 1982.

### The 1970s depreciating dollar

The most notable factor is the effect of a falling dollar (and general currency volatility) on the revenues from commodities denominated in international markets in dollars, notably oil. In 2004, just as in the late 1960s and the 1970s, the value of the dollar is declining. Just as in the 1970s, oil producers are pushing up the price of oil to compensate. (Another compensating effect of a falling dollar for low-income countries is to lower the value of debts denominated in dollars. This compensating effect applies equally to the US's own debts![1])

### The 1970s US deficit

Then as now, the fall in the value of the dollar was related to the US deficit. Then, in the late 1960s the US had built up a deficit, partly as a result of the Vietnam War, and against Bretton Woods rules for balancing imports and exports. When creditors demanded that dollars be exchanged for gold as payment for imports, the US found its reserves of gold (which represented its surplus) run down. To deal with this problem President Nixon's administration took the unilateral decision in 1971 to abandon the Bretton Woods 'adjustable peg' system for fixing exchange rates to gold. From then on, the US would pay for its debts in bank money – dollars or bonds (US Treasury bills).

This decision ensured that the US could continue to borrow and consume, without undertaking the necessary 'structural adjustment' to its economy that would have been required if it had been obliged to restore balance to its

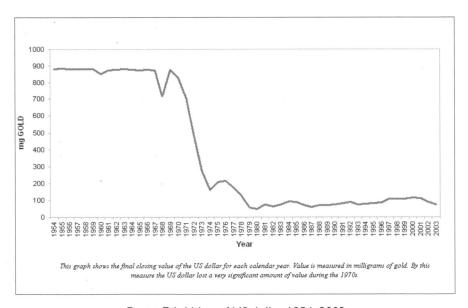

*This graph shows the final closing value of the US dollar for each calendar year. Value is measured in milligrams of gold. By this measure the US dollar lost a very significant amount of value during the 1970s.*

#### Figure 7.1  Value of US dollar, 1954–2003

Source: http://en.wikipedia.org/wiki/USdollar

external account by cutting back on consumption and imports, and building up a surplus of gold, earned from its exports. Furthermore, the US has been able to borrow and depend on the savings of others without losing policy autonomy – the right to determine its own destiny – to foreign creditors. This has not been true for poor, indebted nations.

While the abandonment of the Bretton Woods 'adjustable peg' system for currencies enabled the US to grow and consume by borrowing from the rest of the world, the lower dollar had a severe impact on the oil-producing countries. This was because the delinking of the dollar from gold led to a fall in the value of the dollar.

### Oil price hikes

Revenues earned (in dollars) by producer countries now purchased less in international markets. Oil producers, closing ranks as the Organisation of Petroleum-Exporting Countries (OPEC) cartel, responded by dramatically raising the price of oil in 1973. This was the start of a decade of successive shocks. Rocketing prices for a vital resource, oil, placed a huge burden on poor countries. At the same time, massive earnings from Middle Eastern oil sales flooded into Western banks and institutions. Banks in most of the developed world were reporting net average annual growth rates of deposits of between 25 and 30 per cent (Stambulil 1998).

### Inflation threat: low-income-country debtors to the rescue

While these monies were welcome, they also posed a substantial threat to the stability of Western economies: that of runaway inflation. To deal with this threat, finance ministers, bankers and officials of the IMF and World Bank actively encouraged the disbursement of these excess funds in the form of loans to developing countries. It can be argued that developing countries, by borrowing, rescued industrial countries from the crisis of runaway inflation. In the autumn of 1981, Sir Geoffrey Howe, Britain's Finance Minister, praised the virtues of private banks in recycling funds to low-income countries. He described lending to these countries as 'the best form of recycling' on account of the fact that external loans 'enabled them to finance their external payments and to raise their living standards'. In March 1980, just 18 months before Mexico's default, Paul Volcker, chairman of the Federal Reserve Bank of the USA, also endorsed the rise in bank lending to low-income countries. He dismissed fears of a debt crisis, arguing that

> The impression I get from the data I have received is that the recycling process has not yet pushed exposure of either borrowers or lenders to an unsustainable point in the aggregate.[2]

### Negative real interest rates – at first

The oil-price hike injected huge sums of money into the international financial system, which in turn caused the price of money – interest rates –

to fall, until they effectively became negative. In real terms, banks were paying people and sovereign governments to take their money – to borrow. Then as now, the world engaged in a binge of lending and borrowing.

> One of the reasons for the debt build-up from US$260 billion in 1975 to US$1,265 billion in 1984 was the administrative complacency among monetary authorities that turned a blind eye to the unprecedented expansion of credit to the low-income countries. (Stambulil 1998)

The advent of the syndicated loan led to the belief among financial institutions that they could minimise their credit risk by spreading loans to a variety of countries across the world among several banks, in such a way that the exposure of each bank was minimal.

## Debtors: emerging from colonialism

The need to stabilise Western economies and protect them from the threat of inflation coincided with the need of developing countries for development finance. Zambia was a prime example. At the time of independence in 1964, Zambia, a landlocked country, was wholly dependent on one commodity, copper, and had only one major road for transporting this commodity to the nearest port. A handful of its citizens had university degrees; there were very few schools and no adequate health system. When IMF staff encouraged the newly elected Zambian President to borrow funds for development (at what were, effectively, negative interest rates), Zambia's politicians were quick to sign loan contracts.[3] These politicians were assured by IMF staff that there would always be a demand for copper, and that the price would never fall so low as to prevent Zambia earning the revenues needed to repay these low-cost debts. These confident predictions were to prove very flawed.

Some countries, like Mexico and Venezuela, took out loans to repay previous debts. But for others, this was the first time they had borrowed from *commercial* banks. Many intended to use the money to improve standards of living in their countries. But, in the end, little of the money borrowed benefited the poor. Across the range, about a fifth of it went on arms, often to shore up oppressive regimes. Many governments started large-scale development projects, some of which proved of little value. All too often, the money found its way into private bank accounts. The poor were the losers.

### Commodity price recession worse than the Great Depression
As Maizels (1992) demonstrates, commodity prices in the 1980s 'showed a drastic downward trend, with relatively small annual fluctuations', suggesting that the general commodity terms of trade fell as much as 35 per cent between 1978–80 and 1986–8. Thus he concludes that 'the commodity price recession of the 1980s has been more severe and considerably more prolonged than that of the Great Depression of the 1930s'. It is this commodity crisis that explains most conclusively the protracted debt crises

that befell commodity-dependent, low-income countries from the 1980s onwards. Nissanke and Ferrarini (2004) argue correctly that

> Commodity-dependent poor countries started experiencing a series of severe liquidity crises for debt payment in the early 1980s. Creditors judged this as a temporary condition, and kept reluctantly financing by rescheduling debt through the Paris and London club negotiations. This was an act of *defensive* lending so that their existing claims were paid at least on a regular basis. Based on the diagnosis that the low-income-country debt crisis was a result of government *dirigiste* economic policy failure, creditors thought that structural adjustment policies (SAPs) attached as policy conditionality would arrest the crisis situation. However, despite acceptance of SAPs by debtor countries in order to gain access to official aid, their debt crises continued to deepen, giving rise to the serious question as to whether the debtor countries were facing a solvency crisis rather than a liquidity crisis. (Nissanke and Ferrarini 2004)

However, it was not just low-income countries that were to be the victims of commodity price volatility, the inflationary impact of oil revenues and the accumulation of foreign debts.

### Tightening the noose: higher interest rates

By the late 1970s, inflationary pressures – the result, as we have seen, of the liquidity pumped into the global economy by oil producers – led to action by Western governments. In an attempt to curb wage price inflation at home, they began to raise interest rates. As a result, 'total outflows of dividends, profits and interest payments (from developing countries) rose from US$15 billion in 1978 to $44 billion in 1981 (Lever and Huhne 1982). UNCTAD has calculated that between 1976–9 and 1980–2 the rise in interest rates added $41 billion to the stock of low-income-country debt (Inter-American Development Bank 1985)' (Stambulil 1998: 12). Meanwhile oil prices rose again.

### Loosening the grip: deregulated capital flows

But perhaps most dangerously, leading Western governments began to liberalise capital flows. Led by Prime Minister Thatcher and President Reagan, and supported by central bankers and academic economists, exchange controls over the movement of international capital flows were lifted. Middle-income countries like Chile, Uruguay and Argentina followed suit.

> As a result of financial deregulation in the late 1970s these economies experienced a surge in capital outflows hitherto restricted by regulations on capital exports. The fact that the 1982 crisis occurred when there was a steep rise in interest rates in the US underscores the significance of the capital outflow element of a financial crisis. The appreciation of the dollar at this time also means that repayments magnified the capital outflow in domestic currency terms. At the same time, the accompanying drop in

dollar prices of internationally traded commodities undermined inflows derived from exports. (Stambulil 1998: 5)

Low-income countries were earning less than ever for their exports and paying more than ever on their loans and on oil – a vital import. Furthermore, helped by the removal of exchange controls (encouraged by the IMF through its SAPs) rich elites were effectively given permission to export capital from where it had been earned – out of poor countries, depositing these savings with rich countries. Developing-country governments *had* to borrow more money just to stay afloat.

## The crisis breaks: Mexico on the frontline

In August 1982 Mexico announced to its creditors that it could not repay its debts. The announcement was made after Mexico had failed to raise a large enough loan to repay external debts that were falling due.

> Between 1975 and 1980 four countries had to postpone amortisation payments while servicing interest only. By 1983 the number of countries defaulting on their repayments reached 21 and some low-income countries had instituted state criminal proceedings against public figures on account of alleged negligence and mishandling of public money. (Stambulil 1998: 5)

This pattern was repeated over and over in the following years as other countries found themselves in similar situations to Mexico's. But their debts continued to rise, and new loans added to the burden. Essentially, the poorest countries had become insolvent.

### *Enter the trouble shooters: the Baker Plan of 1985*
When Mexico defaulted on its debt repayments in 1982 the whole international credit system was threatened. Mexico owed huge sums of money to banks in the US and Europe, and they didn't want to lose it. So they clubbed together and gained the support of the IMF for a scheme to spread out or reschedule the debts.

In 1985, President Reagan's second Treasury Secretary, James Baker launched his so-called 'Baker Plan', the first of several attempts by the US Government to tackle the exploding Latin American debt problem. It was managed day to day by Baker's close associate, former Undersecretary of the Treasury David C. Mulford, who later became Chairman of Credit Suisse First Boston's International Group, and just recently was designated by President G. W. Bush as the new US Ambassador to India.

The Baker Plan, which relied heavily on a combination of tougher IMF/World Bank conditions in exchange for a modest amount of new loans from the multilateral agencies, wrongly assumed that, with the right policies, developing countries could grow themselves out of their excessive debts.

## Once more to the rescue: the Brady Plan of 1989

By 1989 debts to commercial banks were no longer worth their value on paper because the banks had written off large chunks of them in theory, assuming they would never be repaid. US Treasury Secretary Brady argued that the banks should reduce the actual value of the remaining debt for larger debtor countries, so that they had less to pay.

According to the World Bank,

> the idea was to restructure bank debt into liquid, tradable and safe securities, the repayment of which (principal and sometimes interest) was secured against US Treasury zero-coupon bonds that were to be held in a trust until the restructured bonds matured. In addition, countries were to undertake economic reform to work their way out of economic and financial stress. (World Bank 2004a: 49)

Debt service was lowered to levels that were already being paid, so no actual benefit accrued to the debtor country. In terms of total debt stock this plan did not help debtor countries. As commercial debts have fallen, multilateral debts have risen. At the same time, the Brady Plan laid the foundations for today's era of low-income-country access to international bond markets. Although bond issuance by developing countries dates back to the early 1800s, its importance in the 1980s was minimal, averaging only US$3 billion per year. Bond issuance increased from US$4 billion in 1990 to a peak of US$99 billion in 1997.

This massive expansion of debt came to an abrupt end with the financial crises beginning with Thailand in 1997, followed by the Russian Federation (1998), Brazil (1999), Turkey (2000) and Argentina (2001). Furthermore, the economic conditions imposed on countries provoked bloody riots (Venezuela, 1989) and debt moratoria (Brazil, 1987; Argentina, 1988). And by the year 2000, the real level of low-income-country debt was 150 per cent higher than it had been in 1985.

## Trinidad/Naples terms

Nigel Lawson and then John Major, both British finance ministers, originally proposed (through Paris Club negotiations) that creditor countries cancel half the debt owed to them by the lowest-income countries, while rescheduling the rest. This could have resulted in debt relief worth £18 billion to the poorest countries. Later Major went further and proposed two-thirds debt remission. In the end, 67 per cent cancellation was agreed at the G-7 Summit in Naples, in 1994.

In practice, however, this level of reduction was only applied to a small proportion of poor countries' debts – the 'eligible debt', with eligibility defined arbitrarily by creditors. Creditors remained very reluctant to offer substantial debt relief to return poor countries to solvency and sustainability. Countries had to keep to stringent SAPs to get debt relief and were not exempt from any repayments to the IMF or World Bank.

## The Jubilee debt campaign and the birth of the heavily indebted poor country initiative (HIPC 1)

In October 1996, largely as a result of pressure from NGOs in the South as well as the North, a major shift by the IMF and the World Bank resulted in a debt relief initiative that contemplated, for the first time in the history of these institutions, the cancellation of debts owed to them. The agreement also recommended a strategy to enable countries to exit from unsustainable debt burdens. The initiative proposed 80 per cent debt relief by the key creditor governments only after countries had fulfilled two three-year stages of structural adjustment conditions. The World Bank announced the establishment of a trust fund to finance the initiative.

In reality, the initiative proved to be completely ineffective. Uganda and Bolivia received debt cancellation in April 1998 and September 1998 respectively – but within a year they were back where they started with unsustainable debt burdens. They had fallen victim to falling commodity prices and impossibly optimistic forecasts (made by World Bank and IMF staff to justify lower levels of debt relief) for their future export and economic growth. Mozambique, after treatment under the initiative, ended up paying only 1 per cent less in debt payments than before it was declared an HIPC. As a result no money was released for spending on health and education. Growing pressure from debt campaign groups, under the Jubilee 2000 umbrella, forced the creditors to admit that HIPC 1 was failing to deliver. In January 1999 Chancellor Schröder of Germany announced that 'radical and bold' steps were needed on debt relief, prompting other G-7 creditors to support calls for an 'enhanced' HIPC initiative. This was launched at the Cologne G-8 Summit (with Russia now included as the eighth country), as 50,000 people formed human chains in Germany to call for the `chains of debt' to be broken.

### Cologne debt initiative/HIPC 2

HIPC 2 was launched at the Cologne G-8 Summit in June 1999 to great fanfares of publicity and promised to provide 'broader, faster and deeper' debt relief, and an improved link with poverty reduction. Creditors talked of a headline figure of US$100 billion of debt relief for HIPC countries, which included US$25 billion of additional relief in the 'enhanced' initiative.

By the end of 2000, 22 countries had received some relief on debt service payments and a total of US$12 billion had been cancelled – but only Uganda had reached the completion point in the HIPC process. In some countries, debt relief had made a tangible difference. For example, in Mozambique, US$60 million had been released into various areas, all vital to sustaining development. Budgets for health, education, agriculture, infrastructure and employment training had all benefited. Overall, however, the level of debt relief had failed to deliver the necessary resources to tackle deep-rooted social and economic problems built up through the debt crises of the 1980s.

Haiti, for example, is not eligible for debt relief under the initiative even though it is the poorest country in the Western Hemisphere and nearly half of the debt was contracted under the Duvalier dictatorship. It will receive no debt cancellation even though it has 50 per cent adult illiteracy, 70 per cent unemployment and an infant mortality rate that is more than double the Latin American and Caribbean average.

As noted above, by the end of July 2004, 14 countries had reached 'completion point' and had stocks of debt cancelled. Few of these countries had reached levels of debt sustainability, thanks to the failure of the HIPC initiative to pursue this objective. Instead, it continued to seek to limit losses for creditors by providing over-optimistic projections for growth, and by focusing on debt-to-export ratios instead of debt as a share of government expenditure.

## What is the way forward?

The new economics foundation and many other NGOs propose the following changes to the international financial system to stabilise financial flows, end the global dependence on US debt, reduce volatility and end the injustice of the poor financing the rich. These changes are necessary, and additional to the mobilisation of resources needed to achieve the MDGs.

Governments should take action, as they did in 1944, to claw back from financial markets their right to policy autonomy. This must be done if democratic institutions are not to be hollowed out, and democratic representation made a sham. As things stand, most governments have given up vital powers to manage investment, economic growth and employment. These are the powers to fix the exchange rates of their currencies, and to set interest rates for their economies. As these are both vital tools for the management of economies they should be in the hands of democratically elected governments, and not in the hands of the unaccountable and often irresponsible financial sector.

A starting point for such a transformation will be to reverse the most pernicious elements of the 'globalisation' experiment. This will mean taming financial markets through

- the reintroduction of capital controls;

- restraints on the growth of credit, through increased regulation by central banks and governments;

- increased control over the rate of interest;

- the establishment of an International Clearing Agency for managing international payments, and global exchange rates. This body would be tasked with maintaining stability in the international financial system by correcting deficit or surplus imbalances, as proposed by J. M. Keynes at the Bretton Woods Conference in 1947 (D'Arista 2003).

- The International Clearing Agency would ensure that the holding of reserves would be in a basket of currencies, not a single currency as today.

It will be vital in rich and poor countries for governments to take action to ensure the availability of cheap, not easy money. Just as the British government was able to establish low interest rates for the whole duration of the Second World War, when Britain was facing one of its greatest crises, so all governments should have the power to maintain low interest rates. Control over the movement of capital is a major corollary of control over interest rates.

Third, it will be vital to empower governments to respond to democratic mandates by returning to governments and parliaments the power to allocate resources for pensions, health, clean water, public transport, the arts, public service broadcasting, energy and other resources for the vulnerable and the poor.

It is our view that Gordon Brown's proposal for an increase in OECD aid by US$50 billion per year will prove ineffectual in achieving the MDGs in the HIPC countries unless there is also 100 per cent debt cancellation in these countries. Besides full debt cancellation, development assistance has to be increased to reach the 0.7 target agreed by donors. Even if the first Goal (eradicating extreme poverty and hunger) is not achieved, meeting the others – which include achieving universal primary education, reducing child mortality, promoting gender equality and combating HIV/AIDS – would require additional expenditures.

The international Jubilee movement is calling for an end to creditor-dominated control over debtor nations. Instead we propose a new, just, transparent and accountable framework for the resolution of sovereign debt crises, based on Chapter 9 of the US Legal Code. (The proposal for such a framework originated with Professor Kunibert Raffer of the University of Vienna, and we at nef are deeply indebted to him for his scholarly leadership on this issue.)

The proposed Jubilee Framework would operate under the key legal principles underlying all insolvency procedures, namely that:

- public debt represents losses to taxpayers in both debtor and creditor nations; therefore any process for resolving debt crises should be open and accountable to these taxpayers;

- all processes should be based on the application of justice and reason;

- any process should protect the human rights and the human dignity of the debtors, as well as the rights of creditors; and

- neither creditors nor debtors can decide on their own claims or payments.

Under the Jubilee Framework, countries could declare themselves insolvent if it became clear that repayments of foreign debts were being made at a cost to the human rights or dignity of the people of that country. Debtor countries would then be able to negotiate with their creditors in front of an independent arbitration panel consisting of nominees from both debtors and creditors.

There has been substantial support for some form of international insolvency process from the IMF and other key players such as the Bank of England. In 2001 the IMF proposed a Sovereign Debt Re-structuring Mechanism (SDRM), which unfortunately gave the IMF a key role in determining, in advance of negotiations, the appropriate level of debt cancellation required to achieve sustainability. NGOs considered this unacceptable, because as a creditor the IMF could not be independent, and furthermore had an interest in setting the level of sustainability (see Raffer in this volume). In addition the IMF applied the SDRM only to middle-income countries such as Argentina. Nevertheless, the SDRM was a step in the right direction. The application of a framework of justice has proved very necessary in the case of Argentina. The failure, after almost four years of default, to resolve Argentina's debt crisis has hurt both Argentina's creditors and its people.

## Conclusion

Globalisation – a term that embraces the liberalisation of capital and trade flows, the removal of policy autonomy from democratic governments, and the failure of international coordination and cooperation – is leading our world towards more and more financial instability and crisis. It is vital that this headlong descent into exchange rate and trade chaos be arrested, to prevent further instability and volatility.

Furthermore, if we are to prevent the growth of right-wing authoritarian political parties, it is vital that we restore policy autonomy to democratic governments, and a belief that something can be done about high levels of economic degradation and suffering. In the 1930s, capital liberalisation and government by markets meant that no one appeared accountable for the growth of unemployment, unpayable sovereign debts (Germany) and the spread of poverty and suffering. As a result, victims of this system turned to authoritarian and fascist political parties who offered jobs and stability.

To prevent this happening again, it is vital that policy autonomy is restored to governments all over the world – so that elected politicians may be empowered to protect the interests of their people and their environments. Central to such policy autonomy is the right to control the money markets and to set interest rates.

The Helsinki Process could play a vital role in promoting such ideas and in supporting politicians in their struggle with unregulated capital markets, thereby helping prevent crises on the scale that occurred in the 1930s.

## Notes

1 Staff at the new economics foundation have calculated that India lost US$12 billion as a result in the fall of the value of her dollar reserves in 2003. To the US, this is a fall in US$12 billion of monies owed to India.
2 Source: private conversation between author and ex-President Kaunda of Zambia.
3 *Ibid.*

## References

D'Arista, J. 2003. 'Financial Architecture in the Twenty-first Century?' in Ann Pettifor (ed.), *Real World Economic Outlook: Debt and Deflation – the Legacy of Globalisation*. London: Palgrave Macmillan.

Eichengreen, B. and P. H. Lindert. 1991. *The International Debt Crisis in Historical Perspective*. Cambridge, MA: MIT Press, Chapter 1.

Greenhill, R. and E. Sisti. 2003. *The Real Progress Report on HIPC*. A report from Jubilee Research at the new economics foundation. September. Retrieved at www.jubileeresearch.org.

Hudson, M. 2003. 'The Dollar Bill: Who Picks up the Tab?' in Ann Pettifor (ed.), *Real World Economic Outlook: Debt and Deflation – the Legacy of Globalisation*. London: Palgrave Macmillan.

IMF. 2004. *IMF World Economic Outlook*, 15, 22 (April).

Maizels, A. 1992. *Commodities in Crisis*. Oxford: Clarendon Press.

Nissanke, M. and B. Ferrarini. 2004. 'Debt Dynamics and Contingency Financing', in A. Addison, H. Hensen and F. Tarp ( eds.), *Debt Relief for Poor Countries*. London: Palgrave Macmillan, p. 35.

Pettifor, A. 2003. *Real World Economic Outlook: Debt and Deflation – the Legacy of Globalisation*. London: Palgrave Macmillan.
Retrieved at www.jubileeresearch.org or www.palgrave.co.uk.

Pettifor, A. and R. Greenhill. 2002. *The US as HIPC – a Heavily Indebted Prosperous Country*. A report from Jubilee Research at the new economics foundation. April. Retrieved at www.jubileeresearch.org.

Stambulil, P. K. 1998. *Causes and Consequences of the 1982 World Debt Crisis?* Pre-doctoral Research Paper, Department of Economics, University of Surrey, Guildford, pp. 5, 12.

World Bank. 2003. *Debt Relief for the Poorest – an OED Review of the HIPC Initiative*. Washington, DC: World Bank.

—— 2004a. *Global Development Finance: Harnessing Cyclical Gains for Development*. New York: Oxford University Press and World Bank, pp. 18, 23.

—— 2004b. *Global Economic Prospects*. New York: Oxford University Press and World Bank.

# 8

# Beyond HIPC:
## Secure, Sustainable Debt Relief for Poor Countries[1]

### NANCY BIRDSALL and BRIAN DEESE

In 1999, the United States and other major donor countries supported an historic expansion of the heavily indebted poor country (HIPC) debt relief initiative. HIPC had two primary goals: to reduce poor countries' debt burdens to levels that would allow them to achieve sustainable growth; and to promote a new way of assisting poor countries focused on home-grown poverty alleviation and human development. Three years after the initiative came into existence, we are beginning to see the apparent impact that HIPC is having, particularly on recipient countries' ability and willingness to increase domestic spending on education and HIV/AIDS programmes. Yet it has also become clear that the HIPC programme is not providing a sufficient level of predictability or sustainability to allow debtor countries (and donors) to reap the larger benefits, particularly in terms of sustained growth and poverty reduction, originally envisioned. An adequate amount of predictable debt relief can be an extremely efficient way of transferring resources to poor countries with reasonable economic management (indeed, more effective than traditional aid). But the full benefits of the transfer, in improved capacity to manage their economies, and in increased investor confidence in an economy's future, require that creditors, investors and committed recipient-government officials have confidence that the improved debt situation will be sustained over the medium term. After reviewing some of the main critiques and proposals for change, we offer here a new way forward – a proposal to deepen, widen, and most importantly insure debt relief to poor countries. We focus on the insurance aspect of our proposal, which would safeguard countries against external shocks for a decade, and on the advantages of financing such insurance by limited mobilisation of IMF gold. We see this proposal as a practical way of making debt relief more predictably sustainable in HIPC countries and of focusing the near-term efforts of international donors.

## The case for debt relief

Jubilee 2000 – a worldwide citizens' movement supported by the pop star Bono, Pope John Paul II, and millions of ordinary churchgoing people in the United States and Europe – was the most successful developed-country movement aimed at combating world poverty for many years, perhaps in all recorded history. It succeeded not just in changing official policy, but in arousing an unusual measure of concern among the world's rich about the state of the world's poor. Jubilee campaigners argued convincingly that the debts owed by poor countries to rich institutions like the IMF and World Bank and to the governments of industrial countries were an unjust burden on their citizens, who were paying obligations mostly assumed by corrupt past leaders. And this debt was sabotaging the ability of even the most reformist, well-intentioned governments to provide minimal social services to their citizens. Jubilee's success was embodied in the enhanced HIPC initiative, agreed to by all the major donors in 1999.

While the political momentum behind the initiative was new, the 1999 agreement represented only one more step – a big one, admittedly – in more than a decade of international negotiations aimed at reducing the debt burden of the poorest countries of the world (Box 8.1 on p. 152 catalogues this history). For the donors, HIPC was not just good politics. Donor countries had another reason to swallow hard, organise, and cancel some of the debt owed to them by the world's poorest countries. Two decades of official lending at cheap rates had failed to catalyse the increased growth and new economic activities needed to finance the resulting debt. Donors had therefore become locked into 'defensive lending'. Unwilling to let poor countries explicitly default, especially to the multilateral creditors, they were stuck with endless rounds of rescheduling debt and negotiating new grants and loans to help poor countries pay back old loans, sometimes independent of recipient countries' ability to use any external resources well.[2]

Debt relief seemed to hold out the promise of getting both the donors and the debtors back on track. Since 1999, more than US$1.3 billion has been released annually in the 26 countries already approved for debt relief, with some apparent impact. The World Bank has been able to track an increase in social expenditures in these countries of nearly the same amount (some countries used external debt relief to write down domestic debts). About 40 per cent of the debt savings are being directed to education and 25 per cent to health care. Nearly every HIPC is using a portion of debt relief to create or expand HIV/AIDS prevention and education programmes. Tanzania ended fees for grade school, and Benin ended fees in rural areas – giving millions of children the chance to go to school. Honduras will offer three more years of free schooling, so that public school students can go up to the ninth grade. Uganda has put every child in grade school, and will hire more teachers and pay for more classrooms and textbooks. Mali, Mozambique and Senegal will increase spending on HIV/AIDS prevention, to slow the spread of the pandemic. But it has also become clear that the current programme is not providing a sufficient level of predictability or sustainability to allow debtor countries (and donors) to reap the full benefits originally envisioned. Many countries will continue to have unsustainable levels of debt after HIPC relief, owed particularly to multilateral donors like the World Bank and IMF.

We begin this chapter by presenting an analytical argument why debt relief can be a more efficient resource transfer than just more new aid. We then turn to the current HIPC framework, and review some of the main critiques and proposals for change. Building on the critiques and proposals, we conclude by offering a new way forward – a three-pronged proposal to deepen, widen and insure debt relief to poor countries. We focus on the third of these proposals, as the most critical and practically feasible debt relief reform around which international donors could consolidate their efforts in the near term.

## Debt relief is effective aid

Debt relief can be more efficient than traditional aid, particularly in countries with a record of responsible government and reasonable respect for the rule of law. Why?

### Debt relief helps correct the traditional bad habits of international donors

First, *debt relief cannot be tied to wasteful donor practices*. Aid is said to be 'tied' when recipient countries are required to purchase goods or services from donor country contractors and suppliers. The practice is highly inefficient, reducing the value of aid by an estimated 15 to 30 per cent (Chinnock 1998). Donors pledged, in the spring of 2000, to end the practice, but exempted food aid and technical assistance from that decision. Technical assistance (mostly consultant advice and training) makes up as much as 25 per cent of total development assistance. In a country like Mozambique, US or German consultants can cost 10 to 20 times as much as their competitors from Brazil or South Africa. Assuming that poor countries could get only twice (not 10 times) as much value for each dollar spent in a competitive world market for technical assistance, and adding to that the cost of continuing to tie food aid, we estimate that donors will continue to waste some US$7 billion per year in aid resources, even after the OECD countries have implemented their pledge. In contrast to new aid disbursements, which may be inefficiently 'tied', debt relief comes in the form of direct budget support to developing country governments.

Second, *debt relief liberates donors from inefficient 'defensive lending'*. Research shows that aid works better in countries where responsible governments are pursuing sensible economic policies. But in the 1990s, donor behaviour was characterised by defensive lending – transferring more resources to those countries with the highest debt, regardless of how well they were performing. This behaviour was, in a peculiar sense, well-intentioned. Donors wanted to avoid the negative multiplier effects on poor countries of falling into arrears with multilateral creditors. But it nonetheless created a debt trap for donors as well as recipients, and made aid less effective. With sufficient debt reduction for the poorest countries, donors would be freed to make sound policies and institutions the sole basis for future decisions on where to spend.

*Debt relief allows for poor country ownership of development strategies*
First, *debt relief reduces the huge transaction costs of conventional foreign aid programmes.* Acquiring and managing aid has high transaction costs for recipient countries. Talented government officials in aid-dependent countries must meet daily with local and visiting missions of the World Bank, the IMF, the European Union, UNDP, the United States Agency for International Development (USAID) and other bilateral aid agencies, as well as with representatives of non-governmental organisations. All of these aid institutions have different, even competing approaches to health, environment, or financial sector reform, and each has different procurement, disbursement, and monitoring rules and customs. In contrast, debt relief has the peculiar advantage of being like cash – it comes without significant transaction costs. This allows recipient countries to streamline the management of aid resources and, with greater control and ownership over their use, it makes them fully accountable for results.

Second, *debt relief provides flexible budget support and makes governments accountable to citizens.* Tanzania received about US$700 million in new donor funding in 1999, and owed US$230 million that year in debt payments, resulting in a net inflow of aid. But most of the new aid money was linked to specific projects or priorities favoured by donors, so the Tanzanian government had to set aside US$230 million of its limited tax revenues for debt repayment. (Typically, HIPC countries spent – before debt relief – about 25 per cent of tax revenue to repay existing debts.) Donors prefer supporting projects to providing cash for budget support because project outputs can be monitored and measured, and projects often provide contracts for donor country consultants and suppliers. So even when countries have positive net transfers of aid (new aid minus payments on old debt), their ability to direct resources where it might be most effective is limited.

Debt reduction allows governments to spend precious tax revenue on their own budget priorities, instead of on debt repayments. This makes governments more accountable to their citizens. A shift of some aid resources from new projects to debt relief would give a boost to countries struggling to strengthen honest and democratic governance.

## Debt relief can foster private investment
A large amount of debt, and perpetual dependence on the beneficence of donors, creates uncertainty about a government's finances and its ability to deliver macroeconomic stability. Investors worry about heavy future tax burdens imposed to sustain or write down public debt. Entrepreneurial energy is directed into less risky projects promising quicker returns – such as

retailing, small construction, and marketing – rather than into major new businesses. Debt reduction that is irreversible and provides a reasonable guarantee of debt sustainability can restore investor confidence.

## Critique of the HIPC initiative

The compelling case for debt relief *per se* has not isolated the enhanced HIPC initiative from criticism (Birdsall and Deese 2002; Eurodad 2001a; Roodman 2001; Oxfam 2001; Drop the Debt 2001; Jubilee Plus 2001). Its design and implementation have been closely scrutinised, in large part as a result of the success of the Jubilee movement in broadcasting the promise of debt relief as an alternative mechanism to change the development assistance business for the better.

The many critiques can be put into two broad categories, representing two different perspectives on the underlying causes of the failure of development assistance programmes in the poorest countries.

### The 'foreign aid down the rat hole' camp

These critics argue that debt relief and other forms of aid have been too great and too easy to get. Recipient governments are often wasteful and corrupt. Even in the best cases of reasonably adequate governance, aid and debt relief simply relieve countries' immediate budget constraint, allowing them to persist with bad economic policies. The official donors and creditors share some blame for providing too many loans, driven by a combination of political, commercial and bureaucratic motives (Easterly 1999; Thomas 2001; Burnside and Dollar 2000).

For these critics, enhanced HIPC retains some traditional conditionality. The IMF must still give the nod affirming that macro policies are adequate for a country to reach the first step in the process, the decision point. And the new Poverty Reduction Strategy Papers (PRSP), announced in 1999, was meant to address deeper concerns about poor governance and over-eager donors. The PRSP envisaged a process whereby governments (aided by World Bank staff) would convene extensive consultations with civil society and non-governmental actors, and prepare holistic, country-owned strategies that would form the basis for both HIPC and future donor assistance.

But the requirements for the PRSP process have themselves provoked a fair amount of cynicism. For critics of aid they seem no different from business as usual – in which much that is written and agreed is never implemented. Another complaint – this time from friends of greater aid, not just foes – is that in some countries parliaments have been largely bypassed in the process of popular consultation. There is an inherent tension between the focus on participation and the connection between the PRSP and release of HIPC debt relief proceeds, the second representing a form of donor-mandated conditionality that hinders the first. While few argue that increased spending on education and health is a bad idea, many southern NGO and civil society advocates caution us not to confuse the pre-set goals of the PRSP process with country ownership. In May 2001, a group of 39 regional networks in 15 African countries argued that the PRSP is simply 'window dressing' (Ranis and Stewart 2001).

Concern has also been expressed that the emphasis on poverty reduction via increases in social expenditures is primarily a donor-owned view, and would not necessarily be the optimal path for a country to attain sustainable growth and thus sustainable reductions in poverty (Addison and Rahman 2001; Burnside and Fanizza 2001).

A final – and critically important – critique is that the PRSPs are not adequately addressing the task of monitoring, and that even if countries buy into the new donor conditionality, it will be impossible to tell where the proceeds of debt relief are really going. The IMF (2002) found that only two of the HIPC countries will have the capacity to track spending related to debt relief transactions within the next year.

## The 'poverty trap' camp

Under this argument, debt reduction is too small and tied to conditionality that is onerous and misguided. Given the complex challenges that many poor countries face – conflict, ethnic fragmentation, dependence on primary commodities with declining and unstable prices, tropical disease, and often small size – debt relief and other forms of aid have been far from adequate to allow them to escape poverty and put them onto a growth path. In this perspective, much more of the blame goes to creditors and donors. Too much of the lending was wasteful and *inefficient*, sustaining donors' own bureaucracies and financing purchases of their own goods and use of their own high-cost consultants (Sachs *et. al.* 1999; Jubilee Plus 2001; Oxfam 2001). Worst of all, much was politically motivated, incurred in dubious situations that call its legitimacy into question. Should countries be expected to service such debt? Does elementary justice not demand that it be cancelled?

The structure of the enhanced HIPC initiative responds more directly to this set of critics – it is bigger (more costly for donors), and faster than previous debt relief efforts. Yet three central criticisms remain to be answered. The *first* is that the basic criterion for HIPC eligibility – a country's stock of debt as a share of its exports – is inappropriate (Eurodad 2001a; 2001b).[3] The criticism is that this ratio is not really germane to whether a debtor country can afford to divert resources away from key social expenditures in order to service outstanding debt. Limiting such diversions was proclaimed to be an underlying purpose of the HIPC initiative: that is reflected in the conditionality attached to HIPC, which is designed to ensure that the freed resources are indeed used for social programmes and for other investments most likely to reduce poverty. An alternative approach is to calculate the maximum affordable level of *debt service* and use that to calculate what percentage of the debt stock needs to be cancelled, rather than deciding to cancel a part of the stock of debt based on a comparison with exports.

A second criticism is that the HIPC initiative needs a truth-in-accounting lesson. Forgiving unpayable debts is simply accepting reality, not doing the debtors a favour (Roodman 2001). Daniel Cohen (2000) has used a model estimated on data from the Latin American debtor countries to infer what HIPC debts would be worth in a secondary market, if the donors hadn't continued to lend defensively to help cover debt service. He finds that some 90 per cent of the debt reduction ought to be counted as a loss (bad debt), and only the remaining 10 per cent as ODA. Other comparisons suggest a figure in the same ball-park.[4] These calculations imply that deeper debt relief, to the point where it accepts the reality of what the debt is really worth, would not actually cost the donors anything much.

A third criticism relates to the debt sustainability analyses that the World Bank/IMF team has been conducting in order to decide whether HIPC debt relief is enough to make the countries' debt burdens sustainable. These are projection exercises, designed to test whether the proposed debt reductions are large enough to enable countries to keep their debt/export ratios below 150 per cent in the longer term (interpreted as up to the year 2017). Projections from 2001 have been harshly criticised as over-optimistic, defying both reality and the past performance of HIPC countries (Birdsall and Deese 2002; Eurodad 2001a; Jubilee Plus 2001; Culpepper and Serieux 2001).

For example, Uganda and Ethiopia are projected to grow at 6 per cent a year for the next decade. That is a record achieved in the past by only a few countries like South Korea, Singapore and Ireland. In Africa, the rate has been more like 1 per cent. The projections assume increases in the prices of primary commodities on which these countries depend. Yet in the last two decades the trend in world prices for agricultural and natural resources has been at best erratic and, at worst, consistently down. Moreover, the projections ignore the poorest countries' vulnerability to drought and floods. A three-year drought has contributed to the collapse of agriculture in Southern Africa this year (though so have civil conflict and political instability).

This matters because many of the efficiency gains for countries from debt relief (explained in the previous section) rely on a predictably manageable stock of debt over the medium term. If an HIPC country receives relief and then immediately falls back into a state of over-indebtness because of an exogenous shock, much of the potential benefit of that debt relief is lost.

## Review of proposals

In the light of these criticisms, many alternatives or additions to the HIPC framework have been proposed, some of which are discussed below.

### *One hundred per cent write-off for all HIPC countries*
Some Jubilee debt campaigners and scholars have argued that the donors should completely forgive the debts owed by HIPC countries. Indeed, the notion of the Millennial Jubilee embodies this principle.[5] A complete write-off

for the 26 decision-point HIPC countries would cost an estimated US$27 billion in net present value (NPV) terms. This figure includes US$5 billion in additional bilateral relief that has already been committed.[6]

But when considering a complete write-off, one must ask the question whether that debt relief will be additional to current aid, and, if not, which other developing countries will pay. Most of the remaining debt held by HIPC countries is owed to multilateral creditors, since most bilateral creditors have already cancelled 100 per cent of the debt owed to them. Unless bilateral donors are willing to reimburse the multilateral creditors (with completely additional money) for the lost debt service as a result of 100 per cent cancellation of the remaining multilateral debt, other poor countries are likely to end up footing the bill.

Consider the case of the World Bank's International Development Association (IDA). How would the World Bank group adjust if IDA's HIPC assets were to be wiped out?[7] Drop the Debt argues that this would not involve the Bank sacrificing its triple-A credit rating. This may be true but is nonetheless misleading in that one would still have to expect its borrowing costs to rise. If the World Bank's reserves are in fact higher than optimal, then the Bank should certainly contribute more of its profits and use less of them to accumulate reserves, but the World Bank is likely incapable of making more than a marginal additional contribution. It would therefore be necessary to respond in one of three ways:

- raise charges to the World Bank's regular borrowers;

- reduce future lending to IDA countries to match the reduced reflow of IDA funds; or

- invest World Bank funds in income-earning assets and use the interest to make grants to poor countries (Meltzer Commission 2000; Lerrick 2000).

The first option would make it more expensive to borrow from the Bank, so the burden would fall on regular borrowers – primarily the middle-income developing countries but also relatively low-income countries such as China and Indonesia. It would be possible to make this cost transitional by rebuilding the Bank's reserves over time, but that would imply either cutting back the Bank's lending or else adding further to the cost of borrowing. In either event, it is the Bank's regular borrowers who would pay. The idea that the World Bank (let alone any of the other development banks) sits on a heap of functionless cash is just wrong.

The second approach requires that other IDA borrowers bear the cost of forgiving HIPC debts. It is true that the fall in lending would be exactly equal to the reduction in amortisation payments due from the HIPCs, so that there would be no collective benefit or cost to IDA's clients. But while there would be no cost to IDA borrowers taken collectively, one again needs to ask whether there would be distribution effects. Suppose the Bank arranged for its IDA lending to each borrowing country to contract by the amount of the country's reduced repayment obligations? That would imply reduced new grants or lending to HIPC countries, and would provoke furious criticism that it was deliberately denying countries the benefits of debt relief.[8] Otherwise, the presumption has to be that loans to non-HIPC IDA borrowers would contract. But that means IDA-only borrowers like Bangladesh and blend borrowers like India and Indonesia would be the ones paying for HIPC! Given that IDA has based its lending quite consciously on taking into account countries' needs given their poverty levels (Burnside and Dollar 2000), there is a strong likelihood that such a redistribution would have a perverse effect on the global fight against poverty.

The Meltzer–Lerrick plan is to have reflows into IDA invested in income-earning assets, and then use the income generated to make grants. The disadvantage of this is that, unless IDA reflows were to be supplemented by large additional donor contributions, the initial impact would be a severe reduction in the flow of IDA money. (If the assets in which IDA invested yielded 7 per cent, then the flow would initially decline by 93 per cent in the absence of additional donor funding.)

The African Development Bank (AfDB) is even less able to write off the debts it is owed without undermining its financial position than is the World Bank. The cost of the HIPC initiative (in NPV terms) represents 102 per cent of the AfDB's reserves and loan loss provisions. Comparable figures are 23 per cent for the World Bank, 13 per cent for the InterAmerican Development Bank, and 20 per cent for the IMF. Financing the HIPC initiative is even more problematic for some of the small subregional development banks.

There are two morals to this discussion. The first is that additionality matters. The second is that it is wrong to think of the multilateral banks' reserves as 'additional'. Raiding reserves to forgive HIPC debt would penalise other developing countries, perhaps equally poor and making better headway in combating poverty. The result could well be a reduction rather than an increase in the rate at which global poverty declines, and a further threat to the achievement of the Millennium Development Goals.

### Change the ratio for calculating debt relief

Oxfam (2001) proposed that no low-income country should be expected to spend more than 10 per cent of government revenue on debt service. This proposal responded to the criticism that a country's debt-to-export ratio was an ill-suited measure to address the needs and constraints of poor countries. This idea forms the foundation for a proposal that is currently being considered by the US Congress. The Debt Relief Enhancement Act of 2002 (DREA), which has been introduced in both the House of Representatives and the Senate, would establish an additional revenue-based criterion for debt relief – limiting HIPCs' debt service to 10 per cent of revenue or to 5 per cent in cases where a 'public health crisis' exists as defined by a high HIV/AIDS infection rate.[9] The new criterion would result in a total of more than US$1 billion in additional annual debt service relief.

We agree with the spirit, though not the letter, of this proposal. It makes more sense to link debt relief to needs than exports. However, the difficulty with revenue-based debt relief criteria is the incentive that they give to a government to limit its search for tax revenue. Under the proposed legislation (which embodies the Oxfam formula), 10 per cent of any extra tax revenue is immediately siphoned off for debt service. Perhaps 10 per cent is not a high enough figure to generate a severe disincentive effect, but it is hard to be sure. And even if there is no disincentive effect, there is surely an equity effect: a country is rewarded for having failed to collect enough taxes to pay for a decent level of social expenditures.

The basic problem with the revenue-based approach is the likelihood that it would divert funding away from other low-income countries toward the HIPCs, irrespective of the relative quality of countries' tax efforts and spending allocations. This is much more than a hypothetical danger. The increasing dependence on aid of the heavily indebted poor countries, primarily in Africa, has played a role in reducing aid to India, from 1.5 per cent of its GNP a decade ago to as little as 0.1 per cent currently, despite the fact that India's tax and spending programmes are relatively reasonable and its record in reducing poverty much better than that of most of the HIPCs. Below, we refer to what we see as a more efficient though perhaps less politically appealing formula, one that is needs-based.

## A three-pronged solution: deepen, widen, and insure

In our book, *Delivering on Debt Relief*, we detail a three-pronged proposal to improve the enhanced HIPC initiative. In this paper we will briefly mention the first two components and then expand on the third, which has become more clearly necessary (as well as politically and practically feasible) in recent months.

### Deepen debt relief

It is clear that HIPC countries need more resources for basic education, health – particularly the AIDS crisis – and infrastructure investments to lift them out of poverty. There is political momentum to do more in this group of countries — mainly small African countries highly dependent on primary commodities and severely affected by AIDS. Additional debt relief is a sensible mechanism for transferring additional resources.

We agree with Oxfam, the sponsors of the DREA, and others, that additional debt reduction should be based on the relation between a country's debt payments (or service) and its social and other needs (to escape a poverty trap, for example). Since using a country's tax revenue in the denominator builds in a potentially unhealthy incentive structure, we recommend a formula that keys the debt service ceiling directly to GNP. That is one variable that no government is going to suppress in order to minimise its debt service bill, and which provides the best single estimate of the ability to afford social services.

Most HIPCs in 1999 collected about 20 per cent of their GNP in tax revenue, and a reasonable proportion of revenue to spend on debt service is 10 per cent; 10 per cent of 20 per cent implies spending 2 per cent of GNP on debt service. That 2 per cent is sustainable, in the sense that it does not require unusual sacrifices by citizens.

The proposal is not very different from the DREA in terms of cost. It would relieve an additional US$700 million of debt service in 2003 for key development needs in 11 HIPCs that have not already attained a 2 per cent debt-service-to-GNP ratio. The 2 per cent threshold could be revisited in the context of the DREA and other initiatives, but the logic of using a debt-service-to-GNP ratio as the criterion for additional debt relief should be employed.

### Widen eligibility to include other low-income countries

Some very poor countries with substantial official debt burdens are not eligible for the HIPC initiative – for the odd reason that they have (or had) good enough credit to gain some access to private capital markets. The official debt of Indonesia, Nigeria, Pakistan and another 16 poor countries is undermining their ability to get back on a growth track. If and when they meet the conditions of an IMF programme, reducing their debt stock to a sustainable level would cost between US$20 billion and US$70 billion, depending on whether Indonesia is included.

Including these countries in a debt relief initiative would dramatically increase the cost to donors. It also brings up the difficult question of selectivity. Making a country like Nigeria eligible for debt relief on its acceptance of an IMF programme may release significant resources to the Nigerian government before it is clear that it is able or willing to use those resources for the benefit of the country's citizens. Including the large poor countries in a debt relief initiative could bring benefits to hundreds of millions more poor people, but could also undermine the positive institutional changes that HIPC and the PRSP are meant to catalyse.

This tension exists in the current HIPC framework, as pressure from activists to expedite the process of getting countries to decision point has diluted the standard (to the extent that the Democratic Republic of Congo may soon reach decision point). The original HIPC goal embodied selectivity, requiring significant measurable progress before decision point (and, of course, additional progress between decision and completion points). The process has now slid towards traditional conditionality, with decision point contingent on reforms to be undertaken in the future. The DRC is still in arrears to all its major creditors, despite recent supportive action by the IMF, World Bank and AfDB. With a projected decision point of January 2003, a component of interim HIPC relief to DRC will be used to pay off remaining arrears.

### Insure HIPCs against external shocks

In *Delivering on Debt Relief*, we suggested that low-income countries' vulnerability to shocks in weather and export prices could be addressed by granting additional relief whenever shocks that are clearly exogenous to the country result in a new erosion of debt sustainability. This proposal was meant to address not only poor countries' unique vulnerabilities, but also the tendency of the World Bank and IMF to choose optimism over reality when conducting HIPC debt sustainability analyses.

A programme that offers adequate insurance to HIPC countries that their debt sustainability will not be undermined by clearly exogenous circumstances is the key to capturing the many benefits of debt relief outlined in the first section of this chapter. Private sector investment, the ultimate key to poverty reduction and growth, is wary of the multiple risks of investing in HIPC economies. If enlightened leaders, in coordination with legislatures and civil society, hold up their side of the compact – adhering to the priorities of the PRSP, attacking corruption, and building strong institutions – then it is in the global community's interest to ensure that these countries maintain a sustainable debt profile to catalyse growth.

This concept has become more important as new data for countries currently within the HIPC framework have become available. The IMF recently reported that as many as half the countries receiving debt relief will be thrown back into an unsustainable debt situation by next year. Of the four countries already to reach completion point, two – Uganda and Bolivia – are projected to have debt-to-export levels above 150 per cent in 2003. In most cases, the increases in the debt indicators were the result of shortfalls in predicted export growth, due to the global economic slowdown and the continued decline of a number of primary commodity prices. New borrowing does not seem to have contributed to the ballooning debt-to-export ratios.

Given this new outlook, one might assume that the projections for future performance would have been revised downward, thus highlighting the need for deeper relief to ensure ongoing debt sustainability. What we see in the IMF report, instead, are revised projections that still assume an average of almost 6 per cent GDP growth rate, an early 'recovery' to that high rate, and greater optimism about primary commodity prices, despite the bleak outcome in 2001–2 (see Figure 8.1).

The current enhanced HIPC initiative has built-in mechanisms to address the issue of exogenous shocks, but they fall short in three critical ways.

*Time horizon*
The HIPC framework does allow a procedure whereby a new debt sustainability analysis is conducted at the completion point and a country that has suffered a severe exogenous deterioration in its circumstances between decision and completion points might be entitled to additional relief (World Bank and IMF 2001b). This procedure, known as 'topping up', provides some measure of insurance to HIPC countries for the period between decision and completion points.[10] That interim period, originally envisaged to average three years, has now been condensed to less than 18 months. As mentioned above,

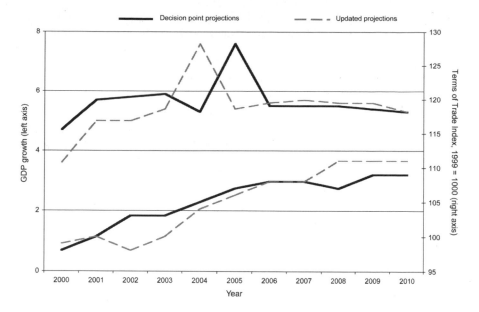

**Figure 8.1 HIPC growth and terms of trade projections**

Source: IMF 2002.

ensuring an adequate period of predictably sustainable debt is a critical component of the success of debt relief in catalysing poverty reduction and growth. Reasonable people can argue about what length of time is 'adequate' (we suggest 10 years as explained below) but it is clear that the topping-up mechanism does not achieve this objective.

The case of Uganda illustrates this point. Uganda was the first country to qualify for debt relief under the original HIPC initiative, and the first to reach the enhanced HIPC completion point, in May 2000. Often considered the HIPC poster child, Uganda's successful national dialogue on poverty reduction in the 1990s was one of the models in designing the PRSP. But in 2002, Uganda's debt was projected to rise to 254 per cent of exports, well above its 1999 levels and more than double the projected level of 117 per cent. The culprit? Not economic mismanagement but a secular decline in world coffee prices, due primarily to Vietnam's entrance into the world market. To quote the 2002 IMF report, 'while the importance of ensuring adequate adjustments in domestic policies in the face of external shocks cannot be overstated, it is equally important to complement such policies with external support, including adequate funds to help deal with cashflow problems arising from exogenous shocks'. We agree. But there is no reason why this virtue should not apply to Uganda over the medium term, solely because it was successful in jumping too early through the HIPC hoops.

*Burden of proof*

While the granting of additional assistance to Burkina Faso at completion point was a welcome signal that topping up was more than lip service, there is still considerable uncertainty as to when and under what circumstances the IMF will agree to grant additional resources. The criteria as stated in the IMF paper of 2001 addressing this issue are 'a fundamental change in a country's economic circumstances ... clearly due to an exogenous development'. But the paper emphasises that topping up is reserved for 'exceptional' circumstances, and that part of the reason for changing the debt-to-GDP criterion from 200 to 150 per cent was to give countries a cushion that would make topping up unnecessary. The comprehensive assessment undertaken to identify fundamental change and exogenous factors is based on IMF and World Bank projections (already shown to be over-optimistic) and require demonstrating that the disruption will be felt for a minimum of 3–5 years. While we certainly want to avoid creating moral hazard with an insurance facility that is too generous, the current system hardly provides the kind of predictability and certainty necessary to reassure potential investors of minimal debt sustainability in HIPC countries.

*Perverse incentives?*

By limiting access to additional funds to the period between decision and completion points, the HIPC framework may compel interim countries and those yet to reach decision point to delay their completion date and increase their interim borrowing, in an attempt to squeeze all the benefits out of the HIPC initiative before they are thrown to the wolves. Indeed, we have already seen overborrowing (beyond what was projected) in Ghana, Ethiopia, Benin and Honduras in the interim period.

A more predictable and sustainable insurance facility for HIPC countries' debt would address these shortcomings. The facility would need to cover a substantial period into the future, at least a decade,[11] if it were to serve the role of reassuring investors that the public sector's debt burden is sustainable. Each year the IMF would calculate whether each HIPC's debt/export ratio exceeded the 2 per cent of GNP proposed above. If it did, then the IMF would examine whether the excess (or how much of the excess) could be attributed to shocks to the terms of trade, bad weather, or other factors that could reasonably be considered exogenous, as compared to a more realistic set of baseline projections. The IMF would make this calculus available for public scrutiny, and provide enough money to reduce the debts to a sustainable level.

How much would such a facility cost? It is, of course, impossible to cost such a facility *ex ante*, since the outlay will depend upon the particular size and sequence of shocks to which the countries are subjected. Nevertheless, the cost of topping up in 2003 for the current decision-point HIPCs – estimated at US$500 million – gives some idea of what the actual cost would be, admittedly during a world recession that has weakened commodity prices. Thus US$5 billion would be a pessimistic estimate of the cost for these 26 countries over ten years. Considering that 10 of the remaining 12 eligible HIPC countries yet to reach decision point are highly dependent on commodity exports, a cost of US$5 billion for the entire set of HIPCs over ten years is optimistic (see far-right column, Table 8.1).[12]

Another way to get a sense of the hypothetical cost of such a contingency facility is to suppose that the value of each HIPC's exports for the next decade were to rise only at the same rate as in the 1990s (or were to remain flat, for countries whose exports declined in the past). Suppose also that this were to occur because of much less favourable developments in the terms of trade than were assumed in the World Bank/IMF study, which would qualify as an exogenous development. Our calculation as to how much this would cost is shown in Table 8.1, where it can be seen that the cost would be some US$5.2 billion for the 24 countries that had reached decision point by March 2002. Of course, it is not likely that all countries would end up mirroring the experience of the 1990s – perhaps equally as unlikely as their achieving 8.2 per cent annual export growth – but the estimate again suggests that US$5 billion may be an optimistic figure for the cost of such a procedure for all HIPCs. And it would cost nothing at all if the IMF and World Bank's rosy projections prove right for every country!

Such contingent facilities are not completely new to the international system. The IMF has for many years operated a Contingency Financing Facility that lends (though it does not grant) money to IMF member countries experiencing a shortfall in export proceeds due to circumstances outside their control. Similarly, the Mexican bonds issued under the Brady Plan included contingent payments to their holders that allowed them to benefit if the price of Mexican oil exports exceeded a benchmark level.

## Financing

In this section, we focus on the financing mechanisms for the insurance facility. In *Delivering on Debt Relief* we propose ways to finance both the deepening and expanding of an HIPC-style debt reduction programme. In the time since publication, more bilateral creditors have moved to 100 per cent cancellation of debt owed to them by HIPC countries, which has lowered the potential cost of deepening. For example, the DREA to bring HIPC countries to the 10 and 5 per cent of debt-service-to-revenue levels would only cost the US $43 million in 2003. The issue of debt in HIPC countries – and thus of additional debt reduction – is increasingly becoming a multilateral debt issue. On the issue of expansion, the cost has made serious consideration politically unfeasible, although some US congressmen have expressed interest in taking up the issue in subsequent years.

To finance the insurance facility for HIPC country debt, we propose tapping an important undervalued resource that belongs to the world community – IMF gold. The IMF currently has substantial holdings of gold on its

Table 8.1 Hypothetical cost of contingency procedure (US$ million)

| | HIPC export projections | | Ex. growth | Revised export projections, 2010 | 2010 debt stock, HIPC | Debt-to-export ratio | Stock goal at 150% | Reduction |
|---|---|---|---|---|---|---|---|---|
| | 2001 | 2010 | 1990–9 av. | (based on 1990s growth) | projection | revised | | |
| Benin | 392 | 791 | 2.5 | 489 | 795 | 1.63 | 734 | 62 |
| Bolivia | 1442 | 3108 | 3.6 | 2054 | 3333 | 1.62 | 3081 | 252 |
| Burkina Faso | 305 | 751 | -2.6 | 305 | 1024 | 3.36 | 458 | 567 |
| Cameroon | 2586 | 4248 | 0.0 | 2586 | 4248 | 1.64 | 3879 | 369 |
| Chad | 242 | 1978 | 0.6 | 255 | 934 | 3.66 | 383 | 552 |
| Ethiopia | 952 | 1815 | 2.6 | 1199 | 2439 | 2.03 | 1799 | 641 |
| The Gambia | 128 | 233 | 2.7 | 163 | 301 | 1.85 | 245 | 57 |
| Ghana | 2416 | 4597 | 11.1 | 6180 | 3503 | 0.57 | .. | .. |
| Guinea | 860 | 1647 | -1.0 | 860 | 1565 | 1.82 | 1290 | 275 |
| Guinea–Bissau | 71 | 181 | 7.5 | 136 | 248 | 1.82 | 204 | 44 |
| Guyana | 718 | 1037 | 5.0 | 1114 | 736 | 0.66 | .. | .. |
| Honduras* | 2673 | 5456 | 8.5 | 4361 | 3323 | 0.76 | .. | .. |
| Madagascar | 1046 | 1811 | 6.5 | 1731 | 1929 | 1.11 | .. | .. |
| Malawi | 480 | 763 | 2.1 | 579 | 1148 | 1.98 | 869 | 280 |
| Mali | 662 | 1190 | 2.3 | 812 | 1520 | 1.87 | 1218 | 302 |
| Mauritania** | 433 | 528 | -2.5 | 433 | 656 | 1.52 | 650 | 7 |
| Mozambique | 805 | 3451 | 6.8 | 1455 | 1611 | 1.11 | .. | .. |
| Nicaragua* | 932 | 1570 | 10.0 | 1651 | 1712 | 1.04 | .. | .. |
| Niger | 279 | 484 | -4.5 | 279 | 768 | 2.75 | 419 | 350 |
| Rwanda | 126 | 367 | -3.0 | 126 | 541 | 4.29 | 189 | 352 |
| São Tomé | 18 | 42 | 5.0 | 28 | 59 | 2.11 | 42 | 17 |
| Senegal | 1692 | 2765 | -1.0 | 1692 | 2364 | 1.40 | .. | .. |
| Sierra Leone | 121 | 330 | -5.0 | 121 | 127 | 1.05 | .. | .. |
| Tanzania* | 1194 | 2274 | 7.9 | 1884 | 3525 | 1.87 | 2826 | 699 |
| Uganda | 801 | 1953 | 11.5 | 2134 | 1320 | 0.62 | .. | .. |
| Zambia | 1038 | 2207 | -3.0 | 1036 | 2575 | 2.49 | 1554 | 1021 |
| Total | | | | | | | (without Chad) | 5292 |

Note: We exclude Chad from the total because of the likely increases in exports due to exploitation of oil reserves.   * Stock in 2007;   ** 2006.

books that are valued at the old official price of SDR35 per ounce (currently about US$45), compared to the market price of about US$290 per ounce. In 1999, it mobilised 14 of the Fund's 103 million ounces of gold, the interest from which helped finance the IMF's portion of HIPC debt relief. At the current price, this would yield something over US$20 billion if the whole of the Fund's undervalued gold were to be mobilised.

Since gold has long since ceased to serve any serious monetary function, IMF gold could be used to pay for the annual cost of the HIPC insurance facility. It is true that this would amount to reducing the IMF's reserves, but, unlike the multilateral development banks, the IMF does not need a reserve to reassure lenders and thus permit it to borrow cheaply. The only function of the IMF gold stock is to reassure central bankers that their funds are safe with the IMF.[13] We believe that the needs of the HIPCs and other poor countries are many times more compelling than safeguarding against the contingency of central bank irrationality.

Some would argue that despite the possible resistance in the US Congress to IMF gold sales (or the complication that the Congress would insist on other reforms at the IMF in exchange for its approval), gold sales are all too easy and cheap an escape for the donors. We do not think this logic warrants rejecting gold sales altogether. Debt relief and new transfers have large potential benefits for reducing poverty, especially if the amount of relief is predictably sustained. This is true even if an insurance facility does not appear to 'cost' the traditional donors anything.

## Box 8.1 Debt initiatives

- 1987: *Special Programme of Assistance for Africa.* Informal donor association managed by the World Bank to provide bilateral debt relief, IDA credits for IBRD debt service relief, and funding for commercial debt buybacks. Available to African IDA-only borrowers with a debt-service-to-exports ratio of above 30 per cent (initially 21 countries).
- 1988: *Paris Club: Toronto Terms.* First agreement by Paris Club creditors to implement new treatment on the debt of low-income countries. The level of reduction was defined as 33.33 per cent.[14]
- 1989: *Brady Plan.* World Bank- and IMF-facilitated debt and debt service reductions by commercial bank creditors. Most Brady deals went to middle-income countries.
- 1989: *IDA Debt Reduction Facility.* Established to restructure and buy back commercial debt with IDA credits (average 88 per cent discount). Available to low-income countries (heavily indebted IDA-only borrowers). Funded from IBRD net income transfer.
- 1990: *Paris Club: Houston Terms.* Agreement to implement a new treatment of the debt of the *lower-middle-income* countries. Houston terms had three components: repayment periods lengthened to or beyond 15 years and ODA repayment periods lengthened up to 20 years with a maximum of 10-year grace; ODA rescheduled at a concessional rate, and the introduction of bilateral debt swaps.
- 1991: *Paris Club: London ('Enhanced Toronto') Terms.* Debt service reduced 50 per cent on non-concessional bilateral debt (12-year grace, 30-year maturity).
- 1995: *Paris Club: Naples Terms.* Debt service reduced 67 per cent on non-concessional bilateral debt (16-year grace, 40-year maturity). Option of debt stock cancellation (5 stock deals processed).[15]
- 1996: *Heavily Indebted Poor Countries (HIPC) Initiative.* Debt stock reduction to bring debt/export ratio under 200 per cent for 41 heavily indebted and poor countries. Participation of multilateral creditors.
- 1996: *Paris Club: Lyon Terms.* Agreement within HIPC framework for 80 per cent relief on non-concessional bilateral debt for HIPC-eligible countries.
- 1999: *Enhanced HIPC (HIPC 2) Initiative.* Increased stock reductions to bring debt-to-exports ratio of HIPCs to under 150 per cent. Interim debt service reduction between decision and completion points. Relief conditioned on the completion of comprehensive Poverty Reduction Strategy Papers (PRSPs).
- 1999: *Paris Club: Cologne Terms.* Agreement within HIPC framework, where non-ODA credits are cancelled up to a 90 per cent level or more if necessary in the context of the HIPC initiative (including topping up). ODA credits are rescheduled at an interest rate at least as favourable as the original concessional interest rate applying to these loans (40 years with 16-year grace and progressive repayment).

## Notes

1 This chapter builds upon and expands the ideas presented in *Delivering on Debt Relief: From IMF Gold to a New Aid Architecture*, by Nancy Birdsall and John Williamson, with Brian Deese (Washington, DC: Institute for International Economics/Centre for Global Development, 2002).

2 Birdsall, Claessens and Diwan (2001) show that in subgroup African countries with unusually high multilateral debt as a share of total debt, the donors collectively (with the important exception of IDA) appear to have channelled resources independently of country capability.

3 The specific 150 per cent benchmark used is also essentially arbitrary, being based on no more than a rule of thumb. The rule of thumb is based on a certain empirical regularity: the finding that defaults become much more common when debt/export ratios exceed something like 200 per cent. But that empirical regularity is based on the experience of a different group of countries, most of which were much richer than the HIPCs.

4 For example, in the 1980s the commercial bank debt of Bolivia (now an HIPC) was quoted at under 10 cents on the dollar prior to the Brady Plan. And the US government, which is mandated by Congress to estimate the present value of its loan portfolio and expense reductions in value as they occur, applies a 92 per cent discount to its HIPC debt (GAO 2000).

5 A recent proposal by Jeff Sachs proposes that all post-HIPC debts be immediately converted into grant aid to address the HIV/AIDS crisis. Sachs argues that there is no financial justification for keeping the remaining debt servicing obligations on these impoverished countries and that the few billion dollars per year in remaining debt service should be rechannelled as grants into urgent social needs.

6 NPV equals the sum of all future debt-service obligations (interest and principal) on existing debt, discounted at the market interest rate. Since much HIPC debt was contracted on concessional (below market) interest rates, NPV is a more appropriate measure of the burden that a country's debt stock imposes.

7 For the partial write-off under the enhanced HIPC initiative, the approach incorporated in present plans is to draw on a trust fund, which is partially funded by donors and partially by contributions from World Bank profits (the latter already a slight tax on non-HIPC borrowers). But even now donor contributions to the trust fund are not adequate to finance fully the enhanced HIPC initiative (the money presently in the trust fund will only last until 2005), let alone full debt cancellation.

8 One could expect many more comments like: 'In an almost cynical game of bait and switch, countries like Mozambique have seen the benefits of debt relief cancelled out by corresponding reductions in aid, resulting in no net gain for social development activities in the national budget'. Edmund Cain, 'Helping Poor Nations Lifts All Boats', *Atlanta Constitution*, 23 August 2001.

9 The term 'public health crisis' has been defined as a nation in which 5 per cent of women at prenatal clinics or 20 per cent of individuals in groups with high-risk behaviour test positive for HIV/AIDS, according to data compiled by the Joint United Nations Programme on HIV/AIDS.

10 The first case of topping up occurred in April 2002 when Burkina Faso was granted an additional US$128 million at completion point.

11 But probably it ought not to cover much more than a decade, so as not to create a moral hazard by destroying a country's incentive to diversify its economy to reduce its vulnerability to exogenous shocks.

12 The extra countries that we are suggesting to be added are mostly much less vulnerable to commodity shocks.

13 The IMF thinks that holding a lot of undervalued gold 'provides fundamental strength to [its] balance sheet' and 'provides the IMF operational maneuverability' (www.imf.org/external/np/exr/facts/gold.htm). More specifically, the Fund argues that its gold holdings matter in allowing even conservative central bankers to treat quota increases as an asset swap rather than a donation, since they know that if necessary the Fund could sell some gold to keep its balance sheet whole if some of its loans to distressed debtors were to sour. While the Fund does indeed lend to countries with major macro problems, its record in recovering debts on its own balance sheet – as opposed to that of the Poverty Reduction and Growth Facility (PRGF) which has a separate balance sheet – is sufficiently sound to make it perfectly sensible for its members to treat quota increases as asset swaps, with or without the Fund's extra 'gold' security.

14 Paris Club debt reduction decisions are made according to five principles: case-by-case decision making, consensus, conditionality (the existence and continuation of an IMF programme), solidarity, and comparability of treatment.

15 Option of stock treatments was/is implemented 'on a case-by-case basis, for countries having established a satisfactory track record with both the Paris Club and IMF and for which there is sufficient confidence in their ability to respect the debt agreement' (Paris Club website).

## References

Addison, A. and A. Rahman. 2001. *Resolving the HIPC Problem: Is Good Policy Enough?*. Paper presented at the WIDER Conference on Debt, Helsinki, August.

Birdsall, N., S. Claessens and I. Diwan. 2001. *Will HIPC Matter? The Debt Game and Donor Behaviour*. Carnegie Endowment for International Peace Economic Reform Project, Discussion Paper No. 3, March.

Birdsall, N. and J. Williamson, with B. Deese. 2002. *Delivering on Debt Relief: from IMF Gold to a New Aid Architecture*. Washington, DC: Institute for International Economics/Centre for Global Development.

Birdsall, N. and B. Deese. 2002. 'What Ever Happened to Debt Relief for Africa?' *International Herald Tribune*, 27 June.

Burnside, C. and D. Dollar. 2000. 'Aid, Policies and Growth'. *American Economic Review*, 90, 4 (September).

Burnside, C. and D. Fanizza. 2001. *Hiccups for HIPCs*. Paper presented at the WIDER Conference on Debt, Helsinki, August.

Cain, E. 2001. 'Helping Poor Nations Lift All Boats'. *Atlanta Constitution*, 23 August.

Chinnock, J. 1998. *In Whose Benefit? The Case for Untying Aid*. London: ActionAid.

Cohen, D. 2000. *The HIPC Initiative: True and False Promises*. Working Paper, Paris: OECD Development Centre.

Culpepper, R. and J. Serieux. 2001. *Journeys Just Begun: From Debt Relief to Poverty Reduction*. Ottawa: North–South Institute.

Drop the Debt. 2001. *Reality Check: The Need for Deeper Debt Cancellation and the Fight Against HIV/AIDS*. Washington, DC: Drop the Debt.

Easterly, W. 1999. *How Did Highly Indebted Poor Countries Become Highly Indebted? Reviewing Two Decades of Debt Relief*. Policy Research Working Paper Series, 2225. World Bank.

Eurodad. 2001a. *Rethinking HIPC Debt Sustainability*. http://www.eurodad.org/

—— 2001b. *Putting Poverty Reduction First*. http://www.eurodad.org/.

GAO. 2000. *Debt Relief Initiative for Poor Countries Faces Challenges*. Washington, DC: United States General Accounting Office.

IMF. 2002. *The Enhanced HIPC Initiative and the Achievement of Long-Term External Debt Sustainability*. http://www.worldbank.org/hipc/Long-Term.pdf

Jubilee Plus. 2001. *HIPC: Flogging a Dead Process*. London: Jubilee Plus Press Release, 17 July.

Kremer, M. and S. Jayachandran. 2001. 'Odious Debt'. Unpublished draft.

Lerrick, A. 2000. 'HIPC: the Initiative Is Lacking'. *Euromoney*, IMF/World Bank Issue.

Meltzer Commission (International Financial Institutions Advisory Commission). 2000. Report to the US Congress. http://www.house.gov/jec/imf/ifiac.htm.

Oxfam. 2001. 'Debt Relief: Still Failing the Poor'. Oxford: Oxfam International.

Pettifor, A., B. Thomas and M. Telatin. 2001. *HIPC – Flogging a Dead Process*. London: Jubilee Plus.

Ranis, G. and F. Stewart. 2001. *The Debt-Relief Initiative for Poor Countries: Good News for the Poor?* Paper presented at the WIDER Conference on Debt, Helsinki, August.

Roodman, D. 2001. *Still Waiting for the Jubilee: Pragmatic Solutions for the Third World Debt Crisis*. Washington, DC: Worldwatch Institute.

Sachs, J., K. Botchway, M. Cuchra and S. Sievers. 1999. *Implementing Debt Relief for the HIPCs*. Working Paper. Centre for International Development, Harvard University.

Thomas, M. 2001. 'Getting Debt Relief Right'. *Foreign Affairs*, September/October.

World Bank. 2001a. *Financial Impact of the HIPC Initiative: First 23 Country Cases*. www.worldbank.org/hipc.

—— 2001b. *Global Development Finance*. Washington, DC: World Bank.

World Bank and IMF. 2001a. *The Challenge of Maintaining Long-Term Debt Sustainability*. www.imf.org/external/np/hipc/2001/lt/042001,htm.

—— 2001b. 'Enhanced HIPC Initiative – Completion Point Considerations', mimeo, 17 August.

# 9

## Debt Work-Out Mechanisms: Debt Arbitration

### KUNIBERT RAFFER

*When it becomes necessary for a state to declare itself bankrupt, in the same manner as when it becomes necessary for an individual to do so, a fair, open, and avowed bankruptcy is always the measure which is both least dishonourable to the debtor, and least hurtful to the creditor.*

Adam Smith, *Wealth of Nations*, 1776

The extremely poor historical record of debt management so far highlights the need for a fundamental change. The rule of law, fairness, and economic efficiency must finally be respected by sovereign debt management. Arguing that a neutral, totally disinterested entity is absolutely necessary to find a proper solution, this chapter demands debt arbitration as the sovereign equivalent of domestic insolvency procedures. After a brief analysis of past debt management and its failure, the chapter shows that debt reduction is urgently necessary to reach all Millennium Development Goals (MDGs) that require financial resources. Developing a global partnership for development with regard to dealing comprehensively with the debt problem, which is part of Goal 8, does not need such financing, but a substantial redesign of present North–South relations. Of all proposals made so far, my international Chapter 9 is the only viable response to this challenge. It would finally transform and civilise international creditor–debtor relations by extending the rule of law and the protection of human dignity to the poorest of the globe.

After presenting the cornerstone of my model, arbitration, the chapter explains how it accommodates debtor protection and finances needs in order to reach the MDGs; how sovereignty is safeguarded in a way fair to *bona fide* creditors; and why multilateral debts must not be given preference. Finally, concrete recommendations for actors willing to campaign in favour of an international Chapter 9 are presented.

## Past failures aggravating present problems

In spite of decades of debt management the crisis persists. The IMF started its first adjustment measures in sub-Saharan Africa (SSA) some 30 years ago, without any tangible success, as data on the region prove. Sustainable recovery of debtors could not be achieved, and the debt crisis has lingered on. Regarding the poorest countries for which the highly indebted poor country (HIPC) initiatives has been designed, suffice it to refer to the Zedillo Report, written at the request of the UN Secretary-General. It concluded that HIPC 2 had 'in most cases' (Zedillo *et al.* 2001: 21) not gone far enough to reach sustainable debt levels, suggesting a 're-enhanced' HIPC 3 (*ibid.*: 54). Present data on HIPCs fully corroborate this conclusion. By proposing its Sovereign Debt Restructuring Mechanism (SDRM) for relatively richer countries, the IMF itself admitted that its own and the World Bank's debt management could not solve the problem.

This failure is no surprise. All historical cases of sovereign debt overhang prove that debts must eventually be reduced by substantial amounts. The IMF (2003c: 140) presented research results for the period 1970–2002 that

> suggest that while large debt reductions have often occurred in conjunction with debt defaults there are cases where they have been brought about by a combination of strong economic growth and fiscal consolidation.

Nineteen out of 26 cases 'were associated with a debt default'. Obviously, reductions were insufficient. The IMF suggests that a 'sustainable public debt level for a typical emerging economy may only be about 25 per cent of GDP' (*ibid.*: 142), much less than present problem cases. Further reductions are necessary, as the IMF acknowledges by proposing its SDRM. This passage recalls well known facts from insolvency procedures: while some debtors believed to be insolvent can overcome their problem, most cannot.

There were steps in the right direction: various Paris Club terms, the HIPC initiatives, and debt reductions such as the Miyazawa–Brady initiative, which failed, as Ecuador or Argentina convincingly prove. Invariably, the problem has been the same: creditors granting too little too late, thus prolonging the problem. Trying to avoid smaller write-offs for the sake of their budgets, official creditors allowed debts to grow further, thus forcing themselves to accept much bigger write-offs later. Short-run bookkeeping formalities have been preferred over workable solutions. Creditors have known that most claims in their books are worth only a fraction of their nominal value. The *Washington Post* (16 March 1999) reported that US$3 billion of 'forgiven' debt would actually mean a 'maximum budget cost' of only US$190 million (or 6.33 per cent of its face value), as the rest had been 'essentially written down or written off as uncollectable'.

At the Cologne summit Chancellor Schröder said in an interview that essentially those debts were forgiven that could not have been collected. I call these lost claims 'phantom debts'. They accumulate and exist only on paper –

in the books of creditors. Economically they are unreal because they are technically irrecoverable (cf. Raffer 2002b). They cannot be cashed. Caused by creditors unwilling to grant a timely reduction, debts have been boosted to ever more unrealistic levels. Debt reduction to sustainable levels appears costlier and costlier on paper. But, as deleting phantom debts simply acknowledges facts, this does not really cost creditors a single cent. One cannot lose money again that was already lost. Deleting phantom debts simply means putting an end to playing the Emperor's New Clothes, acknowledging the naked economic truth. It is 'generosity for free'. On the other hand, debtors get no real relief as this part of their debt could not have been paid anyway. The present practice of including phantom debts at face value when estimating the 'costs' of debt reductions exaggerates real, economic costs substantially, especially so for SSA. Appropriate debt relief looks more expensive and difficult than it actually is. Secondary market prices would be a better and economically more appropriate indicator.

The World Bank (1997: 42) acknowledged that a substantial share of present debts was caused by creditors delaying necessary reductions over the years:

> The surge in borrowing, coupled with increasing reliance on rescheduling and refinancing, increased the nominal stock of debts of HIPCs from $55 billion in 1980 to $183 billion in 1990 ... by the end of 1995 it had reached $215 billion.

Slower growth during the period 1990–5 reflects shifts towards grants, higher concessionality, and the effect of debt cancellations. UNCTAD (1998: 127) estimated that two-thirds of the increase in SSA debt since 1989 was caused by arrears.

After a considerable delay, the World Bank (1992: 10ff., stress in original) acknowledged that insolvency, not illiquidity, was the problem:

> In a solvency crisis, early recognition of solvency as the root cause and the need for a final settlement are important for minimising the damage ... protracted renegotiations and uncertainty damaged economic activity in debtor countries for several years.... It took too long to recognise that liquidity was the visible tip of the problem, but not its root.

The World Bank failed to act on this conclusion, nor did it recall that the Bretton Woods institutions had been the most ardent advocates of the illiquidity theory after 1982, positing that countries would grow out of debts, and that debt reductions would therefore be unnecessary. The HIPC initiative went on delaying, granting 'completion' after six more years instead of at once. More than a decade after calling insolvency the problem the World Bank has still not started to advocate an appropriately swift solution.

Southern debtors have been denied the obvious and humane solution – some form of insolvency procedure, as already suggested immediately after 1982 by a British banker, David Suratgar. Instead, new creditor groups were brought into the game, prolonging unnecessary suffering by debtors, and increasing total debts in a huge Ponzi scheme (cf. Raffer, forthcoming publication 1). Multilateral money bailed out commercial banks during the 1980s. New lenders, institutional investors and the public at large allowed 'old' creditors to reduce their exposure in the 1990s. The IMF (2003c: 139) rightly recalls that switching to bonds occurred 'largely on account of official encouragement and guarantees' as well as 'regulations in financial markets'. Official encouragement and euphoria were in stark contrast to official data available before the 1994–5 crisis: the World Bank's own data, for example, did not justify official statements (Raffer 1996). Latin America's substantial debt overhang persisted; the 'end of the debt crisis' was explained by the toleration of extremely large non-payments, or breaches of contract in spite of new inflows. Both waves of new money increased the debt burden rather than reducing it. Now economic reality has to be faced as no new group of creditors is available, no further shift possible. The game of financial musical chairs is over. Losses have to be recognised and distributed.

Creditors as a group will have to accept larger losses than would have been necessary some 20 years 'ago in order to regain the sustainability of debtor economies. But not all creditors will necessarily be worse off. The structure of creditors has changed dramatically over the last two decades. Bondholders, practically non-existent in 1982, are now an important class of creditors in quite a few cases, while banks have been able to reduce their exposure. Argentina is a good illustration: the share of bonds in public and publicly guaranteed long-term debt rose from 8.2 per cent to 74.23 per cent, and the share of commercial banks declined from 59.6 per cent to 8.3 per cent between 1980 and 1999. Quite noteworthy distributional effects exist, exacerbated by the fact that IFIs were able to secure the privileged status of *de facto* preferred creditors, mostly in breach of their own constitutions. This undue privilege is especially problematic for the poorest countries, where multilateral claims are a substantial percentage of sovereign debts and IFIs have influenced economic policies substantially.

Recognising economic facts long denied by IMF personnel, Krueger (2001: 8) finally declared: 'At the moment too many countries with insurmountable debt problems wait too long, imposing unnecessary costs on themselves, and on the international community that has to help pick up the pieces'. She failed to mention that creditors, most notably the IMF itself, had blocked this sensible solution, forcing debtors to 'wait too long', thus damaging debtor economies severely. Substantial shares of present debts exist only because of prolonged, unsuccessful debt management by official creditors refusing necessary debt relief over decades. The debt burden has grown, impoverishing people further. This is creditor-caused damage – both in middle-income and in HIPC countries. One has to agree with Krueger that this damage should have been avoided.

While debt management has not provided a solution, it has affected North–South relations fundamentally. It provided political leverage to the

North, also allowing creditors to change the policies of debtors. The economic sense behind a 'solution' such as the debt service option – under which Cologne Terms apply, and 90 per cent NPV reduction on eligible debts is achieved 'through concessional interest rates and a repayment period of 125 years, including 65 years of grace' (World Bank 2000: 171) – remains unclear at best. Similarly, the 'bullet option', with an interest rate of 0.0001 per cent (the World Bank does nor dare write over how many years) would be ridiculed in the case of all other debtor–creditor relations. Politically, though, such solutions provide long-term leverage over poor countries.

Rodrik (1996: 17) pointed out that the debt crisis was seen as an opportunity for a 'wholesale reform of prevailing policies', a chance 'to wipe the slate clean and mount a frontal attack on the entire range of policies in use'. A crisis brought about by overspending and overlending in globalised credit markets, and the sudden change in Northern economic policy that sent interest rates skyrocketing around 1980, was simply declared to stem from too little globalisation: import substitution and 'inward-looking' policies. Distinctions between bad and proper import substitution were not made, even though the Asian tigers had used these discredited policies to good effect before they started neoliberal globalisation. The crash of the globalised credit market provided leverage for further globalisation in the South and for enforcing policies the IMF or other creditors wanted debtors to pursue, so much so that 'ownership' of reform programmes has been discussed. In plain English: it is doubtful whether countries actually want to implement what are officially declared to be 'their own' policies.

Meanwhile, continuing as before has become impossible. At present four proposals are on the table (cf. Raffer 2003 as well the other papers of this panel at the DMFAS homepage). These are collective action clauses (CACs), a voluntary Code of Good Conduct for debt renegotiation first proposed by the Banque de France, and two models of sovereign insolvency: the IMF's SDRM and the proposal for internationalising the basic features of US municipal insolvency, so-called Chapter 9 (of Title 11 US Code, Bankruptcy). The latter model has been widely supported by NGOs. In 1990 the Working Group Swissaid/Fastenopfer/Brot für Alle/Helvetas/Caritas submitted the idea of international insolvency to the Swiss Bundesrat, supported by two papers written by Professor K. W. Meessen (Augsburg/Geneva) and myself. The Swiss Parliament discussed it. Switzerland tried discreetly to discuss this proposal internationally, but finally stopped these attempts as no other creditor government signalled any interest. NGOs often prefer to call it the Fair and Transparent Arbitration Process (FTAP). Jubilee 2000 UK was the first Jubilee organisation to advocate it; others followed, such as the German Jubilee movement and Red Guayaquil in Ecuador. The Tegucigalpa Declaration, the platform of Latin American Jubilee movements, explicitly calls for an international Chapter 9 insolvency.

Often it is alleged that the first two of these four proposals contradict or preclude sovereign insolvency. This is fundamentally wrong. Helping creditors to organise, to be able to act more quickly and efficiently, CACs are a helpful component rather than a contradiction of any insolvency. The proper functioning of fair insolvency procedures depends on the full ability of parties to defend their legal and economic interests. Creditors must be able to act efficiently – whatever helps them to do so is welcome. The Code of Good Conduct demands fair representation of creditors, an expeditious and co-operative process, fair burden sharing, preserving the debtor's financial situation, reaching debt sustainability as soon as possible, and also arbitration – briefly, many of the elements to be found in Chapter 9 insolvency.

CACs or the Code should be welcomed whenever these measures are able to prevent formal insolvency procedures. Equally, the very existence of an insolvency mechanism would be helpful in making these options more efficient. Sovereign insolvency is a solution of last resort, an emergency exit necessary and useful, but better avoided. Any sane interceptor pilot insists on having an ejector seat and on making sure it works perfectly. But no sane pilot uses it for ending routine flights, or if (s)he can land the plane. Insolvency is not an easy way out. It is a thorny choice, not least to the debtor.

Two options *do* contradict each other, however: the two models of sovereign insolvency, the IMF's SDRM and my Chapter 9-based debt arbitration.

## The essence of insolvency

The basic function of any insolvency procedure is the resolution of a conflict between two fundamental legal principles. In a situation of over-indebtedness, the right of creditors to interest and repayments collides with the principle recognised generally (not only in the case of loans) by all civilised legal systems: that no one must be forced to fulfil contracts if that leads to inhumane distress, endangers one's life or health, or violates human dignity. Briefly put, debtors cannot be forced to starve themselves or their children to be able to pay. Although their claims are recognised as legitimate, insolvency exempts resources from being seized by *bona fide* creditors. Human rights and the human dignity of debtors are always given priority over unconditional repayment, unless debtors happen to be developing countries and their inhabitants. It is important to emphasise that insolvency only deals with claims based on solid and proper legal foundations. In the case of odious debts, for example, no insolvency is needed. These are null and void. Demands for cancelling apartheid debts are therefore based on the odious debts doctrine.

## Arbitration – the cornerstone of any fair and efficient solution

The acronym FTAP characterises the cornerstone of my proposal. All legal systems demand that a neutral and totally disinterested entity must decide which percentage of debts insolvent debtors are able to repay. Even during the period of debt slavery and debt prisons judges – not creditors – decided on the debtor's fate, which compares favourably with present international debt management. Past initiatives could not solve the problem because of absolute creditor domination. Creditors have been judge, jury, experts and bailiff all in one, sometimes even the debtor's lawyers. This is a grave violation of the very foundation of the rule of law barring parties from also being judges: one must not be judge in one's own cause.

As the long and successful record of national insolvency laws shows, establishing neutral disinterested entities is not only fair, but also the only economically wise and workable arrangement. Refusing to do so is the main cause of unsuccessful debt management. The powerful position of official and especially multilateral creditors *vis-à-vis* poor countries such as HIPCs or most of SSA makes an independent entity all the more urgent. Neutral arbitration is not only a solution for emerging markets but equally if not more appropriately for poor countries. Insolvency relief is not an act of mercy but of justice and economic reason. Yet a difference of attitude shows, all the way down to negligible details such as the fact that the word 'forgive' is not normally used if and when insolvency procedures reduce debts. This relief is a *right* of insolvent debtors. Only developing countries' debts, it seems, need to be 'forgiven'. They remain the only debtors to be refused insolvency protection.

In my model the neutral entity would preferably be an *ad hoc* arbitration panel established by the debtor and creditors. Each party would nominate one or two persons. These nominees would elect one further member for an uneven number, as is traditional practice in international law. Ironically, this procedure is also foreseen pursuant to Section 10.04 of the World Bank's (1985) *General Conditions* determining how to establish arbitration panels. They further provide that the third person shall be appointed if the parties do not agree. Arbitration is foreseen to settle disagreements with borrowers, be they members or not, *inter alia* for 'any claim by either party against the other' not settled by agreement. One might therefore be surprised that the Bank does not show more sympathy for debt arbitration.

Naturally, the debtor government can choose to leave the task of nominating panel members either to the parliament or to the people. Arbitrators could be elected from a roster by voters. Anyone reaching a minimum of supporting signatures by voters would have to be on it. Alternatively, one arbitrator might be chosen by parliament, the other by voters. My model offers a wide range of possibilities to allow democratic participation by the affected. Or, the parliament might establish a special committee for this purpose, including members of the cabinet, as proposed in a bill drafted on the initiative of Congressman Mario Cafiero by the Argentine opposition party ARI. The bill would establish a Comisión Representativa del Estado Nacional. Consisting of members from both Houses and the executive power, it would nominate panel members and represent Argentina during the proceedings. In the case of a change of government, which has occurred quite often in indebted countries, a new, incoming government might be prepared to opt for one of these very democratic possibilities.

The main principles of domestic US Chapter 9 – such as protection of the debtor's governmental powers, the right of the affected population to voice their views, and the best interest of creditors – would form the base on which the arbitration process would rest. Evidently, some important and necessary details of domestic Chapter 9 are unnecessary and inapplicable internationally. The question of eligibility and authorisation to be a Chapter 9 debtor – fundamental and useful within the US for constitutional reasons – is one example.

Arbitrators would have to mediate between the parties; chair negotiations and support them by offering advice; provide adequate opportunities for the affected population to voice its concerns; and, if necessary, decide. This is important because mediators without any authority to decide will normally be less successful in mediating as well. Decisions – if needed – are unlikely to affect substantial sums of money but rather to solve deadlocked situations, because all facts will be on the table. For obvious reasons justified opposition by creditors should not be simply overruled. 'Agreements between debtor and creditors would need the confirmation of the arbitrators, in analogy to Section 943' (Raffer 1990: 305; similarly Krueger 2002: 7) They would have to take particular care that fairness and a minimum of human dignity of the poor is safeguarded – in analogy to the protection enjoyed by a municipality's inhabitants.

Sovereigns could 'file' for 'insolvency protection' or debt arbitration by depositing their demand at the UN. Acting as a registration office or 'post box' the UN, for instance the Secretary-General, would make this demand publicly known and serve as the place creditors can contact. It could also help to organise the panel. Filing would automatically trigger a stay. The panel must endorse the standstill immediately on being formed. The IMF first proposed that it be given the authority to approve standstills. Attempting to placate private creditors, the Fund later made several proposals, including clumsy procedures whose economic result would at best be the same as a general stay (cf. Raffer 2002a, forthcoming publication ?) Thus it is preferable to allow the neutral entity to decide whether to endorse the stay, as is usual in all domestic laws,.

Naturally, the panel would have to reject the debtor's demand if unfounded, denying this debtor any advantage from starting the procedure. The panel would have to deny approval of a plan if the debtor had the means to honour all its obligations subject to debtor protection. It should verify claims, as is routine in any domestic case, in order to apply the same legal standards as in the North. In many discussions representatives of official creditors, especially of IFIs, had declared this proposal too utopian and impossible to implement (Raffer 1990: 309). Meanwhile it became part of Krueger's 'new approach'. The IMF (2002b: 68) demanded specific checks regarding 'for example, the authority of an official to borrow on behalf of the debtor', echoing, almost in the same words, what had been demanded some ten years before (Raffer 1993b: 68).

Should disagreement regarding the implementation of the debtor's plan arise after the panel is dissolved, the panel could reconvene. There is no need to involve the IMF by creating new debts with the IMF to obtain 'an appropriate means for the Fund to signal its disapproval' (2002: 26). Nor for a new IMF mandate to sanction debtors if and as the IMF might think it appropriate (2002: 54).

Clearly, arbitration panels could sit anywhere, including the debtor's or its neighbouring country. To facilitate participation of the representatives of the population it should be in the debtor country or close to it. I have never demanded that the panel 'be headquartered in a neutral country that is neither an active international lender nor a borrower', as Eichengreen erroneously suggests when characterising my proposal (1999: 126). One may suppose this error to stem from the passage: 'The reason why no court, whether located in a creditor or debtor country, should chair the procedures is self-evident: its impartiality is not guaranteed' (Raffer 1990: 304), which refers to courts, not courts of arbitration. Language apart, the illustrating example – the US Court of Appeal for the Second Circuit of New York, definitely no court of arbitration – proves this beyond doubt. However, if a distinguished economist misunderstands this point, it should obviously be clarified.

Unsurprisingly, the IMF tries to find an argument against *ad hoc* panels (2002: 63). As claims would have to be verified first

> to be recognised for participation in decision making ... the selection of a panel would have to follow, not precede, the verification process. But then who would resolve disputes arising from verification if there was no panel already in place?

The answer is simple: all registering creditors nominate their arbitrator(s) who immediately decide(s) on the recognition of claims. CACs would be helpful in organising this process more quickly. Recognised creditors could either confirm their nominees or replace them. The latter course could theoretically become necessary if so many claims are excluded that different arbitrators would have been nominated by the remaining creditors, which – though possible – seems unlikely. As creditors are known and organised, endorsing or replacing could be done quickly. Creditors whose claims are dismissed are party and should have the same right to nominate arbitrators to judge their case as anyone else. To back up a weak point, the IMF adds that creditors might all wish to appoint their own arbitrators, which would make the case unmanageable and 'could distort the balance of power between the debtor- and creditor-selected arbitrators'. This only holds if the nominees are not impartial arbitrators but actually represent and defend the interests of certain groups, an erroneous perception shared by Rogoff and Zettelmayer (2002a). Whatever such a procedure might be, it would no longer be arbitration. In this case, of course, anyone would like to have their own 'defenders' or 'lawyers'. This problem has never occurred in the few cases when private creditors and sovereign debtors have agreed on arbitration on debt issues so far. Compared with having to accept the IMF's choice, my proposal definitely confers more rights on creditors.

Both in my model and under the SDRM, private creditors – but not official creditors – are equally subject to the entity's decisions. Although having no authority to challenge decisions made by the IMF's Executive Board, the Dispute Resolution Forum would be vested with substantial powers over private creditors and debtors. It would decide on the validity and value of claims, the right to vote or the classification of creditors, all of which can have grave financial consequences. It may choose not to recognise a claim. Initially, its decisions could not be challenged. The appeal panel suggested later would still be part of the Forum. Within its mandate this IMF body would have no less authority than the arbitration panel established by the parties. In contrast to debt arbitration, the parties would not be allowed to negotiate necessary reductions but would have to accept the IMF's decisions.

## Protecting sovereignty

The need to deal satisfactorily with sovereignty was used as a powerful argument against the first generation of proposals advocating the application of corporate insolvency (Chapter 11) in the early 1980s. As corporations are not sovereign, it was argued, Chapter 11 would be inapplicable. To counter this legalistic argument I proposed US Chapter 9, Title 11 – municipal insolvency – as the model in 1987 (Raffer 1989). Solving the problem of governmental powers, it is tailor-made for sovereigns. Forgetting its own important objection, the IMF itself now proposes Chapter 11 as the blueprint for its SDRM. None of the Fund's SDRM documents mentions any measure to protect the governmental powers of debtors.

In the US the court's jurisdiction depends on the municipality's volition, beyond which it cannot be extended, in similar fashion to the jurisdiction of international arbitrators. This makes Chapter 9 especially suited for sovereign cases. The concept of sovereignty does not contain anything more than is protected by paragraph §904 (entitled: 'Limitation on Jurisdiction and Powers of Court'):

> Notwithstanding any power of the court, unless the debtor consents or the plan so provides, the court may not, by any stay, order, or decree, in the case or otherwise, interfere with –
> (1) any of the political and governmental powers of the debtor;
> (2) any of the property or revenues of the debtor; or
> (3) the debtor's use or enjoyment of any income-producing property.

Unlike in other bankruptcy procedures, liquidation of the debtor or receivership are not possible. No trustee can be appointed (§926, avoiding powers, if seen as an exception, is very special and justified). Paragraph 902 (5) explicitly confirms: '"trustee", when used in a section that is made applicable in a case under this chapter ... means debtor'. Change of 'management' of US municipalities (removing elected officials) by courts or creditors is not possible – nor should it be in the case of sovereigns. If any regulatory or electoral approvals are necessary under non-bankruptcy law in order to carry out a provision of the plan, §943 (b) (6) requests that this must be obtained before the court can confirm the plan, a point clearly adaptable to sovereigns.

During the Great Depression, Chapter 9 was introduced precisely to avoid prolonged and inefficient negotiations and rescheduling, allowing a quick, fair, and economically efficient solution for over-indebted US municipalities. A first draft by municipalities that did not bar creditor intervention into the governmental sphere was rejected by lawmakers as unconstitutional (Spiotto 1993). Creditor interventions such as those usual in developing countries nowadays were considered unacceptable. A new version containing §904 was allowed to pass. This demonstrates the appropriateness for sovereign debtors. Technically, Chapter 9 offers the legal possibility of implementing an economically sensible solution. It became law for the very purpose of avoiding the kind of 'debt management' practised internationally for decades. Of all other OECD countries only Hungary has insolvency laws for public debtors – adopted on the advice of private Western consultants after the demise of communism. Other governments seem to assume quietly and against historical evidence that public debtors cannot become insolvent.

The powerful position of the debtor might make people, especially non-economists, doubt whether Chapter 9 actually works. Some 500 cases within the US so far show it does. Needing a solution, the debtor must offer something that is acceptable to creditors. Composition plans should be fair, equitable, and feasible. Furthermore, to be confirmed the plan has to be reasonable and, pursuant to §943(b) (7), also in the best interests of creditors, who must be provided with the 'going concern value' of their claims. The note to §943, 11, USCA specifies:

> The going concern value contemplates a 'comparison of revenues and expenditures taking into account the taxing power and the extent to which tax increases are both necessary and feasible' ... and is intended to provide more of a return to creditors than the liquidation value if the city's assets could be liquidated like those of a private corporation.

A court decision further clarified that a plan can only be confirmed if it 'embodies a fair and equitable bargain openly arrived at and devoid of over-reaching, however subtle'. This openness and transparency of procedures are of particular interest for sovereign debtors.

## Debtor protection, human rights, and MDGs

Debtor protection, one main principle of all civilised insolvency laws, remained totally absent in international debt management over many years. HIPC 2 finally introduced the idea of debtor protection, although still in a rudimentary form. Nevertheless its anti-poverty programmes are a move in the right direction and a change from the position held more than a decade ago, in discussions on Chapter 9, that debtor protection would be impossible. By contrast with the HIPC initiatives, none of the IMF's documents mentions debtor protection. Private creditors accept that there are politically uncollectable debts, another way of describing the principle of exempt resources. Unlike the Fund, they have repeatedly granted substantial debt reductions. Speaking of 'bailing in' the private sector is therefore misleading and absurd.

Chapter 9 knows two instruments to protect debtors:

- exempting a minimum of resources to allow debtors to go on functioning;

- the right to be heard of the affected population.


*Exempt resources – the means to protect human rights*
Insolvency laws guarantee insolvent debtors a modest yet humane standard of living, and usually a fresh start, by exempting resources that could be seized by *bona fide* creditors. Domestic Chapter 9 in the US exempts resources necessary to finance minimum standards of basic health services, primary education, and an economic 'fresh start', as insolvency laws put it. The debtor population is protected by the right to be heard and legal limits to tax increases. A public interest exists in the continued functioning of municipalities. Tax increases that would depress the standard of living of the municipality's population below the minimum guaranteed to private debtors are clearly illegal. Feasible tax increases have actually been much lower. In the 1930s, when some creditors insisted on higher payments by the City of Asbury Park – financed by tax increases – the US Supreme Court clearly stated, in refusing to agree to the plan, that 'the notion that a city has unlimited taxing power is, of course, an illusion. A city cannot be taken over and operated for the benefit of its creditors, nor can its creditors take over the taxing power'. (Malagardis 1990: 68)

By contrast any protection has been denied to the poor in the South. The case of Malawi discussed in the Treasury Select Committee (2002) illustrates this difference clearly. Malawi was forced to sell maize from her national food reserve to repay loans. In a BBC interview Malawi's president said the government 'had been forced [to sell maize] in order to repay commercial loans taken out to buy surplus maize in previous years' (Pettifor 2002; cf. Treasury Select Committee 2002). After harvest problems in 2002 famine struck. Seven million of a population of 11 million were left severely short of food, according to Action Aid. This priority of creditor interest over survival – nowadays uniquely possible in the case of Southern debts – must be abolished. My proposal would make incidents such as Malawi's maize sale impossible. The life and the human dignity of people must be equally respected and protected everywhere, be it North or South.

The situation of debt-distressed countries shows clearly that resources necessary to finance the MDGs must be freed. Money that has to be paid to creditors cannot be used to improve maternal health, to reduce child mortality or the proportion of people without sustainable access to safe drinking water or suffering from hunger. It is not available to finance primary schooling for all boys and girls, or to finance the elimination of gender disparities in education. One cannot have one's cake and eat it as well. The introduction of user fees and their effects on the poor prove this point clearly and sadly. In analogy to the protection enjoyed by the population of indebted US municipalities, the money to service a country's debts must not be raised by destroying basic social services and the debtor's future. The principle of debtor protection demands exempting resources necessary to finance humane minimum standards for the poor, and a sustainable economic recovery.

This exemption can only be justified if exempt money is demonstrably used for its declared purpose (cf. Raffer 1990; 2001). A transparently managed fund financed by the debtor in domestic currency would do so. In a discussion with public servants of the G7 and representatives of the Bretton Woods Institutions, Ann Pettifor (1999) proposed a Poverty Action Fund as a means to guarantee that the money is actually used for the poor and for expenditures necessary for a fresh start of the debtor economy. This idea was taken up in a Bill put forward on Capitol Hill. The Debt Relief and Development in Africa Bill (HR 2232), sponsored by Representative Maxine Waters in 1999, required a Human Development Fund organised in a similar way, which would get money freed by HIPC debt relief. This Bill was referred to a subcommittee but did not pass Congress.

The management of this fund could be monitored by an international board or advisory council consisting of members from the debtor country as well as members from creditor countries. They could be nominated by governments (including the debtor government), creditors and NGOs. Naturally, financing MDGs would be a prime task of any such fund. This should be written into its statutes. As this fund would be a legal entity of its own, checks on and discussions of its projects would not concern the government's budget, which is an important part of a country's sovereignty. Furthermore, aid financing MDGs could also be channelled through this fund, changing its character of money just set apart from the ordinary budget towards a normal fund for the poor. However, unless one assumes unrealistic increases in Official Development Assistance in the near future, most MDGs cannot be reached without freeing resources presently used for debt service. In contrast to phantom debts this is money that could technically be taken away from debtors to be used for payments in the same way that a winter coat could be taken from a debtor to recover a larger share of creditor claims. As in the case of private debtors, this must not be allowed to happen. Safeguarding the human right of debtor protection and MDGs would thus mean real losses. As most if not virtually all debt service goes to public creditors in the case of the poorest countries, debtor protection and exempt resources logically mean losses by public – bilateral and multilateral – creditors.

Freeing resources in favour of the MDGs and development is particularly important for SSA, where human distress caused by debt pressure is most pronounced. Sub-Saharan debts differ from Latin American debts in their structure. But there is even less reason to allow creditors to go on being judges. Quite the contrary: as creditors, especially multilateral institutions, have swayed if not dictated debtors' policies, there exists an additional reason why official creditors have to accept financial accountability for their actions. As will be argued in more detail below, debt arbitration is a viable option that will allow both debtors and creditors to share the burden equally. The present victim-pays principle is a unique arrangement, which cannot be justified by economic or legal reasoning (cf. Raffer 1993a). It must be replaced by decent legal arrangements. My Chapter 9 proposal does so. If anything, the foundation of the rule of law and neutral decision making is all the more necessary in SSA, a region where creditor domination is one important root of present problems.

*Right to be heard*
In a domestic Chapter 9 case the affected population has a right to be heard. Internationally, this would have to be exercised by representation. Trade unions, entrepreneurial associations, religious or non-religious NGOs, or international organisations such as UNICEF could represent the debtor country's population. Depending on the country, Christian organisations in Latin America, for example, or Muslim organisations in Muslim countries could be formal representatives. Besides preserving essential services to the population my proposal gives the affected population and vulnerable groups a right to be heard. In a most powerful way it gives voice to those who have been denied participation.

Errors regarding this part of my proposal in the literature suggest a need for clarifications. The brief description of my panel by Rogoff and Zettelmeyer (2002a) – an impressively comprehensive but not always accurate survey of publications on sovereign insolvency before Krueger's (2001) 'New Approach' – is fundamentally wrong. In analogy to domestic Chapter 9, I proposed a population's right to be heard. Pointing out that the principle of representation is known in US domestic cases, I argued: 'Exactly as in Rule 2018, this could be done by trade unions or employees' associations' (Raffer 1990: 305). Unlike domestic US laws I suggested further organisations, such as UNICEF, churches, 'Catholic NGOs, or similar organisations of other creeds (especially in countries with non-Christian majorities), NGOs without religious background ... last, and by no means least, grassroots organisations of the poor'. In Rogoff and Zettelmeyer (2002a: 10) this boils down to 'trade unions, NGOs or churches could function as arbitrators speaking on behalf of the citizens in the debtor countries'. Clearly, a right to be heard does not make someone an arbitration panel member. This right is a useful instrument in domestic Chapter 9 to allow affected people, such as special taxpayers affected by the plan, to voice their views. But like witnesses they are not judges. Nor should arbitrators speak on behalf of any interested party. In a fair procedure they must be totally disinterested and neutral. Rogoff and Zettelmeyer (2002b) corrected this misunderstanding later.

In contrast to the late 1980s, when giving voice to the affected was first demanded (Raffer 1990), the idea that stakeholders should be allowed to voice their views is meanwhile more accepted, at least in theory. Civil society participation is officially part of HIPC 2, although practical results are lagging behind. Recently the IMF (2003b) stated:

> creditors are likely to express views as to the appropriate dimensions of the programme's adjustment and financing parameters. While such input would be welcome, directors emphasised that it would be inappropriate for private creditors to be given a veto over the design of the financing plan or the design of the adjustment programme.

This sounds slightly more participatory than earlier ideas under the SDRM, where the IMF's Executive Board would take all important decisions, especially on the adequacy of a member's policies and the sustainability of the member's debt. As the IMF determines sustainability and economic policies, only one practically important decision is left to creditors. Creditor majorities can refuse to accept the result, however, leaving the problem unsolved and possibly encouraging the IMF to support the debtor. All remaining decisions on terms can only affect relatively minor issues, such as repayment schedules of $n$ or $(n+k)$ years. In practice there is very little substance on which private creditors can actually vote, in spite of IMF rhetoric about empowering creditors and the debtor. They could vote on how to share losses among themselves. Theoretically, they could also grant more reduction than the Fund suggests.

## Sustainability

As facts would be presented by both parties and the representatives of the population in a transparent procedure before the arbitration panel, the debtor's capacity to pay and sustainability would emerge fairly reliably from this process. Defending their legitimate self-interests, anyone could present data and arguments to corroborate their views, thus narrowing down the set of feasible options considerably. By contrast, under the SDRM the IMF alone would continue to decide. Apart from the fact that decisions by a creditor violate the rule of law and are very likely to be unfair to other creditors, the record of IFIs in estimating sustainability urgently calls for change. Their overoptimistic estimates have been one main cause for the failures of the past. They have damaged debtor economies gravely.

Debt sustainability analysis highlights the inefficiency of IFI programmes most clearly. Over decades, too-optimistic forecasts have inflicted damage on member countries, rendering strategies based on such forecasts, especially debt reductions, useless. Recently, the IMF and the International Development Association (IMF and IDA 2004: 13) conceded that theirs was a

> past experience suggesting a systematic tendency toward excessive optimism ... a common theme behind the historical rise in low-income countries' debt ratios was that borrowing decisions were predicated on growth projections that never materialised. This experience points to the need for well-disciplined projections, including by laying bare the assumptions on which they are predicated and by subjecting them to rigorous stress tests that explicitly incorporate the impact of exogenous shocks.... [A]nalysis of projections made by Fund staff over the period 1990–2001 suggests a bias toward over-optimism of about 1 percentage point a year in forecasts of low-income country real GDP growth. The bias in projecting GDP growth in US dollar terms, however, was considerably larger, at almost 5 percentage points a year.

A need for such well-disciplined projections certainly exists. This passage admits that the Bretton Woods institutions have routinely presented over-optimistic forecasts, imperfectly disciplined projections whose assumptions were not explained and which were not stress-tested over decades. Any normal clients could successfully sue their consultants and get financial compensation. But basic legal principles cease to apply whenever their function is to protect Southern debtors and poor people in the South.

Assessing HIPC 2 at the request of Congress, the US General Accounting Office (GAO 2000) corroborates doubts about the reliability of IFI estimates and thus the professionalism of IFIs. Debt sustainability was asked to depend on annual growth rates above 6 per cent in US dollar terms over 20 years – in four cases including Nicaragua and Uganda even above 9.1 per cent. Understandably, the GAO doubted whether such rates could actually be maintained for that long, warning also about the volatility of commodity prices. It pointed out that additional money would be necessary. Like so many creditor initiatives before it, HIPC 2 seems to have been built on fragile, optimistic assumptions and forecasts. Its failure is a logical result. The need for changes in the way sustainability is calculated is obvious.


## Fairness, equality of creditors, and multilateral debts

Unlike the IMF's SDRM, my proposal is fair to the private sector and to debtors. Debtors would no longer be under the thumb of any one creditor, but – as is usual in all other cases – be one party. My model demands inter-creditor equity and safeguarding of the best interest of creditors. All debts, including multilateral claims, must be treated equally. There is no legal nor statutory base for preferred treatment of IFIs as granted *de facto* by creditor governments and mostly accepted by the private sector. In September 1988, for example, the Interim Committee urged all members to treat the Fund as a preferred creditor within the limits of their laws. Aware of the situation, the IMF tried to use its SDRM to legalise this IFI preference in a self-serving way.

Accepting the IMF's sustainability level for emerging markets' public debts of 25 per cent of GDP (2003c: 142), and plausibly assuming that it cannot be higher for the poorest countries, one can immediately calculate the extra losses other creditors would have had to take to bail out IFIs if the SDRM had been established.

IFIs insist on full repayment, even if damages negligently caused by their staff occur and have to be paid by borrowers. This has created a perverted incentive system totally at odds with any market economy: a high rate of IFI failures is bound to render adjustment programmes necessary, which are again administered by IFIs, just as failed programmes are likely to call for new programmes, as long as unconditional repayment to IFIs is upheld. An institutional interest was allowed to develop that is at odds with efficiency, economic logic, and even the statutes of IFIs themselves. Debt management must deal with the unsurprising results.

Like any other creditor IFIs must carry the risk of losses. Like consultants they must be financially responsible for their decisions. Decisions must be connected to risks. The most basic condition for the functioning of the market mechanism demands this. If this link is severed market efficiency is severely disturbed, as former communist economies clearly prove. Economic efficiency, but also fairness to debtors and other creditors, demands that IFIs, at least co-responsible for the present mess, should no longer be treated with preference. Equal treatment of all creditors when debtors, acting on IFI advice, become insolvent: this is the easiest way to introduce financial accountability. As IFIs have influenced economic policies of debtors to the extent of sparking the 'ownership' discussion, this is economically mandatory.

Argentina provides a telling example of the difference between the market and IFIs. *Clarin* (29 November 2003) reported that a German court had ordered a bank to compensate a client whom it had advised to buy Argentine bonds as safe yet high-yielding investments. The court followed the plaintiff's argument that the bank did not explain Argentina's already known difficult situation sufficiently, ordering the bank to indemnify its client fully because of the advice it gave. In sharp contrast, any protection is totally absent when it comes to IFIs, which benefit even from their own negligence and errors. If normal accountability standards applied to Southern debtors, there would be no multilateral debt problem.

The statutes of all multilateral development banks foresee default of sovereign borrowers and appropriate ways of recognising losses. These banks have to form provisions pursuant to their statutes. All have the authority to modify the terms of loans other than the currency of repayment after or to avoid defaults. Article IV (6) of the World Bank's Articles of Agreement demands a special reserve to cover what Article IV (7) calls 'Methods of Meeting Liabilities of the Bank in Case of Defaults'. Detailed rules governing how to proceed follow. The Agreement Establishing the Inter-American Development Bank provides for 'Methods of Meeting Liabilities of the Bank in Case of Defaults' (Article VII (3)). Charges should first be made 'against the special reserve provided for in Article III, Section 13', which is to meet the Bank's liabilities in the case of debtor default. The statutes of the Asian Development Bank similarly demand a special reserve to meet liabilities in the case of default (Article 17). Article 18 gives the detailed description of how to proceed already known from the World Bank and the Inter-American Development Bank. In the case of the African Development Bank these rules are apparently enshrined in Articles 20–22. As the AfDB's homepage does not grant access to the text of its own statutes – an absolutely unique case – this can only be inferred from the headings displayed. Clicking the links, though, brings one straight to the Bank's 'visions', rather than its statutes (an e-mail describing the problem and asking for the legal text was received, according to AfDB's computer, but not answered). The European Bank for Reconstruction and Development recognises losses and survives.

Initially, IMF drawings provided short-term emergency finance without any conditionality to allow members to stay within the exchange rate limits set by the Agreement. Loan loss provisions were therefore unnecessary for the IMF. When conditionality was introduced, no appropriate changes making the Fund financially accountable were made. Nevertheless, although at first it refused to accept reality, the Fund has built up loan loss provisions for quite some time. This was because economic facts asserted themselves. The 1986 audit raised the possibility that the next one might have to be qualified if the Fund did not take clear steps to recognise the poor quality of some assets and claims (IMF 2003a). Forced by external auditors, the IMF started to provide for non-payment. These resources, however, are not called loan loss provisions.

The IMF's 'precautionary reserves consist of General and Special Reserves and the [Special Contingent Account] SCA-1' (IMF 2003a: 3). Its Articles of Agreement do not demand it, but provisioning is not prohibited. The Fund's margin includes a surcharge to 'generate resources for a SCA-1, established specifically to protect the IMF against the risk of loss of principal resulting from arrears' (*ibid.*). The Fund has already considered the use of value-at-risk models. It had precautionary balances of about SDR6 billion, or 8.5 per cent of credit oustanding, at the end of October 2003 (IMF 2004: 26). It has decided to bring these reserves to SDR10 billion. The IMF is prepared to take losses, charging members the costs of defaults but refusing, like all IFIs, to apply the money to the purpose for which it has been accumulated. All other IFIs have much higher 'precautionary balances', ranging from slightly more than 20 per cent (World Bank) to over 30 per cent (Inter-American Development Bank) of credit outstanding. As current countries have already paid for provisioning, using these resources cannot mean that costs of borrowing increase.

This should not be misunderstood as criticising IFIs for provisioning. On the contrary – this course is economically sound and financially very prudent. What *must* be criticised, though, is that these reserves are not used sensibly. At present, clients have to pick up the bill, but do not get relief when needed. This is comparable to an insurance company charging necessary fees but refusing to cover damages. Of course, no private firm would be allowed such behaviour.

The Articles of Agreement of IDA, which are especially important for SSA, are somewhat vague. Pursuant to Article V (3), titled 'Modifications of Terms of Financing', IDA may 'agree to a relaxation or other modification of the terms on which any of its financing shall have been provided'. In the case of maturities of 35, 40 or even 20 years with 10 years grace periods and 'no interest charge' (IDA 2004: 2) this leaves few realistic alternatives beyond outright grants. Meanwhile, IDA 13 foresees between 10 and 25 per cent of grants depending on absorptive capacity and country performance. The argument that amortisations needed to refill IDA funds would preclude debt relief is thus no longer valid. Grants to finance basic education or health, as recommended by Raffer and Singer (1996: 209ff.), like cancelled IDA debts, do not create re-flows. If grants for projects are possible without harming the functioning of IDA, granting debt relief is logically possible too.

The important contribution of the HIPC 1 was finally breaking the taboo of multilateral debt cancellation, a very commendable step taken by James Wolfensohn. The need to reduce multilateral claims is now accepted. The argument that IFIs cannot do so is no longer upheld. Member countries tolerating provisioning are obviously prepared to face economic reality. Under HIPC the IMF already, though reluctantly, reduces its claims via grants. IFIs still enjoy unjustified preferred treatment, though. Multilateral development banks should finally obey their own statutes. Other creditors would no longer have to pay for the consequences of wrong or negligent decisions by multilateral institutions. The market mechanism must be brought to IFIs, including the IMF, by subjecting them to financial accountability in the same way consultants already are (Raffer 1993a). This market incentive would improve the quality of operations substantially. As SSA proves, this is urgently needed. Furthermore, the poorest countries with little debt to private creditors but substantial multilateral shares cannot benefit meaningfully from debt reduction schemes if multilateral debts are excluded.

## Best interest of creditors

As in the US, the outcome of any internationalised insolvency procedure must also be in the best interest of creditors. The important point of fairness apart, no biased mechanism would be generally accepted, and rightly so. For a sovereign wishing to have new access to credit markets the way the debt overhang is dealt with is critical. If creditors feel that they have been treated fairly, they are likely to be as willing to provide new loans for economically promising projects in the future as creditors usually are after corporate insolvency cases. This might be less important for very poor countries, but is fundamental for countries such as Argentina.

Unlike present Paris Club practice or under the SDRM, Chapter 9 would confer the full rights of a party on all creditors. The Paris Club expects private and non-Club creditors to implement the Club's decisions, although they had no say and were not even heard. This is unjust, and refusals to implement other people's decisions must be understood. Furthermore, the weakest actor, the debtor, is told to gain comparable treatment from other, excluded creditors. Should a recalcitrant creditor take debtors to court in a Paris Club member country, debtors will not be protected by the creditor government but lose the case. Putting an end to such absurdities and injustice is thus in the best interest of all *bona fide* creditors. An international Chapter 9 would do so. It would also prohibit any creditor discrimination in order to finance bail-outs of IFIs, improving recovery rates for the vast majority of creditors.

Although the introduction of Chapter 9 would not automatically abolish legal norms making debt management unduly difficult – called 'legal risk' in the literature – it would provide an opportunity to do so, and thus to stabilise the international financial architecture further than the mere existence of a sovereign Chapter 9 would. Signalling that lending may be risky and fostering solutions 'in the shadow of the law' as Anne Krueger put it, Chapter 9 would provide the right incentives. But, in addition, the universal introduction of tax-deductible loan loss reserves, as practised on the European continent, would allow an economically virtually costless stabilising feature to function. Tax authorities in countries restricting tax deductibility are implicitly of the opinion that losses occur when the entry correcting a loan's nominal value is made in the creditor's books. But loans still kept at face value in the books will have lower factual or real values once the creditworthiness and economic standing of debtors have become doubtful, as the existence of secondary markets proves.

From an economic and factual point of view, money is actually lost before nominal claims are finally adjusted in the books. Recognising diminished values of claims is just another way of stating that the sum of net assets, and thus the tax base, has declined. To the extent that provisions reflect actual losses in the values of loans already suffered but not yet booked – if loan loss reserves set aside during one year are equivalent to the change in factual values during that year – they do not economically constitute taxable income. Increasing reserves continuously in line with declining factual values would not really cost taxpayers a single cent. Should the economic outlook of the debtor improve, these reserves would have to be reduced accordingly, of course, to keep provisions in line with actual values. Tax regimes without deductibility of reserves thus tax illusory profits 'existing' only due to accounting practices. Creditors are forced to grant an interest-free loan to the Treasury by shifting losses to the future.

In practice, uncertainty will not allow a precise estimate of probabilities of losses (and thus factual values). One might therefore discuss whether reserves actually match losses already suffered. If reserves are larger than these losses banks get a loan by tax authorities equivalent to the difference between reserves and changes in the real values of loans; if reserves are smaller this difference is taxed as illusory income. The costs for reserves of $100 are (t)-times this difference. Or, more formally,

$$\$[100(1 - p) - \text{reserves}]ti \quad (1)$$

where (t) is the tax rate, (i) the interest rate at which either the government or the private creditor can borrow (depending on whose costs are calculated), (p) is the probability of repayment – and 100p, hence, is the expected value. The first term in square brackets expresses actual losses. Assuming that supervisory authorities keep loan loss reserves roughly in line with the decline in value of dubious loans both costs to taxpayers and taxation of illusory profits will be very low or negligible. A substantial stabilising effect can be obtained at no or minimal real cost to taxpayers.

Economically, provisions have the important function of spreading losses over some years, which might ruin creditors if they had to be absorbed in one year. Whether to have a tax system encouraging more prudential provisioning this way is a political question, which should not be decided without considering the alternatives. Bail-outs such as Continental Illinois or the US Savings and Loan institutions (with a price tag of several hundred billion dollars) are sufficient to show that extremely limited tax deductibility does not necessarily avoid costs to taxpayers. The introduction of an international Chapter 9 might be used as an opportunity to make the stabilising feature of loan loss provisioning available to all creditors. Rendering crisis management easier, this is ultimately also in the interest of debtors.

## Speed

In order to avoid further damages to debtor economies a speedy solution is needed. Chapter 9-based debt arbitration adapts functioning national and international procedures. It could be implemented immediately if and when important creditors such as the G7 agree. Without or against them, neither the SDRM nor Chapter 9 could be implemented. No new institution would be created. Panels would dissolve once they had served their purpose, reconvening later on if needed. As insolvency procedures should and hopefully will remain exceptional in the future – the mere existence of sovereign insolvency would contribute to avoiding crises – a standing institution would soon be severely underemployed.

## Campaigning for change

Safeguarding the rights of Southern debtors by debt arbitration based on Chapter 9 would have positive effects on multilateralism, because it would mean a fundamental change from present international relations, where the rights of developing countries have often and repeatedly been infringed. It would reach the MDG objectives of dealing comprehensively with sovereign debts and regaining sustainability, and of introducing a rule-based financial system no longer denying equal rights and correct treatment to the South. Abolishing undue discrimination against Southern sovereign debtors would facilitate global partnership. Real partnership can only be based on equality.

Easy to implement with immediate effect, my proposal needs only to clear political hurdles and to be explained to the private sector. Private creditors have usually been much more open. Leading bankers like David Suratgar or the late Alfred Herrhausen have even proposed publicly to emulate the insolvency regime. Public creditors are much more recalcitrant. For public creditors the rule of law would mean giving up power, becoming one party instead of being the judge. IFIs especially would lose importance as solved crises no longer need to be managed. By contrast, the IMF's self-serving SDRM proposal would increase the Fund's importance, installing it firmly and officially as the overlord of sovereign debt relief on top of averting any possibility of holding multilateral institutions accountable for their decisions regarding the policies debtors have to adopt (cf. Raffer 2002a; 2003).

There is a need to convince decision makers that the civilised standards holding undisputed sway in the cases of all other debtors must finally be applied to the South. Many public creditors will need lobbying. But there are also people within the public sector who wish such change to be brought about. Parliamentarians have supported debt arbitration, especially in Germany and Latin America. Governments in North and South willing to change the present discrimination against Southern debtors and their peoples must build a coalition across the North–South divide with international organisations, parliamentarians, public servants, NGOs and the public at large, as well as private creditors interested in re-establishing the economic viability of debt-distressed Southern debtors or concerned about the present plight of so many people. These efforts can and should build on already existing networks and support. Public pressure and lobbying is the only way to convince recalcitrant public creditors. It was Jubilee 2000 UK that put the proposal on the political table, and several Jubilee movements (especially in Ecuador, Germany and Switzerland) and NGOs have lobbied for it. Thus, it was possible to present it during the UN's *Finance for Development* process. Without public support Chapter 9 (or FTAP) would have remained another academic idea.

For understandable reasons the dependence of debtor governments on the goodwill (or arbitrariness) of their creditors may prevent many of them from speaking up as loudly as they might wish to, and actually should. It is all the more necessary that others speak out strongly and clearly for a just and fair solution that puts human dignity and life before debts. A newborn child's life expectancy must eventually be influenced less than it is at present by whether (s)he is born in a heavily-indebted municipality within an OECD-country or in a heavily-indebted country in the South.

Besides the economic reasons for such a solution already explained by Adam Smith, there exist ethical and political rationales. If one believes in the equality of all human beings, human rights must be protected for anyone, irrespective of nationality or colour. If the rule of law is indeed as important as OECD governments like to think, it must be applied universally – including to the debt issue where creditor governments themselves have manifest interests. All members of the UN agreed to the Millenium Declaration stating their determination to deal comprehensively and effectively with the debt problems of developing countries so as to make their debts sustainable in the long term. Some encouragement for efforts to change international debt management for the better might be taken from reading the declaration of UN member nations:

> We will spare no effort to promote democracy and strengthen the rule of law, as well as respect for all internationally recognised human rights and fundamental freedoms, including the right to development.

## References

Annan, K. 2000. 'Freedom from Want', in: *We, the People, The Role of the United Nations in the 21st Century.* New York: UN 2000.

Eichengreen, B. 1999. *Toward a New International Financial Architecture: a Practical Post-Asia Agenda.* Washington, DC: Institute for International Economics.

GAO (US Government Accounting Office). 2000. 'Developing Countries: Debt Relief Initiative for Poor Countries Faces Challenges' (Chapter Report, 06/29/2000, GAO/NSIAD-00-161) http://www.gao.gov.

IDA. 2004. 'Background', (print-out on 7 April) http://web.worldbank.org/WBSITE/EXTERNAL/EXTABOUTUS/IDA/0,,contentMDK:20051270~menuPK:83991~pagePK:83988~piPK:84004~theSitePK:73154,00.html.

IMF. 2002. 'The Design of the Sovereign Debt Restructuring Mechanism – Further Considerations'. Mimeo, 27 November, International Monetary Fund.

—— 2003a. 'Executive Board Reviews IMF's Income Position'. Public Information Notice No. 03/64, 22 May, http://www.imf.org/external/ np/sec/pn/2003/pn0364.htm.

—— 2003b. 'Selected Decisions and Selected Documents of the IMF, Twenty-Seventh Issue, as updated as of 30 June 2003, Arrears to Creditors and Debt Strategy'. Print-out on 26 April, http://www.imf.org/external/pubs/ft/sd/index.asp?decision=EBM/02/92.

—— 2003c. *World Economic Outlook (September).* Washington, DC: International Monetary Fund.

—— 2004. 'Financial Risk in the Fund and the Level of Precautionary Balances'. Internal document,3 February, International Monetary Fund.

IMF and IDA. 2004. 'Debt Sustainability in Low-Income Countries – Proposal for an Operational Framework and Policy Implications'. 3 February, International Monetary Foundation and International Development Association, World Bank.

Krueger, A. 2001. 'International Financial Architecture for 2002: a New Approach to Sovereign Debt Restructuring'. 26 November, http://www.imf.

org/external/np/speeches/2001/112601.htm.

—— 2002. 'Sovereign Debt Restructuring and Dispute Resolution'. 6 June, http://www.imf.org/external/np/speeches/2002/060602.htm.

Malagardis, A. N. 1990. *Ein 'Konkursrecht' für Staaten? Zur Regelung von Insolvenzen souveräner Schuldner in Vergangenheit und Gegenwart.* Baden-Baden: Nomos.

Pettifor, A. 1999. 'Concordats for Debt Cancellation: a Contribution to the Debate'. Mimeo, Jubilee 2000 Coalition UK, 18 March.

—— 2002. 'Debt Is Still the Lynchpin: the Case of Malawi'. http://www.jubilee plus.org/opinion/debt040702.htm.

Raffer, K. 1989. 'International Debts: A Crisis for Whom?' in: H. W. Singer and S. Sharma (eds.), *Economic Development and World Debt.* London and Basingstoke/New York: Macmillan/St. Martin's [Selected papers of a Conference at Zagreb, 1987], pp.51ff.

—— 1990. 'Applying Chapter 9 Insolvency to International Debts: an Economically Efficient Solution with a Human Face'. *World Development,* 18, 2: 301ff.

—— 1993a. 'International Financial Institutions and Accountability: the Need for Drastic Change', in S. M. Murshed and K. Raffer (eds.), *Trade, Transfers and Development: Problems and Prospects for the Twenty-First Century.* Aldershot: Edward Elgar, pp. 151ff.; also on: http://mailbox.univie.ac.at/~ rafferk5.

—— 1993b. 'What's Good for the United States Must Be Good for the World: Advocating an International Chapter 9 Insolvency', in Bruno Kreisky Forum for International Dialogue (ed.), *From Cancun to Vienna. International Development in a New World.* Vienna: Bruno Kreisky Forum, pp. 64 ff. [in English and Spanish also on http://mailbox.univie.ac.at/~rafferk5].

—— 1996. 'Is the Debt Crisis Largely Over? – A Critical Look at the Data of International Financial Institutions', in R. Auty and J. Toye (eds.), *Challenging the Orthodoxies.* Basingstoke and London/New York: Macmillan and St Martin's Press, pp. 23ff. (Paper presented at the Development Studies Association Conference, Lancaster, 7–9 September 1994.)

—— 2001. 'Debt Relief for Low Income Countries: Arbitration as the Alternative to Present Unsuccessful Debt Strategies'. WIDER Discussion Paper, WDP 2001/113 (October), World Institute for Development Economics Research, UN University, Helsinki/Helsingfors, http://www.wider.unu.edu/ conference/ conference-2001-2/conference2001-2.htm.

—— 2002a. 'The Final Demise of Unfair Debtor Discrimination? – Comments on Ms Krueger's Speeches'. Paper prepared for the G-24 Liaison Office, to be distributed to the IMF's Executive Directors representing Developing Countries, 31 January, http://mailbox.univie.ac.at/~rafferk5.

—— 2002b. 'Schemes for Resolving the External Debt Problem', in OPEC Fund for International Development (ed.), *Financing for Development, Proceedings of a Workshop of the G-24 held at Nigeria House, New York, 6–7 September 2001.* Pamphlet Series No. 33, OPEC Fund for International Development, August 2002 pp. 141ff. (or via link on my homepage).

—— 2003. 'The Present State of the Discussion on Restructuring Sovereign

Debts: Which Specific Sovereign Insolvency Procedure?'. Paper presented at the Fourth Inter-Regional Debt Management Conference, DMFAS, UNCTAD, Geneva, 11 November 2003, http://r0.unctad.org/dmfas/pdfs/raffer.pdf (link on my homepage).

—— (Forthcoming publication 1) 'The Debt Crisis and the South in the Era of Globalisation', in M. Spoor (ed.), *Globalisation, Poverty and Conflict*. Dordrecht: Kluwer.

—— (Forthcoming publication 2) 'The IMF's SDRM – Another Form of Simply Disastrous Rescheduling Management?' in C. Jochnick and F. Preston (eds.), *Sovereign Debt at the Crossroads*. Oxford: Oxford University Press.

Raffer, K. and H. W. Singer. 1996. *The Foreign Aid Business: Economic Assistance and Development Cooperation*. Cheltenham (UK) and Brookfield (US): Edward Elgar.

Rodrik, D. 1996. 'Understanding Policy Reform'. *Journal of Economic Literature* 34, 1: 9ff.

Rogoff, K. and J. Zettelmeyer. 2002a. 'Early Ideas on Sovereign Bankruptcy Reorganisation: a Survey'. IMF Working Paper, WP/02/57.

—— 2002b. 'Bankruptcy Procedures for Sovereigns: A History of Ideas, 1976–2001'. *IMF Staff Papers*, 49, 3: 470ff.

Spiotto, J. E. 1993. 'Municipal Bankruptcy'. *Municipal Finance Journal*, 14: 1ff.

Treasury Select Committee, House of Commons. 2002. 'Treasury – Uncorrected Evidence', Thursday, 4 July, http://www.publications.parliament.uk/cmselect/cmtreasy/uc868-iii/uc86801.htm.

UNCTAD. 1998. *Trade and Development Report 1998*. Geneva: United Nations Conference on Trade and Development.

World Bank. 1985. *General Conditions Applicable to Loan and Guarantee Agreements, Dated January 1, 1985*. Washington, DC: World Bank.

—— 1992. *World Debt Tables 1992/93*, Vol. 1. Washington, DC: World Bank.

—— 1997. *Global Development Finance*, Vol. 1. Washington, DC: World Bank.

—— 2000. *Global Development Finance*, Vol. 1. Washington, DC: World Bank.

Zedillo, E. *et al.* 2001. 'Recommendations of the High-level Panel on Financing for Development'. United Nations General Assembly, 26 June (A/55/1000).

# 10

## Achieving Healthy Urban Futures in the Twenty-first Century: New Approaches to Financing Water and Basic Sanitation

### DAVID C. TIPPING, DANIEL ADOM and ANNA K. TIBAIJUKA

## A new human security challenge: the rapid urbanisation of poverty and ill health

Human security challenges are increasingly sharing the political discourse at the global level with traditional concerns such as foreign affairs, traditional security policies and international development aid. There is an emerging consensus in the global community that new mechanisms have to be found to address global challenges that pose a threat to both the developing and the developed world. *Everyone has a stake in changing the dynamics of globalisation that appear to be going against the global majority.*

Globalisation is played out in cities and the 'decoding of globalisation' can only be undertaken at a local level (Sassen 2001). While the debate on MDGs and global public goods (GPGs) makes frequent reference to globalisation as a major driving force of change, the second seminal global trend – urbanisation – does not always receive the attention it deserves, despite the fact that under MDG 7 – *ensure environmental sustainability* – Target 11 is to achieve a significant improvement by 2020 in the lives of at least 100 million slum dwellers.

It is essential for any strategy on global public goods and MDG attainment to grasp the nature and scale of urban change resultant from world population growth. Over the last 50 years, urban populations have increased explosively. While in 1970 approximately 37 per cent of the world's population was living in urban areas, by 2006/7 this figure is expected to be 50 per cent. At this time there are approximately three billion people living in urban areas, and approximately one billion people now living in slums.

Slums are the most visible manifestation of poverty. As presented in Figure 10.1, the world population is expected to rise to nine billion by 2050. By this time, the total number of people living in urban areas will be six billion. It is

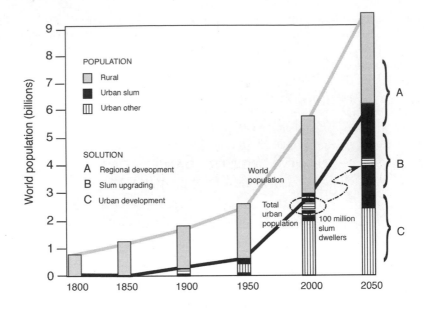

Figure 10.1 Dynamics of the urban slum problem

time, the total number of people living in urban areas will be six billion. It is projected that the number of slum dwellers will increase by another billion (from 2030) to approximately three billion. This crisis is of unprecedented magnitude, and the greatest impact will be felt in the developing world and in turn affect predominantly its most vulnerable populations. With MDG 7, Target 11 (put in place in 2000 and circled in Figure 10.1), which aims to improve the quality of life for 100 million slum dwellers, we are only touching the surface of the real slum challenge.

This exponential growth is taking place without the corresponding ability of many cities in the developing world to expand public provision of basic services. As a result, in nearly all urban centres, there are neighbourhoods with little or no provision of the basic infrastructure and services that are essential for public health and well-being (Helsinki Process 2004: 22). City and municipal authorities must cope with these challenges, therefore, as best they can; few national governments give any sort of priority to increasing resource streams (Helsinki Process 2004: 22). The machinery of governance (good policies and strong institutions) is lacking, access to capital markets is difficult, and market forces are failing to ensure that development is balanced within a sustainable and holistic framework.

### Links between the MDGs and the Habitat Agenda
The *Habitat Agenda*, adopted in 1996 by the governments of 171 countries in Istanbul, Turkey, drew attention to the serious consequences arising from

urbanisation and grouped its aspirations around the notion of livability (UNCHS 2001). Livability refers to those spatial, social and environmental characteristics and qualities that uniquely contribute to people's sense of personal and collective well-being, and to their sense of satisfaction in being the residents of that particular settlement. The aspirations for livability vary from place to place, and evolve and change in time; they also differ among the diverse populations that make up communities. Therefore, conditions for livable human settlements presuppose a working democracy in which processes of participation, civic engagement and capacity-building mechanisms are institutionalised. As identified in Figure 10.2, there are also various preconditions that create the conditions for socio-economic development, including good urban governance and the notions of sustainability and fairness that are central for achieving good health and welfare.

The *Habitat Agenda* recognises that cities need a higher priority in national development strategies. Cities provide most of the infrastructure for national development, and are more effective and efficient at this than rural areas. Jobs in cities are more productive, and higher *per capita* GDPs are achieved. At the same time, urban services benefit more people, and this economy of scale in turn benefits rural persons. Cities thus offer the chance to provide well-being to poor and low-income populations by efficiently and effectively

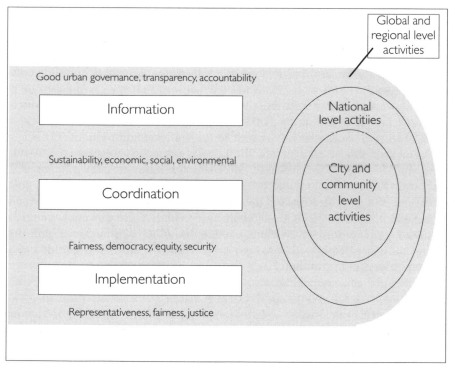

Figure 10.2 Base model of GPG production, delivery and consumption system

harnessing the opportunities of economic globalisation to reduce social, economic and environmental inequalities between regions and reducing social exclusion within them, thus enhancing social cohesion.

The Istanbul Declaration and the *Habitat Agenda* together, by outlining the many principles and strategies in support of socio-economic development, have been described as a 'practical road map to an urbanising world'. They promote a positive vision where all have adequate shelter, a healthy and safe environment, basic services and freely chosen employment (*Habitat Agenda* 1996: Para 21). Health features prominently in the road map, as health problems related to adverse environmental conditions in urban areas – including a lack of access to safe water and sanitation, inadequate waste management, poor drainage, air pollution, and exposure to excessive noise levels – as well as ineffective and inadequate health services exact a heavy toll, not only in lives lost but in quality of life and the overall contribution to society of millions of people in cities, towns and villages. These problems may also aggravate social tension and inequity, and increase the vulnerability of people to the effects of disasters.

The MDGs now provide a powerful organising device for the *Habitat Agenda*. Of particular priority is Target 10, access to safe drinking water and sanitation, not only because it significantly improves quality of life and work (particularly of women and girls), but because it prominently contributes to the achievement of the MDGs that address health: Goals 4, 5 and 6. Clearly, any strategy to improve the lives of slum dwellers is dependent on strategies that address the interface between Target 11 and other MDGs. Members of Track II of the Helsinki Process also make clear that 'advances in health are impossible without simultaneous advances in education (Goal 2) and gender equality (Goal 3). All of these sectoral actions to achieve the health goals (Goals 3, 4, and 5) also contribute to accelerating the rate of poverty reduction (Goal 1)' (Helsinki Process 2004: 14) – and the achievement of the health goals in turn lends significant support to the achievement of other MDGs.

As regards Goal 7, Target 10, the issue is not *access* to water alone, but *adequacy*. Are water supplies safe, sufficient for needs, regular, convenient and available at an affordable price? Similarly, for sanitation, it is not just provision, but rather a *quality of provision* that is (1) convenient for all household members (including women and children); (2) affordable; and (3) insulated from contact with human excreta and other wastewater within the home and wider neighbourhood. Figure 10.3 presents data on urban dwellers without water and sanitation.

Worldwide epidemiological and demographic information suggests that health, health services and survival rates are better in cities than in rural areas. However, intra-urban differentials suggest that poor and low-income urban people are worse off in terms of communicable and non-communicable diseases than the poor in rural areas (UN–HABITAT 2002). Life in urban slums with inadequate shelter is precarious, where women and children are the principal victims of violence, crime, overcrowding and all the health

| Environmental health<br>*Access to good quality drinking water and basic sanitation*<br>• 'Adequacy' is a subjective term, i.e. for the poor<br>• Inequity: poor may pay more (up to 16x)<br>• Constraints: finance, scarcity (increased cost of development)<br>  cost recovery, technical capacity to maintain systems | | | | |
| --- | --- | --- | --- | --- |
| Region | Number and proportion of urban dwellers without *improved* provision for: | | Indicative estimates for the number (and proportion) of urban dwellers without adequate provision for: | |
| | Water | Sanitation | Water | Sanitation |
| Africa | 44 million<br>15% | 46 million<br>16% | 100-150 million<br>35-50% | 150-180 million<br>50-60% |
| Asia and Pacific | 98 million<br>7% | 297 million<br>22% | 500-700 million<br>35-50% | 600-800 million<br>45-60% |
| Latin America and Caribbean | 29 million<br>7% | 51 million<br>13% | 80-120 million<br>20-30% | 100-150 million<br>25-40% |

**Figure 10.3 Slide from presentation on improving living conditions for the urban poor**

Source: WHO and UNICEF 2000 in Tipping 2004.

hazards associated with inadequate living conditions in rapidly growing towns and cities. It is among slum dwellers that malaria, tuberculosis, the opportunistic diseases associated with AIDS, and other epidemics take the heaviest toll.

A growing body of evidence further highlights the increasing impact of trauma, especially violence-related, with mental ill health predicted to become a leading disease burden in developing countries. Health quickly becomes a social justice issue – the urban poor are dying at a much higher rate of both infectious and chronic, degenerative diseases than other groups; socio-economic living conditions are disparate. The most vulnerable subgroups include children, women, the elderly, and indigenous people.

*Where is the greatest need (focusing on slums/urban inequities)?*
Over the last few decades, cities in both developing and developed countries have emerged as the major form of human settlement. Several observers have indicated the inevitability of urban conglomerations, due to a large extent to the nature of people and the positive contributions of these environ-ments. It is predictable that over the coming years, and into the future, more people live in and around cities and urban localities than in rural areas. Cities have in effect become a barometer of humankind's progress into the

twenty-first century. The concentration of the economic, social, political and administrative organs of a nation or region in cities has further made it attractive for the rich as well as the poor, particularly migrants from rural areas.

In 1970, more than two-thirds of humanity lived in the countryside. By 2001, 47 per cent of the world's population was located in urban areas. This figure will rise to 50 per cent by 2007. It is projected that by 2020 approximately 56 per cent of the world's population will be living in cities. Africa, considered the least urbanised continent until recently, is experiencing the most rapid rate of urbanisation at 5 per cent per annum. Between 1990 and 2020, within many of our lifetimes, urban populations in Africa will increase nearly fourfold, from 138 to 500 million.

Figure 10.4 presents data reflecting trends of world population growth, including the individual components for rural populations, urban populations and urban slum populations. In 2000 it was estimated that more than 924 million people, comprising 43 per cent of the urban population of developing countries, lived in slums. Nearly all of the population growth in the world between now and 2050 is in the urban slums of the developing world! It is now clear that almost all (over 80 per cent) of the world's population increase over the years remaining to achieve the MDGs will take place in the urban areas of developing countries. Most of this growth will be absorbed by slums

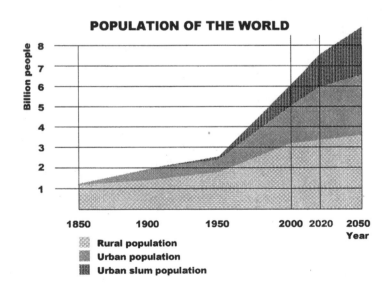

Figure 10.4 Trends of world population growth

Source: Reutersward 2004.

and shanties in the developing world.

Once in the cities, however, migrants find that the housing, jobs, incomes, services and amenities – the things that attracted them to the city in the first place – are not available or are inaccessible to them. As a result, between 30 and 75 per cent of the populations end up in squatter settlements, making a living with minimal resources and the few informal services that are accessible to them. The impacts of inadequate provision of water and sanitation, particularly on health, are usually most evident among the section of the urban population characterised by their low incomes or the particular settlements in which they live.

Figure 10.5 confirms that child mortality is higher in cities where the poor have less access to water; a slum penalty. In fact, access to water in cities has a proven impact on the incidence of waterborne disease. African cities have the highest child mortality rates (12.6 per cent for girls, 15.3 per cent for boys) and the lowest levels of access to water.

There is clearly a need to focus attention on slums and urban inequities. To move forward, cities will need to mobilise/optimise resources (social, political and economic) in a coherent institutional framework (OECD 2004), focusing on the sustainable development of metropolitan regions through rural–urban linkages and area-wide urban strategies to create the right physical, cultural, social and economic environment for improved health,

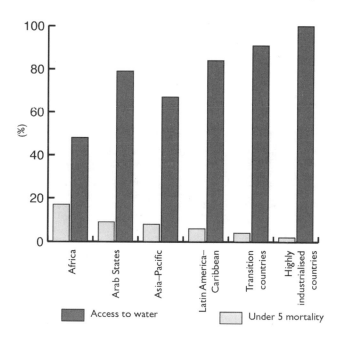

Figure 10.5 Child mortality in cities and poor household access to water

Source: UNCHS 2001.

poverty reduction and subsequent economic growth.

### Current levels of access to water and sanitation (in slums)

An estimated 1.1 billion people were without access to water supplies in 2002, and about 2.4 billion people were without adequate access to sanitation (WHO and UNICEF 2000). It was further estimated that the global percentages of people without access to water supplies were 5 per cent and 29 per cent of total populations for urban and rural areas respectively, with a weighted average of 18 per cent. Corresponding estimates for sanitation were 15 per cent and 60 per cent respectively, with a weighted average of 39 per cent.

Unless urgent action is taken now, there will be over 4 billion people unserved by 2025, a large proportion of them (approximately 57 per cent) in urban areas. In a recent paper that focuses on a financing strategy for poorest countries to meet MDG Target 10, Hua *et al.* (2004) present a typology made up of four quadrants (Table 10.1) to illustrate where the unserved populations are located.

Based on this typology, and using data derived from the 2003 *Human Development Report*, the paper demonstrates that, of the global estimate of about 1.2 billion without access to water supplies, about 705 million live in low- and middle-income countries (UNDP 2003). Of this number, about 416 million live below the poverty line and 320 million are from low-income countries. In a similar manner, of the estimated 2.7 billion without access to sanitation, approximately 1.9 billion are in these low- and middle-income countries and about 633 million, representing about a third of the total, live below the poverty line (see Table 10.2), with 540 million from low-income countries.

Most of these unserved people who live below the poverty line (320 million for water supplies and 633 million for sanitation) are those most likely to be found in the inner-city slums, and are the most likely to be left out if appropriate strategies are not urgently developed to reach them.

#### Table 10.1 Unserved people: where are they?

|  | Low-income countries | Middle-income countries |
| --- | --- | --- |
| Below poverty line | Quadrant I: Unserved people living in absolute poverty in low-income countries | Quadrant II: Unserved people living in absolute poverty in middle-income countries |
| Above poverty line | Quadrant III: Unserved people living above the poverty line in low-income countries | Quadrant IV: Unserved people living above the poverty line in middle-income countries |

Source: Hua *et al.* 2004.

Table 10.2 Distribution of global population of unserved across quadrants for water and sanitation

|  | Low-income countries | Middle-income countries | Total |
|---|---|---|---|
| **Water supplies** | | | |
| Below poverty line | 320 | 96 | 416 |
| Above poverty line | 30 | 259 | 289 |
| Total | 350 | 355 | 705 |
| **Sanitation** | | | |
| Below poverty line | 540 | 93 | 633 |
| Above poverty line | 565 | 730 | 1295 |
| Total | 1105 | 823 | 1928 |

Source: Hua et al. 2004.

The latest data available from the *Mid-Term Assessment of Progress* (WHO and UNICEF 2004) indicate that, while there have been gains in all regions with regard to water coverage, there are still 1.1 billion without safe drinking water. The absolute problem remains in Asia, where nearly two-thirds of the total number of unserved live. However, the very low relative coverage levels found in sub-Saharan Africa, where 42 per cent of the population remain unserved, confirm that this region is lagging behind with regard to the MDG Water Target.

In contrast, global sanitation coverage presents a more alarming story. An estimated 2.6 billion people – half the population of the developing countries – now live without improved sanitation. Again the absolute problem is in Asia, where only a third of the region's population have access; however, both the sub-Saharan Africa and South Asia subregions have the lowest relative rates of coverage. The trends suggest that the MDG Sanitation Target will be missed by 500 million people.

It is important to achieve balance between investments in water and sanitation. An imbalance in these investments can lead to disease outbreaks spawned by water contaminated by sewage – which is particularly relevant to the achievement of Goal 4: reducing child mortality. From a public health perspective, the addition of the sanitation target into the Johannesburg Plan of Implementation at the World Summit on Social Development (WSSD) (UN 2002) and consequently into the Targets to be achieved through the MDGs is of critical importance. Indeed, it has reinvigorated integrated water resources management as a vital component of any strategy for improving health and as a central intervention to reach Goal 4.

*The scope of health conditions in slums*
The UN–HABITAT report *The Challenge of Slums* shows that slum life often entails enduring some of the most intolerable living conditions, which

frequently include sharing toilets with hundreds of people, living in over-crowded and insecure neighbourhoods, and constantly facing the threat of eviction. The urban poor suffer infant death rates 1.5 to 3 times higher than in areas served by piped water and sanitation. Similarly, under-5 mortality rates have been estimated to be 10 to 20 times higher (Helsinki Process 2004), which is 240 times higher than in high-income countries. It is a fact that some 3,560 children under 5 years, mostly from rural villages and urban slums in the developing world, lose their lives daily because their water supplies are contaminated, inadequate or non-existent, or they have

---

### Box 10.1  Examples of the rate and incidence of water- and sanitation-related disease in urban areas

- The existence of a yard tap nearly doubled the chances of a mother washing her hands after cleaning a child's anus, and doubled the chances of her washing faecally soiled linen immediately.

- A study in Salvador, Brazil showed that children in households with no toilet had twice the incidence of diarrhoea of those with sanitary toilets.

- Children in slum areas of Tamil Nadu, India are benefiting from child-friendly toilets. Until now children had to defecate in open drains in front of their houses or walk in search of places for open defecation amidst existing faeces, and return home without washing because there was no water available.

- In the slums of Salvador, Brazil, surface water drainage halved the number of cases of frequent diarrhoea. When combined with low-cost sewerage, the rate was reduced even further.

- The prevalence of roundworm and whipworm is halved by improved drainage, and hookworm infestation reduced by a factor of three.

- In Madagascar, 3.5 million schooldays are lost each year due to ill-health related to bad sanitation.

- Hygienic home environments, contributed to by easy access to safe water and adequate sanitation facilities, decrease children's exposure to infectious disease.

- Health improvements in children resulting from improved water, sanitation and hygiene education lead to higher rates of school attendance and better performance.

- Provision of sanitation and drainage infrastructure has major beneficial effects on child health.

Source: www.lboro.ac.uk, accessed 10 September 2004.

---

no sanitation nor hygiene regime (WHO and UNICEF 2004). Many of these deaths are in the poorest households and communities. For each death there are a multitude of others, including older children, adults and the elderly, who are afflicted by unsafe water and sanitation-related illness.

For the lack of adequate water and sanitation, people carry a heavy health burden that translates into huge national medical bills, reduced productivity, and lost exports and tourism when epidemics break out, particularly in slums. As pointed out by Dr Lee Jong Wook, Director-General of the World Health Organisation, 'water and sanitation are primary drivers of public health ... once we can secure access to clean water and to adequate sanitation facilities for all people, irrespective of the difference in their living conditions, a huge battle against all kinds of diseases will be won' (WHO and UNICEF 2004).

*Infectious disease*

In the last two decades, infectious diseases have emerged as the latest challenge to governments across the globe. Recent outbreaks include West Nile Virus, SARS and Avian Flu. These diseases existed before, but their incidence and geographic range suddenly increased. Contributing factors include globalisation, urbanisation, environmental change (weather patterns, deforestation), internal conflict, mass population movements and the collapse of basic health services. While in some cases the outbreaks originated in rural areas, their effects were mostly felt in cities – cities that in turn are hubs of global interconnectedness. This lesson was clear during the recent SARS outbreak, which particularly threatened urban areas.

Children are particularly vulnerable to most infectious and parasitic diseases. The status of children in poor urban areas is often worse than that in rural areas. Poor children under 5 years in slums suffer and die more often from diarrhoea and acute respiratory infections than rural children. Many of these deaths are preventable, given timely diagnosis and correct treatment. In early life the living environment exerts a powerful influence over survival, as well as both physical and mental development. The WHO states that up to 1 in 10 children under 5 years can die in the poorer urban areas, but there are few reliable data on at-risk urban-poor populations. Table 10.3 presents mortality data for infants and children under 5 years in the urban slums of Nairobi. The data show that mortality risks for these groups are particularly high.

The challenge facing those seeking to implement the Habitat Agenda together with the MDG Agenda is to generate local action for global goals, and to ensure global resources for local development. In order to achieve the MDGs and the overall aim of human security in a rapidly and seemingly irreversibly urbanising world, it is essential to develop the capacity of national governments, local authorities, service utilities, non-governmental organisations (NGOs) and community-based organisations (CBOs) to ensure adequate provision for water supply, sanitation, drainage, solid waste collection and

Table 10.3 Infant and child mortality in urban slums, Nairobi, compared with other areas of Kenya

|  | Infant mortality per 1,000 births | Under-5 mortality per 1,000 births |
|---|---|---|
| NCSS* | | |
| Nairobi slums | 91.3 | 150.6 |
| National** | | |
| Rural | 75.9 | 113.0 |
| Other urban | 56.6 | 83.9 |
| Nairobi | 38.7 | 61.5 |

\* National Cross Sectional Slums Survey 2000.
\*\* Based on 1998 Kenya Demographic and Health Surveys (KDHS) data.

management, electricity supply, surfaced roads and footpaths, street lighting and health care.

### Gender inequalities: women, water and urbanisation

In crowded urban settlements, sanitation can be far more than a public health issue for a girl: it determines her privacy and dignity; it determines whether her potential to become a productive citizen in society will ever be fulfilled. Women today constitute 70 per cent of the world's absolute poor. They pay a heavy price, through daily drudgery and lost opportunities, in procuring water for their families.

In their report on *Health of Children Living in Urban Slums in Asia and the Near East: Review of Existing Literature and Data*, Fry et al. (2002) make a point to the effect that factors such as marginalisation, illiteracy, and gender can determine whether a group lives in urban poverty or not. In cities, poverty is not always absolute, but rather is measured by the opportunity and resource difference between 'haves' and 'have nots' living close to each other.

In most countries, the majority of poor urban households are virtually run by women, who must earn a living, and who as a consequence are obliged to spend long hours working away from home. As Fry et al. (2002) observe, however, available work and adequate compensation for women are often limited by gender discrimination. Thus, when women fall ill, the cost of illness leads to debt, which leads to increased poverty. This situation has consequences on the health and development of small children who are often forced to do all kinds of menial jobs to earn a living. Gender issues also affect poverty levels, by limiting employment opportunities for female heads of households and also affecting access to health facilities among the poorest women. It may be that a high proportion of maternal death rates in sub-Saharan Africa, which are 100 times higher than in developed countries, are indirectly related to the water carrying burden and exposure to waterborne disease when collecting water.

Background papers for the United Nations Environment Programme's Global Women's Assembly on Environment have recently listed the major challenges faced by women in urban settlements, showing clearly how trends in urbanisation and privatisation have affected women in a particular way, increasing gender discrimination and threats to life and health (Dankelman 2004). Yet they also underline that along with the risks come new opportunities for women, as life in the city opens up choices that were not available to them in rural settings, such as access to family planning, access to education and access to work. In consequence, women have been the initiators of many innovative urban projects and environmental initiatives. It will be essential that the role of women at the municipal level is recognised, and that project proposals and financial systems take their particular and central role into account.

## Constraints on water and sanitation provision in developing countries

Ultimate responsibility for adequate services in water and sanitation to urban populations, especially in low-income settlements and in smaller urban centres, lies with national government, which has to provide the appropriate legal and regulatory framework for implementation by subnational government at the local level. Resources for this purpose must be made available from national and subnational tax revenues, user charges, cross-subsidies from users, private sector investment and ODA, or a combination of all of these sources.

Local authorities are usually the implementation entities that carry out the provision of water and sanitation at the local level. The dilemma is that even though they are the main implementers, available resources are inadequate for them to carry out this function effectively. Although different actors have an important role to play, providing an effective legislative, financial and institutional framework for water and sanitation will above all be the result of intense and sustained efforts by national governments themselves.

### Financing gap

The *Global Water Supply and Sanitation Assessment 2000 Report* (WHO and UNICEF 2000) presents financial data on the level of investment in water supply and sanitation from national and external support sources, for Africa, Asia and Latin America and the Caribbean over the period 1990–2000. Despite the constraints inherent in the data sources used in preparing the report, the data provide a good indication of the state of investment in the water and sanitation sector over the period.

Figures 10.6 and 10.7 encapsulate the findings of the report on the level of annual investment in urban and rural water supply and sanitation over the period. As the graphs clearly depict, contributions from national sources

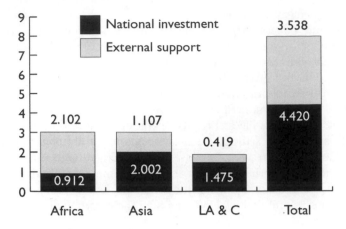

Figure 10.6 Annual investment in urban water supply in Africa, Asia and Latin America and the Caribbean, 1990–2000

Source: WHO and UNICEF 2000.

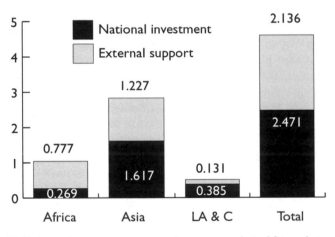

Figure 10.7 Annual investment in rural water supply in Africa, Asia and Latin America and the Caribbean, 1990–2000

Source: WHO and UNICEF 2000.

as a percentage of the total annual investment in the water and sanitation sector tend to be relatively lower in African countries (25–50 per cent) than in Asia and in Latin America and the Caribbean (60–90 per cent). While this clearly demonstrates Africa's dependence on external sources, as against substantially higher local investment levels in the Caribbean and Asia, it should be noted that the absolute problem (of access for urban water) in Asia is receiving the same global investment allocation (see Figure 10.6). It is also evident from Figures 10.6 and 10.7 that except in Asia, where the total annual investment in rural water supply is about equal to that of the urban

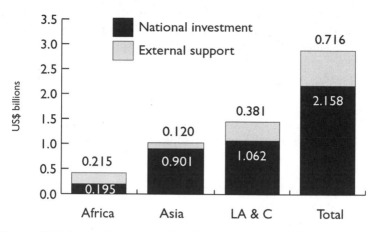

Figure 10.8 Annual investment in urban sanitation in Africa, Asia and Latin America and the Caribbean, 1990–2000

Source WHO and UNICEF 2000.

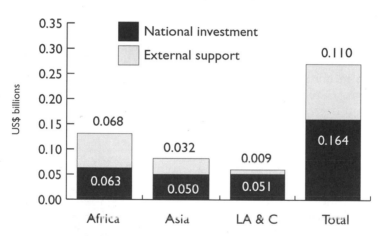

Figure 10.9 Annual investment in rural sanitation in Africa, Asia and Latin America and the Caribbean, 1990–2000

Source WHO and UNICEF 2000.

areas, investments in urban water supply in Africa and in Latin America and the Caribbean tend to be about three times the level of those investments in rural areas, despite the huge gaps in rural coverage.

In Figures 10.8 and 10.9, the ratio of national contributions to total investments is similar in respect of sanitation, except for in Africa where there is a rise of about 50 per cent. It is clear that donors are supporting water developments, while sanitary needs are not being allocated adequate resources. This might reflect the high cost of water storage developments, but may also imply that there is a need to re-prioritise sectoral investments in water and sanitation to meet the challenges developing countries face and to improve the appalling health status of vulnerable populations.

Figure 10.10 presents the median total investment in water supply and sanitation in the three regions as a proportion of overall government investment (1990–2000). Among regions, one can see that the majority of governments in Latin America and the Caribbean give higher priority to water and sanitation sectoral investments. For the majority of governments in both Africa and Asia, funding development in the sector is a far less pressing priority.

*A snapshot of expenditure at the local level*
Figure 10.11 presents data on both '*per capita* local government revenue (annual)' and '*per capita* local government expenditure (annual)' taken from UN–HABITAT's Urban Indicator database. The data – from a sample of 237 cities invited to participate in this UN–HABITAT programme – are limited in terms of sample design, though they allow for reliable comparison between cities and regions. The total local government expenditure in developing nations varies by a factor of 241 when compared with that of highly industrialised countries (HIC). This has major repercussions on how local authorities provide basic services and infrastructure, including access to clean drinking water and basic sanitation. The level of income received by local authorities is highly dependent on the level of independence they enjoy from central government. More independent municipalities are able to raise their own finance, set taxes and levy user fees.

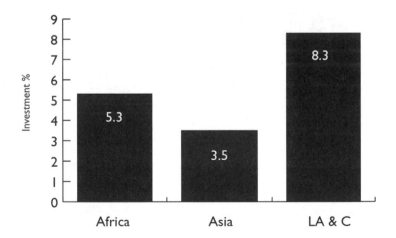

Figure 10.10 Median total annual investment in water supply and sanitation

Source: WHO and UNICEF 2000.

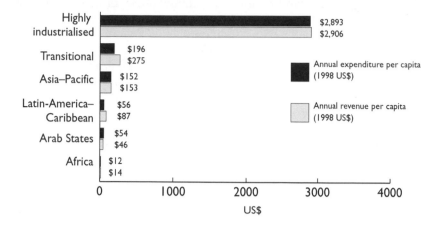

Figure 10.11 How much cities earn and spend

When comparing Figure 10.11 with Table 10.4, which presents data on 'regional *per capita* local government capital expenditure (annual)', the outcome in terms of infrastructure investment is obvious. Low levels of capital expenditure correlate with low levels of household access to infrastructure. This is not true for the economies in transition, which in spite of their low level of investment can generally rely on an adequate existing infrastructure system.

While the case for additional external assistance in the Africa region identified above recurs, though now with added emphasis on investment at the local level, it is noted that local authorities in developed countries spend a lower proportion of their income on capital expenditure. This is probably because the primary infrastructure in these cities and regions has already

Table 10.4 Annual local authority capital expenditure for 1998

| City region | Annual expenditure per capita | Annual capital expenditure per capita | Proportion of income spent on capital expenditure |
| --- | --- | --- | --- |
| Highly industrialised | 2893 | 1133 | 39 % |
| Transitional | 196 | 77 | 39 % |
| Asia–Pacific | 152 | Not reported | Not reported |
| Latin America–Caribbean | 56 | Not reported | Not reported |
| Arab states | 54 | 32 | 59 % |
| Africa | 12 | 10 | 85 % |

been put in place, and expenditures are mainly on extension of systems, upgrade of equipment and processes, etcetera.

## The governance gap

It has become increasingly evident that establishing clear policies and strategies supported by appropriate institutional reforms, and making real commitments to on-the-ground implementation of programmes in the water and sanitation sector, would lead to the efficient and sustainable use and protection of water resources, and to the achievement of the MDGs (Adom 2004). In this context, as further noted by the MDG Task Force on Water, most of the globally relevant examples of success in meeting the water and sanitation Targets have been accompanied by major institutional and policy changes, such as sector policy reform underpinned by national level reform, a shift in the role of central government from implementation to facilitation, and the devolution of responsibility to local governments and communities.

This reflects the growing importance of the principle of subsidiarity – ensuring responsibility for implementation at the level for which it is most suited and where it is most effective, and also ensuring that decisions are taken as closely as possible to the citizen. Nevertheless, there is still substantial debate on what kinds of institutions and policies countries will need to achieve the water and sanitation goals and, on another level, to balance the use of water resources in the system to optimise socio-economic development.

The many solutions to the water, sanitation and human settlement crisis have many dimensions and urgently require significant paradigm shifts towards integrated water resource management and the improvement of urban governance, particularly in the developing countries. This should rest on preconditions for development, such as the sustainability criterion and principles of good governance, which allow all stakeholders to articulate their needs in local-level processes that feed up to higher levels for consideration in planning, programming and budgeting. In this, a level of political commitment and leadership is required that can only come from those with vision and the will to act.

## The policy gap

While poverty reduction remains the overarching object of the MDG/WSSD Targets, there is a need for a more integrated and holistic approach to water, sanitation and human settlements. In responding to the needs of the people, this should take a cross-sectoral approach towards planning and development, aligned with integrated water resources management principles. The policy gaps in this context relate to making sound policies – based on information generation, analysis and feedback, and matched with strong yet flexible institutional and administrative frameworks – that take the following into consideration:

• the involvement of all sectors of central and local government and partners (local and international) in integrated planning and implementation;

- enhancing the capacity of local governments, political leaders and decision makers;

- involvement of the private sector, NGOs and CBOs at all levels;

- support to innovative mechanisms that mobilise and effectively utilise financial resources: examples include the African Water Facility of the African Ministerial Council on Water (AMCOW), hosted by the African Development Bank (AfDB); and the Water and Sanitation Trust Fund of UN–HABITAT for the Water in Cities Programme;

- enhancing the resource base of local governments through political decentralisation and devolution of power to source and control resources;

- using partnership and participation principles to advance the course for meeting the MDG/WSSD targets, with an emphasis on local-level action;

- using regional cooperation and integration within appropriate frameworks – the New Partnership for Africa's Development (NEPAD), for example, or ministerial fora such as AMCOW in Africa – as an important vehicle for solving capacity problems at the level of individual states.

It is increasingly found that the formulation of policies within and across jurisdictions is key, as well as the coordination of policy implementation between the sectors. It is also acknowledged that preventative health measures should be geared towards the social, economic and environmental determinants of health and habitat, and that this is also only possible through work across sectors. There is also a need to complement local policy decision making with participative democracy within forms of governance, decision making and resource allocation that are most responsive to the needs of the poor and positively affect their quality of life.

## The institutional gaps

In most developing countries, it has been widely recognised that the water and sanitation sector has increasingly failed to deliver acceptable levels of service. From various assessments of performance of the sector a number of problems are revealed (online at www.zambia-water.org.zm, accessed on 22 August 2004):

1 Multiplicity of organisations without clear allocation of responsibility, thus leading to duplication, gaps, conflict and competition, and thus constraining the development and implementation of a comprehensive water and sanitation sector policy and strategy.

2 Inadequate financial resources to meet the costs of extending coverage of water and sanitation to the majority of the population, and to meet the costs of essential operation and maintenance of facilities. Conse-

quently, in spite of significant capital investments, mostly financed by external support agencies, the new facilities rapidly decline into disuse.

3 Shortage of qualified and experienced manpower – professionals in engineering, accounts and management – is often exacerbated by high staff turnover from central and local government institutions charged with responsibility for provision of water supply and sanitation services.

4 Poor operation and maintenance of facilities in urban and peri-urban as well as in rural areas. This has been exemplified by high water losses through leakage and wastage, a breakdown in the barrier protection system, and a large number of inoperative mechanical and electrical plants in urban areas, and hand pumps in the rural areas.

5 Low billing and collection efficiencies, especially in urban areas, preventing the possibility of a self-sustaining sector.

Thus, as the MDG Task Force on water points out, there is a need to focus on institutional capabilities and mechanisms for service delivery – on capabilities to deliver water and sanitation services to the poor, and on mechanisms to implement effective channels of delivery. Delivery capacity and domestic capacity to implement are clearly related to income and resources. In this context, particular attention needs to be paid to:

• The role of government in service delivery, and the costs involved in alternative delivery channels. Service delivery by government, the private sector, NGOs, CBOs, or self-help groups can entail very different costs (and, ultimately, communities need to decide which approach they would prefer).

• Calculating life-cycle costs for each infrastructure system and optimising the selected delivery and maintenance system with these in mind.

• Tapping of additional resources.

• Formalising and encouraging the role of small-scale providers.

• Undertaking broader actions comprising social mobilisation, and other actions to promote 'voice' and a sense of ownership at community levels, capacity building and, most importantly, a set of incentives (such as the promotion of competition between service providers) are all conducive to improved service provision.

• Strengthening utilities: while community-based programmes will definitely play an important role in meeting the water and sanitation targets, they will not solve all problems. Since solutions will also come through better-performing formal utilities, strengthening and supporting these will be critical.

The constraints are not insurmountable, and can be overcome with better information, coordination, and supported implementation. In the meantime, it is essential not to delay improvements to water resources management, planning and implementation by lack of concern for an integrative approach.

Clearly, better policies and strategies (livability, economic growth, etcetera) for the development of cities are needed. Satterthwaite (2004) states that 'conventional development systems and processes are not designed for the conditions of the poor nor are they appropriate to the needs of the poor'. It seems that local authorities need to be nurtured to support local initiatives and to ensure that funds are spent effectively.

Institutional reforms could be geared towards efficient and effective provision of infrastructure and basic services, especially to currently unserviced areas of the city. Mechanisms could be devised to improve coordination between national government and local authorities. This way, cities and metropolitan regions might be empowered to respond to complex problems associated with the holistic notion of sustainable development. Optimisation of rural–urban linkages and area-wide urban planning would only serve to enhance the potential of cities and metropolitan regions to contribute directly to the achievement of the MDGs in developing countries.

Local action can contribute to global goals such as poverty reduction. For this to happen, international cooperation needs to move down to the local level. Aid agencies are not geared to work at that level; official bilateral and multilateral agencies were established to channel funding support to central government, and are thus inefficient at targeting the local level at this time (Satterthwaite 2004). While funding can be pre-allocated to local govern-ment through decentralised government, it can also be effectively channelled through intermediary organisations that support diverse, community-driven initiatives.

## Opportunities to mobilise new finance for water and sanitation

There will be approximately 1.5 billion people born and living in slums by 2015, the year the MDGs are to be met; this figure will rise steadily to approximately 3 billion by 2050. It is self-evident that resilient and sustain-able water and sanitation systems need to be installed in view of this challenge. A well-coordinated, efficient and effective global response is needed.

National governments in the developing world, and even more so cities and communities, have encountered significant difficulties in mobilising additional financial resources for water and sanitation – a gap that the new priority assigned to this area through the adoption of the MDGs has addressed. It is necessary, therefore, to reassess priorities in the global public goods agenda, in the ODA agenda and in the agendas of national governments of developing nations, in order to ensure global access to clean drinking water and basic sanitation. Not only will existing financing mechanisms have to be enhanced and re-evaluated for appropriateness and flexibility, but new financial resources and mechanisms will also have to be considered under the guise of international cooperation (a major component of success).

*Prospects for multi-level financing: global/regional*
A range of financing vehicles has been introduced in recent years with respect to water and sanitation. Even though they have not been introduced as an explicit part of a global public goods agenda, they clearly help guide strategic orientation in that direction. Established mechanisms and proposals identified include the Cities Alliance Small Grants Facility, the World Bank Group/International Finance Corporation's Municipal Fund, UN-HABITAT's Water and Sanitation Trust Fund, the AfDB's African Water Facility, UN-HABITAT's Slum Upgrading Facility, and the Emerging Africa Infrastructure Fund. This is not an exhaustive listing. Some are public; many are yet to be fully established. These trust funds are a drop in the ocean.

*The Cities Alliance Small Grant Facility*
The Cities Alliance, established in 1999, is a joint initiative of the World Bank and UN–HABITAT. It is a vehicle for implementation that aims to marshal the resources, experience and knowledge of the international development community to improve livelihoods for the urban poor, by focusing on two priorities for action to reduce urban poverty: (1) helping upgrade slums and squatter settlements in and around most larger cities; and (2) supporting city development strategies, a city-based consensus-building process by which local stakeholders develop strategic plans linked to investment follow-up. Up to December 2002, the Alliance had approved more than US$33 million in funding allocations, in the form of grants in the range US$40,000–500,000 to support development activities in cities, countries and NGOs/CBOs. These allocations were linked to more than US$3.8 billion in investments (including US$2.3 billion World Bank lending) in more than 24 countries. The Alliance is also developing new facilities and investment instruments to expand the level of resources reaching local authorities and the urban poor, including the Community Water and Sanitation Facility (grants of up to US$500,000 from non-core funding), and the Cities Without Slums Facility for sub-Saharan Africa (grants up to US$75,000).

*The Municipal Fund*
The Municipal Fund, established in 2003, is a joint initiative of the World Bank and International Finance Corporation (IFC). It brings together IFC's credit culture and market expertise and the World Bank's public policy and capacity-building experience to address the needs of the municipal financial market. The Fund has full access to IFC's strong credit assessment, financial product line (including local currency financing) and risk management capabilities (swaps, options, forward contracts). Local and state entities that are creditworthy have the opportunity to invest in infrastructure projects without needing sovereign state guarantees. Investments made by states and municipalities are not limited to water, but include electricity, solid waste and urban

transport infrastructure.

### The Water and Sanitation Trust Fund

The Water and Sanitation Trust Fund, established in 2003 by UN–HABITAT, is designed to contribute to the achievement of the MDG water and sanitation goals in urban areas by supporting creation of an enabling environment for pro-poor investment, and providing a vehicle to significantly improve the volume of ODA flows to this sector. As a grant financing mechanism, the Trust Fund provides a fast-track mechanism for reaching out to the poor, facilitating access to benefits from city-wide improvements that often bypass them. The Trust Fund is financed by a consortium of bilateral donors, but other non-traditional sources are being sought. In 2003 the Asian Development Bank announced a US$500-million line of fast-track credit to participating cities in Asia.

### The African Water Facility

This Facility is located in the African Development Bank (AfDB). The AfDB has developed a legal instrument for establishing the Facility Trust Fund, which is in the process of being approved by the Board of Directors and Governors of the Bank. A five-year schedule of implementation has been developed, with commencement of operations planned for 2005. The proposal is to mobilise US$614 million for Facility activities. The Facility would provide support at the subnational, regional and river basin levels in a range of areas including integrated water resource management, policy and institutional reform, design of regulatory instruments and building monitoring capacity.

### The European Union Water Facility (EUWF)

The European Commission has designed a 500-million-euro Water Facility to provide technical assistance and co-finance investment in the water sector of African, Caribbean and Pacific (ACP) countries. The proposed Facility is aimed at promoting public–private partnerships for water development. Seed capital will be used in the form of grants, loans, loan guarantees and other financial instruments to get projects moving and attract private sector cash for large water investments (Reina 2004). By bringing new partners together the Facility becomes an important catalyst for action.

### The Emerging Africa Infrastructure Fund

DfID has launched a unique public–private financing partnership whose area focus is sub-Saharan Africa. Currently valued at US$300 million, the fund is a new approach to financing infrastructure for poverty alleviation, while harmonising development and commercial objectives in pursuit of sustainable development and economic growth. Standard Bank Group of South Africa was contracted to establish the fund, which offers competitive, long-term lending for an array of infrastructure opportunities, such as greenfield developments, privatisation, refurbishments, upgrades and expansions. Given the high risk for companies of investing in Africa, the aim was to share the risk burden and create conditions for economic growth and livelihoods for Africans. There are similar funds bringing in new capital for African development, including the South African Infrastructure Fund and the American Insurance Group (AIG) African Infrastructure Fund.

*Prospects for multi-level financing: national level through bilateral aid*
According to the OECD's *Annual Development Cooperation Report* (2004), the major aid donors have a long way to go if they are to reach the levels of aid pledged at the UN Financing for Development Conference in Monterrey, Mexico in 2002. Aid needs to rise from US$58 billion per annum in 2002 to US$75 billion per annum by 2006. In that report the OECD also evaluated progress in meeting the Millennium Development Goals and Targets in developing countries by 2015, and concluded that many of these would simply *not* be met. This is most apparent for health in most regions, and for many of the other Goals and Targets in sub-Saharan Africa.

Given the importance of water, sanitation and public health for so many of the MDGs, it is most surprising that the average share of bilateral aid for the water and sanitation sector was only 6 per cent of the overall aid allocations made in 2001–2 (OECD 2004). This was a fall from 9 per cent in the 1999–2000 period and immediately prior to the Millennium Declaration being ratified. Table 10.5 presents OECD Development Assistance Committee (DAC) countries' annual average commitments to the water and sanitation sector (1999–2002) and the overall share in total sector-allocable aid.

There was actually a 35 per cent drop in the amount of bilateral aid going to the water and sanitation sector over the period, with the combined bilateral contribution to the sector dropping almost 25 per cent. This was negated somewhat by a 71 per cent increase in allocations by the multilateral donors over the same period. However, there remained a net drop in funding to the sector of approximately US$455 million (14 per cent). As identified in this report, there is a clear need for bilateral donors to reprioritise the overall percentage of ODA budgets targeted at the water and sanitation sector. At the WSSD in Johannesburg in 2002 it was suggested that this would be humanity's best investment in development and sustainability.

Figure 10.12 presents data on ODA flows to the sector. It specifically identifies trends in bilateral grants and loans over the period 1973–2002, using a five-year moving average. This more recent analysis shows that the increase in ODA to water supply and sanitation since 1990 can be attributed to an increase in lending only (OECD 2004: 5). It highlights that there has been no clear trend in grant allocations to overall ODA; and that there has been no pure increase in bilateral funding to the water and sanitation sector. It is noted that the average grant element of total ODA in the water and sanitation sector is inferior to that of other sectors. Further, after the sharp decrease in commitments observed in the 1999–2000 period, and continued in the 2001–2 period, current bilateral commitments now stand at their

Table 10.5  Aid to the water and sanitation sector by donor (1999–2002)

| | US$ million | | % of donor total | | % all donors | |
|---|---|---|---|---|---|---|
| | 1999–2000 | 2001–2 | 1999–2000 | 2001–2 | 1999–2000 | 2001–2 |
| Australia | 48 | 16 | 6 | 3 | 2 | 1 |
| Austria | 35 | 10 | 13 | 6 | 1 | 0 |
| Belgium | 11 | 30 | 4 | 5 | 0 | 1 |
| Canada | 31 | 20 | 5 | 3 | 1 | 1 |
| Denmark | 99 | 24 | 15 | 5 | 3 | 1 |
| Finland | 13 | 16 | 9 | 7 | 0 | 1 |
| France | 175 | 141 | 11 | 8 | 6 | 5 |
| Germany | 314 | 273 | 11 | 10 | 10 | 10 |
| Greece | 0.4 | 1 | 1 | 1 | 0 | 0 |
| Ireland | 6 | 11 | 7 | 7 | 0 | 0 |
| Italy | 35 | 25 | 11 | 10 | 1 | 1 |
| Japan | 1300 | 499 | 13 | 6 | 41 | 18 |
| Luxembourg | 8 | 9 | 13 | 13 | 0 | 0 |
| Netherlands | 54 | 120 | 5 | 8 | 2 | 4 |
| New Zealand | 1 | 1 | 2 | 2 | 0 | 0 |
| Norway | 26 | 36 | 4 | 4 | 1 | 1 |
| Portugal | 7 | 1 | 5 | 1 | 0 | 0 |
| Spain | 68 | 45 | 10 | 6 | 2 | 2 |
| Sweden | 27 | 39 | 5 | 6 | 1 | 1 |
| Switzerland | 27 | 24 | 6 | 5 | 1 | 1 |
| United Kingdom | 131 | 86 | 5 | 4 | 4 | 3 |
| United States | 154 | 267 | 2 | 4 | 5 | 10 |
| Total DAC countries | 2569 | 1692 | 9 | 6 | 81 | 63 |

Source: OECD 2004.

lowest level since 1985. It is clear that we cannot wait for the pledged increased ODA to water and sanitation, and that the MDG/WSSD approach may be the most effective means of increasing funding to the sector.

With regard to aid allocation mechanisms, the OECD continue to report that most of the ODA goes to a small number of large urban projects, with approximately half of total ODA going to just ten countries. In 2000–1 these recipients were said to be mostly middle-income countries; they were also the major beneficiaries of foreign direct investment (FDI) in the water and sanitation sector. More disturbingly, in the same period it was found that approximately 12 per cent of total aid to the water sector went to countries where 60 per cent (or less) of the population had access to safe sources of water supply. It quickly becomes clear that a new vision of what globalisation (in all its forms) aims to achieve needs to be hit upon. If all people are to enjoy the benefits of globalisation, bilateral donors will need to engage in

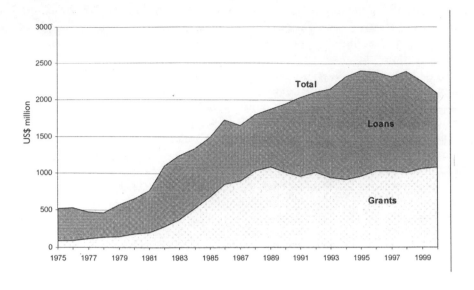

Figure 10.12 Trends in bilateral grants and loans for water supply and sanitation, 1973–2002 (5-year moving averages, constant 2002 prices)

Source: OECD 2004: 5.

significant efforts to increase aid to the 'neediest' countries, and specifically to poor populations living in slums.

*Prospects for multi-level financing: city, community and slum level*
Funding streams are increasingly going local, so support mechanisms must be developed. Cities and communities need to contribute to the development of appropriate solutions, not only to technical solutions, but to governance and finance as well. Part of the solution may be to develop domestic financial systems. Mavrotas (2004) confirms that this has been a neglected area of development, and that much can be done to help move countries towards achievement of the MDGs. Such an approach would enhance national–local linkages, giving local communities more voice, at the same time enhancing local savings and investment in pro-poor growth. This approach would further help to attract FDI to developing countries.

There is much work to do at the local level to identify existing, and nurture new and innovative, funding sources, to construct the support infrastructure for greater private and foreign direct investment, and to maximise the availability and optimise the use of local resources. There is need for funds that facilitate greater access to microfinance and public loan guarantees. Also important at the local level is the introduction of revolving funds and financing vehicles that facilitate access to capital markets.

*Private sector involvement*

It has been shown that the private sector can provide adequate access to water and sanitation by mobilising investment capital faster and more cheaply than the public sector. New models of public–private partnership should be explored for the development of infrastructure and services at the city level. A joint venture model (or special purpose vehicle) is envisioned with public government (a blend of national, cities and community) retaining the majority of equity (greater than 50 per cent ownership) and the private sector given management rights. Ownership of the venture would essentially be structured in the same way as many FDI deals in countries where laws dictate that national interests *must* retain ownership.

Such ventures could construct water and sanitation infrastructure and provide services, through a combination of soft loans from the World Bank (to the government), and possibly land holdings. The private sector investments could be structured to contribute to specific aspects of the project, and might take various forms: syndicated bank borrowings (by both local and international banks) and additional land holdings, with commercial investors given first opportunity to finance other associated developments.

Risks would be apportioned based on the structure of financing. There might be subsidisation of user fees, supported by a global tax or a topic-specific global fund. Investors could then benefit from infrastructure revenue streams. As infrastructure provision encouraged further development, with land values appreciating, potential capital gains would accrue. A key issue would be to structure the investment so that the venture provided reasonable returns, and at the same time affordable and reliable service levels, thus bringing in the private sector but ensuring that social development objectives were met. Such a joint venture could even be structured with a view to listing an equity or debt instrument on local stock exchanges.

The primary benefit of such a set-up for the public is service provision, while the secondary benefits include the fact that local government retains a piece of the action. Whatever the managers of the venture earn, the public would be ensured an equal share. As most city authorities are cash-strapped, this would provide a little cash flow for them and a possible means to finance additional projects or provide other services in the city. The city would also gain capacity and experience, and the confidence to design, finance and implement other capital investment projects. Business models that allow the private sector to make a fair profit, in partnership with a public that would retain a piece of the action, need to be explored. At the same time, efforts must be made to ensure that private sector management of water utilities does not undermine equity concerns, and that strong regulation is enforced to ensure that the poor are not priced out of access to basic services.

## Conclusions and recommendations

Providing access to clean drinking water and basic sanitation can be the most effective and sustainable way to benefit the poor while increasing the overall quality of city life, but water and sanitation are generally under-funded in developing countries. However, given the global benefits of greater disease control, subsequent socio-economic development and ensuing peace and security – all of which transcend national borders – there is a need for global funding streams to be brought down to the local level in support of individual cities and communities in the developing countries. History has shown that the gains will bring prosperity and security, as argued in this chapter, and the opportunities for positive globalisation are clear.

In order to reach the MDGs, water and sanitation need to be at the core of the global agenda. The eight issues set out below are considered crucial for the achievement of Target 10 for water and sanitation.

1  *A focus on urbanisation and slums is necessary.* A global strategy and frame-work on water and sanitation must be oriented more towards solving the problems of slums in poor countries. This implies that a wide range of existing mechanisms in development finance (as may be put forward in Poverty Reduction Strategy Papers) must be adjusted accordingly, to take the urban level and new urban settings into account.

2  *A focus on the poorest is critical.* The MDGs highlight the need to address the poorest and most vulnerable. The proposed strategies need to consider the conditions of both rural and urban poverty and other linkages. All actors should be encouraged to report on the number of people served by their intended and ongoing projects, programmes and other initiatives, to assist with allocation of scarce funding, forecast progress with the MDGs, evaluate effectiveness of interventions – and, in all these ways, ensure that the poor are actually being reached by interventions.

3  *Investment is critical.* Investment in water and sanitation is critical for the achievement of all MDGs. Both the global community and central governments need to give water and sanitation the highest priority for investment, and the annual funds going into the water sector as a whole need to be significantly increased at all levels of governance. The current resource levels of investment for water and sanitation as a global public good are insufficient; doubling the current annual finance flows is just the first step.

4  *Additional finance is necessary.* There are a multitude of potential financial sources that could be adapted for provision of this global public good. No single financing source will be politically feasible and large enough to fill the gap, so a package of measures will be needed. Industrialised countries must meet their commitments by increasing their ODA contributions to 0.7 per cent of GDP. Domestic measures also need to be reconsidered. These would include local regulatory reforms, setting realistic tariffs, ensuring cost recovery and increased management efficiency.

5 *New mechanisms for municipal financing are essential.* This goes beyond ODA into access to the capital markets. Mitigating the risks of lending and investment in the sector will assist in attracting finance, but it means instituting a supportive legal framework and building up local financial systems. The absence of legal foundations makes it difficult to attract finance. Major investments, both in infrastructure and capacity building, need to be made at the community level; and there is demand for new business models for public–private partnerships, as well as fair profit for quality service.

6 *Municipal governance needs improvement.* New financial flows must be complemented by good governance initiatives, including institution building and training of decision makers, implementers and a wide range of municipal-level stakeholders – the how is as crucial as the what. This should include mechanisms of accountability, planning, inclusivity, leadership, transparency and the development of integrated multisectoral approaches. It also implies good regulatory frameworks in the water sector in developing countries.

7 *A cross-sectional approach based on social needs is essential.* MDG strategies on water and sanitation need to move beyond the functional technical sanitary approach into the social and cross-sectional area, involving a wide range of partners and governance mechanisms. Hygiene and health education need to be available alongside broader health promotion strategies. This means working with the education sector, with private companies involved with hygiene products and the like, and of course with local and national media.

8 *New mechanisms of cooperation are essential.* New mechanisms of cooperation must be developed in the international arena that allow for the local voice to be heard and for municipal stakeholders to become important partners in development. It is also critical that the voices of community action groups, slum dwellers' associations and other civil society voices get heard at the global level.

Finally, it is recommended that the Helsinki Process in general engage the municipal level in its governance discussion. The future of the world is urban, and in the discussions over globalisation, this parallel trend – particularly with a focus on urban slums – has been significantly neglected. We would urge that as a follow-up to the discussion of this chapter a working group be established together with UN–HABITAT that looks more systematically at the interface between the local and the global.

## References

Adom, D. 2004. *The Water for African Cities Programme: Potentials for Linkages with the AMCOW Process.* Discussion paper, UN–HABITAT.

Dankelman, I. (ed.) 2004. *Background Papers*. United Nations Environment Programme, Global Women's Assembly on Environment: Women as the Voice for the Environment. Nairobi, 11–13 October.

Fry, S., B. Cousins and K. Olivola. 2002. *Health of Children Living in Slums in Asia and the Near East: Review of Existing Literature and Data*. Activity Report 109, Bureau for Global Health, USAID.

Habitat Agenda. 1996. *Goals and Principles, Commitments and Goal Plan of Action*. UN Conference on Human Settlements (Habitat II), Istanbul, 3–14 June.

Helsinki Process. 2004. *The Planet at Risk: Mobilising Resources for Global Human Security*. Report of Track II (on the Global Economic Agenda) of the Helsinki Process on Globalisation and Democracy, June 2004 Revision, Geneva.

Hua, M., R. Lenton, K. Lewis, G. Schmidt-Traub and A. Wright. 2004. 'Financing Strategies to meet the Millenium Development Goals for Water and Sanitation in Low-Income Countries'. Draft for discussion at the seminar on Water for the Poorest, World Water Week.

Mavrotas, G. 2004. 'Capital Flows for Development: Issues, Challenges and Agenda'. Paper presented at meeting of Track II (on the Global Economic Agenda) of Helsinki Process, Pretoria, October.

Millennium Project. 2004. *Achieving the Millennium Development Goals for Water and Sanitation: What Will it Take?* Interim Report, Task Force 7 on Water and Sanitation, New York.

OECD. 2004. *Aid for Water Supply and Sanitation*, Annual Development Cooperation Report. Paris, Development Assistance Committee, Organisation for Economic Cooperation and Development.

Reina, P. 2004. 'Africa Builds its Funding Framework'. *Water 21*, Magazine of the International Water Association, August 2004.

Reutersward, L. 2004. 'The Challenges of Sustainable Urbanisation'. Paper presented at meeting on UN–HABITAT Strategy and Dutch Cooperation, UN–HABITAT.

Sassen, S. 2001. *The Global City*. New York: Princeton University Press.

Satterthwaite, D. 2004. 'Working with the Urban Poor and their Organisations to Reduce Poverty'. Paper prepared for the Norwegian Ministry of the Environment, Commission on Sustainable Development 12, New York, 14–30 April.

UN. 2002. *Report of the World Summit on Sustainable Development*. New York: United Nations.

UNDP. 2003. *Human Development Report 2003*. New York: United Nations Development Programme.

UNEP. 2004. *Women and the Environment*. Nairobi: United Nations Office/United Nations Environment Programme.

UNCHS. 2001. *The Istanbul Declaration and the Habitat Agenda with Subject Index*. Nairobi: United Nations Office/United Nations Centre for Human Settlements.

UN–HABITAT. 2002. *The State of the World's Cities 2001*. Nairobi: United Nations Human Settlements Programme Publications Unit.

WHO and UNICEF. 2000. *Global Water Supply and Sanitation Assessment Report*. Geneva: World Health Organisation and United Nations Children's Fund, Joint Monitoring Programme for Water Supply and Sanitation.

# 11

## A Political Agenda for Global Economic Governance

### COLIN BRADFORD JR and FANTU CHERU

The world is at a critical juncture: on the one hand, the opportunity to come together to pursue a common agenda; on the other, the danger of breaking into opposing groups based on differences in income, interests, religion or race. Globalisation exacerbates this tension between opportunity and threat. Both the reality and the perception of globalisation embody these tensions, for globalisation contains forces within it for both good and ill. The most keenly felt tension is the sense that globalisation creates greater inequality in an already unequal world. The fact that the wealth of a minority of people is growing rapidly while billions live in abject poverty is one of the major ethical challenges facing humanity today. If the world is unequal, then it must be undemocratic. As a result, globalisation and democracy present simultaneous challenges.

To make a difference in the face of these enormous forces, there is a need to think in terms of transformational change in order to reverse the current pattern of inequality at the global and national levels. In this respect, the Millennium Development Goals (MDGs) provide a powerful organising framework for international actions to change the current pattern of globalisation and generate forces for greater democracy, equity and security. At the core of a transformative development agenda is the need to strengthen global commitment to humane governance. It must be focused on strengthening global ethics and responsibility by bringing the principles of human development and social protection into the concept of global economic governance.

### Ethical norms and principles for a new global economic agenda

The drivers of transformational change consist of value components and instrumental elements. The value components have to do with the power of common aspirations and ethical principles to bind actors to common purposes. The instrumental components provide incentives for individual, institutional and corporate efforts to improve productivity growth, jobs and incomes, thus making resources available for realising human aspirations and specific goals for human security, as well as for enhancing the capacity and dignity of the individual. Responsibility rests with each individual as a citizen of our communities and nations, and all of us as global citizens, to contribute to human solidarity. Small and medium enterprises, large corporations, private sector associations, labour unions and other organised aspects of the private sector have a vital role to play and major benefits to be reaped from a global society of healthy, educated, productive workers. Local, national and global public institutions are also key actors in the common enterprise of improving the human condition in all societies.

Guiding ethical principles are necessary to frame issues clearly. Ethical principles reflect commonly accepted international human rights instruments. The promotion of human rights is of particular relevance in the context of globalisation and its potential for excluding and marginalising weak members of the international community and people with limited power to influence economic decisions. Human rights afford protection against such exclusion and marginalisation. Moreover, international human rights agreements codify the rights of the poor and the obligations and duties of governments to respect, protect, and fulfil these rights. This report is guided by a set of ethical principles which undergird international human rights.

*Human dignity and human freedom*: protecting human dignity and expanding human freedom entail expanding liberties, opportunities and capabilities. Deprivation of human freedom relates to the inability to avoid hunger, poverty, treatable illnesses and premature mortality, as well as the denial of civil and political liberties. The aim of economic globalisation should be to reinforce human dignity and expand human freedoms, not the other way around.

*Responsibility and accountability*: individuals, organisations and governments have responsibilities to respect, promote and fulfil all human rights for all. International financial institutions and private commercial banks are not exempt from general international human rights regulations and must become accountable to the public. Lack of accountability undermines democracy's substance, if not its form. Such accountability requires mechanisms for arbitration when weaker governments have grievances.

*Inclusion of marginalised voices*: an essential principle of the international human rights framework is that every human person and all peoples are entitled to participate in, contribute to and enjoy civil, economic, social, cultural and political development in which all human rights and fundamental freedoms can be fully realised. This means that participation is not simply something desirable from the point of view of ownership and sustainability, but rather that *participation is a right*. The inclusion of marginalised voices in the discussion of the global economic agenda is not only a practical necessity, but is fundamental to the achievement of a just and democratic global order.

*Democratic treatment and equality in sharing losses*: inflation, exchange rate volatility, capital flow surges and hemorrhages, and financial crisis hurt the poor disproportionately. Yet global mechanisms and national programmes are inadequate to protect the poor from financial shocks and to compensate them for the unjust severity of the impact. For globalisation to be fair and more democratic there must be policies, programmes and mechanisms designed to protect the poor from the disproportionate burden they bear of the costs of globalisation.

*Policy choice for self-determination*: in reforming the global economic agenda to achieve a more fair, equal and democratic world, special emphasis needs to be placed on preserving and enhancing the *policy options* open to developing nations to choose their own development path consistent with their values, institutions, history and national priorities. At present, their policy choice is narrowed by loan conditions, structural adjustment programmes, trade rules and financial dependency on developed countries. There is an urgent need to enlarge the range of country policy options and choices. Such expression can best be undertaken by elected local representatives and not by external donor officials.

*Sustainability and a commitment to protect common heritage resources*: development processes should respect the rights of future generations as well as the present. The prevailing economic logic conspicuously ignores the human consequences of resource depletion. Sustainability relies on the conservation of the life-support functions of the ecosphere, which cannot be replenished by technology or replaced through economics. This is considered natural capital. Each generation should inherit a natural capital stock equal to that which the preceding generation inherited and humankind must learn to live on the annual production or interest generated by the existing stocks of natural capital.

These ethical principles are driving forces in determining the concerns and conclusions of this report. They shape and motivate the actions necessary to finance the achievement of the MDGs by 2015. However important this achievement would be, the reforms in processes and institutions vital to these efforts themselves are important dimensions of the trajectory of transformational change. If the global governance institutions and processes were working well, current tensions would not be as acute as they are.

## Sources of dynamism: impetus for transformational change

Transformational change that vaults societies forward to a different level and quality of life requires simultaneous, significant participation of the three major elements of society: *the private sector*, *the development state* and *civil society*. Without the full engagement of these three engines of change, the end result over the next decade will be an extrapolation of existing conditions, or at best incremental improvement which fails to give global society a new sense of itself as just, open and fair.

## The private sector

Business leaders are increasingly interested in shaping global investment, trade, and production in ways that generate social goods such as employment, income growth, environmental benefits, productivity improvements and distributional outcomes that create greater equality and broader participation in the gains from globalisation. In developing countries, entrepreneurship through domestic small, medium and large enterprises is the main engine of job creation, decent work and growth. Foreign investment and enterprises are extremely important supplements to domestic private sector dynamism by enhancing investment, technological change, competitiveness and export potential. But internal dynamism attracts external resources rather more forcibly than foreign investment jump-starts domestic growth. Foreign private sector actors – whether banks, businesses, or investors – have a major stake in developing the missing markets for their services, products and finance, which go wanting due to lack of institutional infrastructure, policy reform and political commitment in poor countries. As a result, the entrepreneurs, executives and leaders from developing countries *and* industrial economies have an immense common stake in poverty reduction, income equality and job growth due to the enormous market potential opened up by transformational change.

Without the private sector, transformational change is dead in the water; without transformational change, the private sector (foreign and domestic) is condemned to slower growth trajectories, failing to realise the potential of missing markets.

## The public sector: the development state

Unrealised market potential in developing countries means, more often than not, market failure, for business cannot rely on market signals alone to guide investment and business decisions. Government failure is also an obstacle to private sector growth. As a result, society and the private sector have a stake in strengthening, not weakening, public sector capacity to govern and to support the functioning of the market. Successful developing countries have been those that have shaped a constructive, mutually supportive relationship between the public and private sectors, rather than those that have opted for the primacy of either the market or the state.

The *development state* is one that has the administrative, legal, and regulatory capacity to support the market and the private sector. It is a capable rather than a crony-capitalist state; it is one that thrives on private–public partnerships rather than fearing or being captured by them. The development state is one pushing for financial system reform to benefit small, medium and large enterprises through broad access to credit and legal frameworks to enforce contracts that buttress capital markets supported by supervisory and regulatory agencies for transparency and accountability. The development state is one that pushes for education and health systems which create a productive and skilled workforce and invests in institutional and physical infrastructure which complements private sector dynamism. The development state is a strong, democratic state which reflects local values and priorities and drives the development thrust from inside outward rather than a weak, submissive state that permits external forces to drive internal priorities and outcomes.

### Civil society

Civil society has created new vehicles, modalities and channels for organising, articulating and transmitting the interests and priorities of communities and sectors to private and public authorities. Civil society organisations have become the indispensable third party to the dialogue and decision making necessary for nation building and for development. It is through public–private partnerships that the development state can engage with the private sector in more dynamic development arrangements, and through partnerships with civil society that both the private and the public sector can be more responsive, efficient and effective in implementing developmental change.

It is very clear that a transformative development agenda requires a unified, compassionate and people-centred approach by governments, international organisations, the private sector and civil society actors. The main economic engines for growth, then, are domestic private sector savings and investment, human capital formation and skills, and the development state; the latter must be capable of selective intervention to create both the economic environment for private sector investment and growth and also the conditions of human security that allow people to be healthy, educated and productive members of society. Productivity is the central dynamic factor in economic growth; it is the productivity of labour, in the end, that drives economic outcomes, enhanced by capital and institutional infrastructure. People-centred human development is an economic as well as a social agenda, not a trade-off; people are the convergence point for the interests of the private sector, the public sector and civil society. It is this convergence on the individual that makes the MDGs a powerful local, national and global framework for action.

## Key priorities for action: what needs to be done?

Achieving the MDGs in all countries by 2015 will require a major unified effort by each of the three main sources of transformational change: the private sector, the development state and civil society. Business as usual will not suffice. Nor will mere incremental efforts translate into the qualitative shifts required. Only simultaneous, substantial effort on all fronts will generate the high-yield outcomes necessary to achieve the MDGs by 2015. The promise of the MDGs is intrinsic synergies among health, education, gender equality, the environment and poverty reduction that generate high returns to simultaneous investment. Inter-sectoral synergy is a source of dynamism that can be realised by moving forward toward all the MDGs simultaneously.

### Public–private sector dynamics

Economic growth remains a crucial determinant of poverty reduction, job growth, and greater income equality. Since (1) the private sector accounts for at least 80 per cent of domestic savings and investment in most developing countries, (2) net private capital flows now outstrip net official development assistance (ODA), and (3) less than 15 per cent of total ODA now finances job generation and GDP growth, the need to catalyse private sector engagement, mobilise private resources and support private sector dynamism is critical to achieving the MDGs. Without the domestic private sector, progress toward the MDGs will be severely constrained. But private sector growth cannot be fostered without proactive effort by the development state and the participation of civil society. Among the policies that national governments must adopt to spur private-sector-led growth are the following:

1   They should create a policy environment supportive of entrepreneurship and private sector development by strengthening the legal and regulatory environment and ensuring that public expenditure is more efficient and transparent. This requires shifting government organisational culture towards development promotion and facilitation and away from regulation and control.

2   Governments must develop clear policies and a long-term vision of the socio-economic and political fabric of the country, with democratic governance as a common framework for formulating and implementing policies. The framework must also define clear policies on the role of different societal actors in achieving the vision: the state, the bureaucracy, civil society and the private sector.

3   Governments should combat corruption through public sector reform and by strengthening accountability institutions, such as the Anti-Corruption Bureau, the Auditor-General or the customs and excise departments. Not only does corruption hamper economic development, but it also undermines democracy and destroys government credibility.

4   The tax base should be broadened to strengthen the financial foundations of the public sector, including public debt management, building the capacity of the development state and increasing private relative to public sector investment.

5   The financial system should be developed through the institutional and legal development of the banking system; it should extend its services to poor communities and the informal sector, while creating greater financial security and reducing risk through adequate oversight and supervisory mechanisms.

6   Governments should expand poor people's access to productive resources: they should work specifically in slums, rural villages and poor communities to secure land tenure and title, to create microfinance and

banking institutions that capture savings and capitalise assets of the poor so there is a dramatic improvement in the access of the poor to credit.

7   Public–private partnerships for infrastructure development should be encouraged in critical sectors such as energy, transportation and communications, where the private sector is more efficient and the public sector has a role as regulator, guarantor and steward.

8   Parliamentary oversight of economic policy, national budgets and institutional development should be strengthened to hold governments accountable for improved resource mobilisation for development as a means of creating pressure to increase domestic savings and public revenues while controlling public indebtedness. This strengthened domestic private sector and internal financial system can be used as a foundation to maximise the contribution of private capital flows to national development goals, and as a framework for attracting foreign direct investment rather than expecting FDI to drive domestic growth.

Despite this domestic effort as the cornerstone of the overall effort, domestic resources in poorer countries will not be sufficient to generate the jobs, economic growth and social investment necessary to achieve the MDGs. New sources of external finance will be necessary, both internal and external. The new consensus reached in Monterrey in March of 2001 on financing for development highlighted Goal 8, identifying the importance of the *development partnership of industrial country actions* for achieving the MDGs and creating a new concept for formulating policy on external resources for achieving national and global goals: policy coherence.

### Strengthening policy coherence

A transformative development agenda requires, at the very least, significant progress in improving policy coherence by developed countries – based on taking the *total* amount of resources available to developing countries as the metric for measuring external finance accruing from trade, debt reduction, foreign investment, private capital flows, remittances or official aid. If, for example, developed-country agricultural subsidies on commodities exportable by developing countries amount to US$365 billion a year, and foreign aid is US$55 billion a year, then the external resources available to developing countries could be six times the level of foreign aid if industrial countries did away with agricultural subsidies. This new metric creates a compelling logic that a failure to act on agricultural subsidies requires compensatory proportional action on debt reduction or aid to make up for the shortfalls in action on trade. Industrial countries themselves have embraced the concept of policy coherence, which now is a powerful new framework for mobilising external resources for the MDGs in the decade ahead. As a result, industrial country actions on trade, debt and aid must be looked at together. The key actionable areas in policy coherence are discussed in the following pages.

*Agricultural trade reform*

Trade cannot facilitate development unless fundamental reforms are made to the underlying global trade structure. Achieving the MDGs would require, at the very least, the introduction of mechanisms to achieve fair and stable prices for commodities and improve market access for exports from developing countries. Without action on agricultural subsidies by industrial countries, the development partnership inaugurated in the Monterrey Consensus is dead.

One of the ways in which poor countries can try to benefit from globalisation is to increase their share of global trade. However, the benefits from such integration tend to be distributed unevenly, and adverse forms of integration into the global economy may increase rather than reduce poverty. Despite the elimination of many of the barriers that have restricted international trade in goods, significant barriers to trade still persist – often to the detriment of the poorest countries.

The main issues of interest to developing countries are on the agenda of the Doha Development Round of trade negotiations. These include basic issues of market access to industrial country economies, terms of trade between developing country exports and imports from industrial countries, commodity price volatility and trade patterns, phasing out export subsidies and trade-distorting domestic support measures in agriculture by industrial countries, especially those that are also cotton growers, and special and differentiated treatment for poorer countries.

But it is now three years since Doha and development dimensions have been ignored in the subsequent negotiations. For example, the July 2004 WTO package failed to reflect the special and differential treatment that the Doha Declaration promised to developing countries. If the WTO talks continue on their present trajectory, they are unlikely to deliver the development benefits promised in Doha. Developing countries have made it clear that without action on agricultural subsidies they will not proceed with the Doha Round, nor agree to its conclusions. This strong stance by developing countries in the international trade negotiations is a reflection of a notion borne out by empirical research: that trade is a key to growth, which in turn is central to poverty reduction; policy coherence requires that, without action on trade, actions on debt and aid will have to be proportionately greater.

*Support for a full cancellation of poor countries' debt*

The debt of poor countries has become so large that most new official aid flows do little more than offset the interest and principal payments on previous debt. In this situation, it is difficult for additional aid to have an economic or social impact, and debt payments by poor countries crowd out private investment and public expenditure on education and health. Significant debt reduction is necessary for the recovery and resumption of growth in many indebted countries, and for achieving many of the MDGs.

Full cancellation of the debt of poor countries by industrial countries is now politically feasible, economically necessary and socially responsible. The

UK, under the leadership of Prime Minister Tony Blair, has proposed a 100% debt cancellation as a way out of this conundrum. His proposal has received widespread support by other governments, international NGOs, and analysts. It was considered seriously at the last G-7 summit in the United States in July 2004 and at the IMF–World Bank ministerial-level Development Committee meeting in autumn 2004. This is an actionable item that deserves the full support of the international community. It must be made clear, however, that debt cancellation can make a huge difference in developing countries only when there is greater policy coherence (integrating the trade, aid, debt, capital flow and macro-policy aspects) within developed countries.

*Doubling the current ODA level*
If trade and private finance supplement domestic resource mobilisation and debt relief buttresses the development state, ODA is the instrument for improving human security and people-centred development, as well as providing budgetary, balance of payments and private sector support. ODA is the most flexible and direct external instrument for achieving the MDGs. In the end, paying for the international component of achieving the MDGs has to come from somewhere; if it does not come from private finance, trade enhancement, or debt reduction, aid is the instrument of last resort.

Several sources have estimated that at least doubling ODA from its current US$50 billion level to over $100 billion is necessary to reach the MDGs, along with increased domestic resource mobilisation within developing countries. This is an achievable goal, but it will require concerted efforts by industrialised country governments, parliaments, civil society groups and the private sector.

*Regulation of international capital flows*
Unlike international trade, there is no global regime applying to international capital flows, including foreign direct investment (FDI). The financial instability and sharp currency fluctuations caused by large inflows and outflows of external funds have led many developing countries into financial and economic crisis, with dramatic and sudden increase in poverty rates. Ilene Grabel of the University of Denver has argued that neoliberal financial reform exposes developing countries to five mutually reinforcing risks, namely the risk of currency collapse; the risk of capital flight; the risk that governments, firms and banks will pursue fragile financing strategies; the risk of contagion from financial crises that originate elsewhere; and the risk that external actors will exercise undue influence over domestic decision making ( Grabel 2002).

A number of proposals have been floated in the aftermath of the 1997 East Asian financial crisis for the creation of international institutions and mechanisms to regulate and stabilise international capital flows. The most ambitious proposals advocate the establishment of fully-fledged global institutions for reducing risks, such as a Board of Overseers of Major International Institutions and Markets with wide-ranging powers for setting standards and for oversight and regulation of commercial banking, securities and insurance (Kaufman 1992). Others advocate less ambitious global mechanisms that involve reforming the mandates, membership and/or governance of existing organisations – such as the IMF, the Bank for International Settlements (BIS) and the Financial Stability Forum (FSF) – that set codes and standards in areas of financial regulation and supervision of macroeconomic policy (Cornford 2002; IMF 2002).

On the domestic side, there is increasing recognition that developing countries should rely on national policy measures to reduce their vulnerability to risks by restricting currency convertibility or by imposing Chilean-style capital control. Through these and similar measures, countries can avoid the excessive build-up of external debt, curb the volatility of the flow of funds, and create greater scope to adopt macroeconomic policies that can counter recession (such as lower interest rates or budget expansion). Grabel (2002) concludes that most financial crises can be avoided and that the potential benefit of increased financial regulation can be as great as the immense human and economic cost of crises.

## Mobilising for common accountability: how to get it done?

It is common knowledge that global decision making in economic and social affairs has become much less democratic, participatory and transparent. Simultaneously the resources, mandate and influence of the UN have been eroded, while the IMF, World Bank and WTO have expanded their power and mandate. As a result, the policy autonomy of developing countries has been narrowed by loan conditions, trade rules and structural adjustment programmes. Recent efforts to shift policy control to developing countries – PRSPs being a case in point – have not been accompanied by the democratisation of multilateral financial institutions. An important element in a transformative agenda is the reform of the decision-making system in international institutions like the IMF, the World Bank and the regional development banks, so that the developing countries can have a fair say in the policies and processes of institutions that so much determine the course of their economies and societies.

The prevalence of wide-scale human deprivation in the midst of a world of plenty can be avoided and the fight against mass poverty won. But this requires significant policy changes by governments in both developed and developing countries. To correct the current global imbalance, the first priority is for the democratic deficits to be rectified by political, judicial and institutional reforms within countries in which the voices of the poor are not heard and their interests are not served. Local values and priorities need to drive policies and resource allocation, rather than the global policy regime setting national development strategies.

Economic reforms following one-size-fits-all models are too narrow and too rigid to achieve transformational change. In contrast to the Washington

Consensus on economic reform, the Monterrey Consensus on the MDGs and the financing for development efforts to achieve them embodies a multi-sectoral development strategy which is more promising as a catalyst for transformation. The complexity and intersectoral linkages of the multi-sectoral MDG agenda provide many more dimensions for choices regarding sequencing, timing and priorities to infuse implementation strategies with local values, preferences and variants than the previous paradigms for economic policy reform.

Since the MDGs echo the human aspirations of all, there is more congruence between local, national, regional and global programmes for achieving them and less sense of an external agenda imposing constraints on national and local decisions. The MDG agenda can be home-grown rather than imported. As a result, the internal mobilisation of political support and financial resources is more energising than trying to create consensus on adjustment and stabilisation efforts supported by international agencies. The infusion of local and national input into the MDG effort drives the global response rather than a global mandate overpowering the local, as in the past.

## Global policy leadership

The new global agenda requires global policy leadership to press the priority of the intersectoral nature of the agenda and provide guidance for the inter-institutional relationships most conducive to implementing that agenda. Issues at the interface are the essential issues that generate the synergies and high-yield outcomes on which success depends. Political guidance at the highest level is necessary to provide a framework for complementary rather than competitive relationships among the major international institutions responsible for the principal domains of the global agenda. If the world anticipates transformational effects from this agenda, the relationship among the international institutions cannot be left to market forces or bureaucratic coordination. Nor is this a matter for ministers of finance alone. Global political leadership at the highest level is required to push the intersectoral and policy coherence elements of this agenda – very different to business-as-usual modes of national governance, which tend to follow the turf-driven division of labour stand-offs rather than coordination and cooperation.

The mechanism appropriate for this kind of role in the international system must by its nature reflect the entire international community. There may be many alternative mechanisms for achieving a high degree of representativeness. But it seems safe to say that the G-8 is not sufficiently global in its membership to constitute a legitimate forum for implementing the new global agenda, since it does not involve developing countries in its membership.

An illustrative alternative would be the G-20, which consists of the G-8 plus Australia and the EU Presidency (when not a G-7 member) and ten of the largest developing countries: China, India, Korea, Indonesia, Turkey, Saudi Arabia, South Africa, Brazil, Mexico and Argentina. The G-20 has been meeting at finance-minister level since 1999. Elevating the G-20 to head-of-state level is being promoted by Canadian Prime Minister Paul Martin, among others. Its legitimacy rests on its demography, diversity and more democratic representation of the world than the G-8 has; the G-20 represents over 60 per cent of the world's population as opposed to 14 per cent for the G-8.

The elevation to head-of-state level of the G-20, or the formation of a similar, more representative body, is a necessary step in providing more legitimate political leadership and strategic guidance to address the intersectoral and inter-ministerial dimensions of the new global agenda required to achieve the MDGs by 2015. It would generate the momentum and the resources necessary to implement the new global agenda.

### Policy coherence and global monitoring

The G-20 type global strategic guidance requires follow-through and follow-up. Beyond global political leadership, three components are necessary to the ongoing process of global governance: a *policy coherence component*, involving OECD member governments; a *monitoring and evaluation component*, tracking progress by both industrial and developing countries; and a *consultation component*, involving diverse organisations from civil society, the private sector, and parliaments. These three components are needed to complement the summit process of political leadership in helping to create a movement for the mobilisation of policies, resources, and efforts to transform globalisation for the benefit of all.

Policy coherence must happen at two levels: within the OECD and between the UN agencies and the Bretton Woods institutions. The current division of labour which assigns 'hard issues' of finance and economics to the Washington institutions, and 'soft' issues of social development to the UN system is no longer tenable, because it is out of synch with current insights into how development actually works.

#### Policy coherence within the OECD

Industrial country governments need to support a process within the OECD that leads to periodic assessments of their national trade–debt–aid efforts and to accountability for achieving policy coherence either through positive reinforcing actions in each domain or by additional increases in ODA to offset backsliding or failure to act positively on trade or debt.

The OECD Development Assistance Committee (DAC) is already the primary forum for industrial country donor coordination. It was the source in 1996 of the seven International Development Goals (IDGs), now the MDGs, and plays a proactive role in the international community, including promoting policy coherence in OECD member countries through peer review of all donor country policies, not just aid policies.

The annual spring High-Level Meeting (HLM) of OECD country development cooperation ministers is the highest-level policy-making body in the donor community. The DAC High-Level Meeting is usually followed by the annual OECD ministerial meeting, with a representation of ministers that reflects the variety of issues on the agenda. The HLM could be charged with preparing the review of policy coherence in development policies (trade, investment, debt and aid) of OECD member countries, to be reviewed periodically at OECD ministerial meetings. Critical issues from the OECD Ministerial could then be referred on to the G-20 Ministerial, to be put before G-20 heads of state in a timely way. This sequence could become the primary path for pressing forward the policy coherence component of the global agenda.

*Policy coherence between UN agencies and the Bretton Woods institutions*
The global agenda is composed of issues at the interface, whether in the social-environmental-poverty-growth agenda for developing countries or the policy coherence agenda for industrial countries. For the first time this now requires priority attention to the inter-institutional relationships necessary to assure that the intersectoral synergies are identified, acted upon and fully exploited. This intersectoral agenda of the MDGs requires that new relationships be forged between the UN agencies, the WTO, the IMF, the World Bank, and the regional development banks for Africa, Asia, Eastern Europe and Latin America.

*Global monitoring*
Monitoring of progress toward the MDGs goes forward in multiple channels. At the IMF–World Bank annual spring and autumn meetings, ministers of finance from industrial and developing countries meet in the Development Committee and the International Monetary and Finance Committee (IMFC). For the spring meetings, the World Bank prepares the World Development Indicators Report, which uses the MDGs as a framework for organising the statistical compendium and highlights the global aspects of tracking progress toward achieving the MDGs. The IMF–World Bank Development Committee itself has played a continuous role in reviewing, revising, and reinforcing the MDG agenda twice a year since the Monterrey Conference and Consensus in 2002. Parliaments of developing and industrialised countries should be part of the global monitoring and evaluation process as a way of scrutinising the work of their own national governments and the international institutions as well.

The United Nations system is charged by the Secretary-General with ensuring that every five years between now and 2015 individual country reports are prepared assessing the degree to which each developing country is on course to achieve the MDGs by 2015. In the UN General Assembly in the autumn of 2005 the Secretary-General will provide the first of three assessments of global progress toward the MDGs based on these national reports. The decade ahead is all that is left of the 25-year period allocated to achieving the MDGs (1990–2015).

The most important track, without doubt, is the set of national monitoring and evaluation exercises undertaken by the developing countries themselves.

Box 11.1 International community: mechanisms for a mobilisation movement

| | | |
|---|---|---|
| Political leaders | G-20 heads of state | **Global strategy** |
| | G-20 ministers | Agenda setting for heads |
| Industrial countries | OECD Ministerial<br>OECD DAC | **Policy coherence**<br>Agenda setting for Ministerial |
| Developing countries | IMF–WB Dev. Committee<br>UNGA 2005-10-15<br>National monitoring | **Global monitoring** |
| International institutions | G-20 summits<br>Chief Executives Board | **Inter-institutional relations**<br>Management follow-up |
| Society | World Social Forum<br>World Economic Forum<br>IPU* and /or PNoWB** | **Engagement of:**<br>Civil society<br>Private sector<br>Parliaments |
| Key priority actions | Helsinki Process | Follow-through |

\* Inter-Parliamentary Union
\*\* Parliamentary Network of the World Bank

However, many developing countries are hampered by low capacity and weak statistical institutions for undertaking comprehensive monitoring of development outcomes. The strengthening of national statistical systems and institutions is the most important element in the global monitoring-and-evaluation exercise because they have spillover effects in buttressing the policy process in developing countries and strengthening national ownership and control of development trajectories.

### Building a global movement for humane governance
The framework put forward here for considering the specific instruments for mobilising resources needed to achieve the MDGs is the notion of a mobilisation movement coalescing interests and instruments into one comprehensive and integrated effort to change the course of globalisation into processes, forces and patterns which benefit all humanity rather than the few. To achieve this noble goal, diverse mechanisms in the global system and different

elements of society need to be marshalled and connected so that each action on one instrument, whether trade, debt, investment or aid, contributes to the achievement of the broad global agenda embodied in the MDGs. An important dimension of this mobilisation effort is the need to ensure that the voices of the marginalised majority are included in the discussion of the global economic agenda. The major benefit of having a single global agenda of internationally agreed upon goals, targets and indicators is that it is a way of keeping the implementation phase and the mobilisation effort *unified*, so as to realise the intrinsic synergies embedded in the new global agenda.

In this unified agenda, the central principles are policy coherence for industrial countries and intersectoral development strategies and programmes for developing countries. No single MDG is achieved without the others. The MDG linkages between environment, health, education, gender, poverty and growth are central for developing countries, just as the policy coherence linkages between trade, debt, aid and capital flows are central for industrial countries.

## Conclusion: the Helsinki Process as a continuous process

The Helsinki Process is one in which process is more important than product. The fundamental purpose of the Helsinki Process is to spur action by identifying key priorities in the global agenda necessary to achieve the MDGs and by creating connections between actors and advocates, policy makers and parliamentarians, private sector and public sector leaders, and between local, national and global actors to implement that agenda. The Helsinki Conference in September 2005 is one event in which leaders will gather to promote the overall agenda and to push specific issues within it. In different venues in different locations involving a variety of actors, the Helsinki Process has already facilitated forward movement on several key issues, such as debt cancellation and the sale of IMF gold to finance the HIPC trust fund. There have also been contacts with UK officials on the cancellation of debt idea and how, when and where to get it enacted. There has been collaboration between US and Canadian think tanks on how to advance the G-20 to head-of-state level. More needs to be done. Other similar endeavours are contemplated as vital steps in the Helsinki Process, conceived as a means of action rather than as a series of reports. It is hoped that the Helsinki Process on globalisation and democracy, like the Helsinki Process on human rights in East–West relations before it, may have an ongoing life in continuously convening, convincing and coalescing interests and actors in implementing the new global agenda for achieving the MDGs by 2015.

## References

Cornford, A. 2002. 'Standards and Regulation', in Y. Akuyz (ed.), *Reforming the Global Financial Architecture: Issues and Proposals*. London and New York: UNCTAD/TWN/Zed Books, Chapter 2.

Grabel, I. 2002. 'Capital Accounts Controls and Related Measures to Avert Financial Crisis'. Paper presented at the Alternatives to Neoliberalism Conference sponsored by the New Rules for Global Finance Coalition, Washington, DC, 23–24 May.

IMF. 2002. *Report of the Acting Managing Director to the International Monetary and Financial Committee on Progress in Reforming the IMF and Strengthening the Architecture of the International Financial System*. Washington, DC: International Monetary Fund, April.

Kaufman, H .1992. 'Ten Reasons to Reform'. *Euromoney*, November.

# Index